WAR OF LIES

When George Washington Was the Target and Propaganda Was the Crime

A news biography of his war years

"Some of the gazettes of the United States have teemed with all the invective that disappointment, ignorance of facts, and malicious falsehoods could invent." ~ George Washington

Jane Hampton Cook

Wheelhouse Lit, Nashville, TN
Valor & Virtue History Mystery

Cover art: George Washington by D-Keine, licensed
from Istock

DEDICATION

To my husband John Kim Cook.

CONTENTS

THE PROPAGANDA TARGET: GENERAL GEORGE WASHINGTON BY CHARLES
WILLSON PEALE 1780, THE COLONIAL WILLIAMSBURG FOUNDATION. GIFT OF
JOHN ROCKEFELLER JUNIOR

BENJAMIN FRANKLIN, FREE SPEECH ADVOCATE & NEWSPAPER EDITOR

SUSPECT 1: GENERAL HORATIO GATES, A CAREER BRITISH OFFICER WHO BECAME A CONTINENTAL ARMY GENERAL

SUSPECT 2: JAMES RIVINGTON, A LOYALIST NEWSPAPER EDITOR WHO
BECAME THE KING'S PRINTER IN NEW YORK

SUSPECT 3: GENERAL CHARLES LEE, A CAREER BRITISH OFFICER WHO BECAME A CONTINENTAL GENERAL

A Second Picture of GENERAL CHARLES LEE, Who Loved Dogs

PEYTON RANDOLPH, THE CLOSEST RESEMBLANCE TO HIS BROTHER,
SUSPECT 4: JOHN RANDOLPH, WHO DID NOT LEAVE A PORTRAIT
BOTH COUSINS OF THOMAS JEFFERSON

ACKNOWLEDGMENTS

Thank you to my agent, Jonathan Clements and to Melody Grubaugh for proofing and editing. Thanks also to Kate Hooten for editing and to Beth Barns for reviewing and providing input.

WAR OF LIES

INTRODUCTION: TRUTH & INTEGRITY

One of America's founders, John Adams, understood human nature better than many in his generation. He may have communicated by writing with a quill pen on parchment paper instead of voice-dictating a message on a smartphone, but he understood that truth and integrity were essential elements for any society's survival.

Adams believed that any institution could be corrupted by lies and disinformation–whether that system was a royal empire entangled with the elite's priorities or a republic whose power was diffused through three different branches and levels of government. Despite this, Adams believed that a monarchy was more naturally tyrannical and corrupt than any other system.

"But kings and nobles have much oftener combined together, to crush, to humble, and to fleece the people," he wrote four years before the Continental Congress issued the Declaration of Independence. To Adams, a commitment to integrity by the people and their leaders was the only real bulwark against tyranny, no matter the institution or era.

"The preservation of liberty depends upon the intellectual and moral character of the people. As long as knowledge and virtue are diffused generally among the body of a nation, it is impossible they should be enslaved. This can be brought to pass only by debasing their understandings or by corrupting their hearts," Adams wrote.

What did Adams mean by debasing people's understanding? He was worried that deception, lies, and corruption would prevent people from having sufficient information to know the truth about important matters affecting them. Debasing people's understanding would prevent the diffusion of knowledge and truth among the majority of society and thus result in corrupting its intellectual character. Falsehoods, especially in the form of propaganda in newspapers, would erode liberty and promote tyranny.

One of the causes for the American Revolution was corruption. King George III corrupted colonial governors and judges when he began paying their salaries instead of allowing the people to pay their salaries through their legislatures as had been the custom before his reign. As a result, governors and judges owed their loyalty to the king, not to the people.

Adams understood that if enough people's understanding of truth was debased, even through no fault of their own, then the system would become unjust and fall apart. He knew that the Judeo-Christian virtue of integrity, combined with courage, was necessary to preserve a healthy and free society.

George Washington also understood that moral integrity was the glue that kept the culture intact. "Of all the dispositions and habits which lead to political prosperity, religion, and morality are indispensable supports," he reminded Americans in 1796. During his war years, he frequently was attacked in the news by lies and propaganda that distorted people's understanding of the truth about him. One propagandist despised Washington so much that he wrote letters in Washington's name and published them as authentic. Washington never knew who wrote these counterfeit letters, although he had his suspicions.

Today, recently digitized historical documents, including letters and newspapers, provide new clues for solving the 247-year-old "history mystery" of who wrote Washington's counterfeit letters. *War of Lies* unveils Washington's rise and fall in the media, his battle with internal cabals, and four suspects who may have been responsible for the forged letters. One suspect closely fits the facts and timing behind the counterfeit letters.

War of Lies will reveal what John Adams understood in 1772. When integrity reigns, Americans cannot easily be corrupted. Truthfulness is the bulwark against corruption, historical revision, unhealthy historical perspectives, cancel culture, propaganda, communism, tyranny, and other ills that have crept into society.

Vigilance, which is one of the virtues represented by the color blue in the flag, demands that we once again restore, renew, and elevate the virtue of integrity in our society and institutions.

Though this book is not about slavery, *War of Lies* also uncovers aspects of the incremental journey that George Washington experienced as his views on slavery changed, leading him to free his slaves at his death.

May *War of Lies* enlighten you with a deeper understanding of our nation's history and the challenges our founders faced, including lies and propaganda.

May you see the similarities and differences to life today and appreciate the important role that truth and integrity play in society no matter the era.

Jane Hampton Cook, author

PART ONE

Colonel Washington, Newsmaker, Assassin, & Media Darling

"Be not hasty to believe flying reports to the disparagement of any."

#50 of *110 Rules of Civility and Good Behavior,
Francis Hawkins, 1640*

1 VALLEY FORGE AWAKENING

Great Awakenings. Sometimes awakenings happen all at once. A single shocking, nightmarish jolt is enough to awaken some souls from hazardous slumber. At other times, an awakening comes from restless sleep, with revelations arriving in bits and spurts, such as a lie here or a jealous jab there. These needles may trouble a conscience, but their punctures aren't quite enough to keep some from snoring or dreaming through the tickling torment. When dawn comes, if their own sin is causing the trouble, they can seek peace by praying to God for forgiveness.

But what happens when the sins of others—whether rulers, trusted colleagues, or vicious enemies—are the cause of sleepless nights? What happens when deceivers spin a web of lies or leave a trail of corruption, falsehoods, betrayals, treason, disinformation, or death? Many souls are tossed and turned when clouds of injustice hover over head. What do the masses see during such moments? Tyranny. What do souls seek during these types of great awakenings? Independence. Liberty brings justice, integrity, forgiveness, and peace in its wake.

The Pennsylvania plateau known as Valley Forge was originally a sleepy countryside amplified by the slapping of a river on one side, the rustle of grass on the hilly second side and the fluttering of birds along the tree-lined ridge on the third. New sounds overtook the valley in the winter of 1778. This natural triangle was transformed by the hacks of axes and the grunts of men as they built twelve hundred log huts arranged in neat military rows. The sky was obscured by smoke from continuous camp fires, which they used to keep warm and cook tasteless flour fire cakes, the only food available when they first arrived.

That winter, Valley Forge was transformed into the camp of the Continental Army's main division, which included twelve thousand poorly clad, hungry soldiers and four hundred women and children. These awakened patriots were united in fighting the tyranny imposed on their homeland by the British lion.

Throughout his reign, different actions taken by King George III had awakened British subjects throughout His Majesty's thirteen American colonies. They saw tyranny as he pursued policies that taxed them without allowing them representation in Parliament, corrupted their governors and judges, abolished their local legislative bodies, and implemented martial law. The kinetic jolt had come in April 1775, when the authoritarian British general governing Massachusetts had ordered his red-coated soldiers to seize the colonists' weapons and ammunition stores at Lexington and Concord. From the patriots' point of view, the general's officers had fired the first shots in the War for Independence.

Congress had quickly responded by naming George Washington of Virginia as Commander-in-Chief of the Continental Army. By May 1776, newspapers reported that patriots in Virginia had concluded that King George III and Parliament had responded to their petitions, protests, and objections with "increased insult, oppression, and a vigorous attempt to effect their total destruction." These Virginians had authorized their representatives to call for independence from England at a meeting of the Continental Congress. Their sentiments, which matched those of thousands throughout the colonies, came to fruition when Congress issued the Declaration of Independence on July 4, 1776.

By December 1777, after a few victories, even more defeats, and just as many retreats, General Washington had strategically chosen Valley Forge for the Continental Army's winter encampment. Valley Forge's location and natural barriers would give his army what it desperately needed: protection from the enemy, the better-trained British military and their hired Hessians occupying Philadelphia two dozen miles away.

Valley Forge was far enough away to prevent the Redcoats from launching a surprise attack as they had at Whitemarsh weeks earlier, but it was close enough for Washington to keep an eye on their movements out of Philadelphia. Fortunately, the valley had yet to hear the cacophonous cannonade of combat. Washington was determined to keep it that way. Though highly concerned about their need for clothing and food, Washington was also focused on taking advantage of winter's slumber in the velvet valley to retool his soldiers' skills.

Yet as St. Valentine's Day approached in February 1778,

Washington was hoping for the best surprise of all, the safe arrival of his wife, Martha. Near the huts at the confluence of Valley Creek and the Schuylkill River, he had rented a two-story stone house to occupy with Martha, while also sharing the parlors and living areas with two dozen officers and assistants. Such a claustrophobic arrangement would not surprise her. After all, Mrs. Washington had joined her husband in camp under similar circumstances the previous winters, in New Jersey in 1777 and Massachusetts in 1776. Washington had relied on her to entertain the officers, which enabled her to evaluate their loyalty and motives.

He knew that Martha was a good judge of character, as was Alexander Hamilton, a young upstart and new secretary. As much as he admired Hamilton's zeal for the cause, from Washington's perspective, this energetic officer had recently become concerned—too concerned—about a pesky internal matter called a cabal.

Captain Hamilton was one of Washington's aide-de-camps. A few months earlier in the fall of 1777, Washington had lost the Battle of Brandywine in Pennsylvania while Major General Horatio Gates had won the Battle of Saratoga in New York. Washington had sent Hamilton to Gates in New York in November with an order for Gates to send troops to him in Pennsylvania.

"General Gates had influence and interest elsewhere; he might use it, if he pleased, to discredit the measure there also. On the whole it appeared to me dangerous to insist on sending more troops from hence while General Gates appeared so warmly opposed to it," Hamilton had written Washington about Gates's defiance of Washington's order to send him men. A conspiracy may have also led Gates to stall.

While in New York, Hamilton had also caught wind of a secret coup to replace Washington with Gates as Commander-in-Chief. Though Washington had confronted Gates and those involved in his polite and honorable way and believed that they were now more loyal to him than ever, Hamilton remained worried. He still feared that this monster of a cabal wasn't unmasked but was merely hiding its head.

By February 14, 1778, Martha had not yet arrived. Instead the post brought Washington a different kind of surprise, one that awakened him to a new danger. This correspondence involved Martha, though it was hardly a valentine. Instead, Washington received a handbill published in New York. Circulating among taverns and shops, this flyer featured a letter said to be from Washington to Martha dated June 24, 1776. One line was particularly salacious, especially for the well-mannered Washington and the prim petite Martha.

"How could you imagine that I distrusted either your prudence or your fidelity?" the letter asked. Was this true? Did George Washington doubt his wife's loyalty to him or to the cause?

Another damaging assertion was also implied in the letter: Had the commanding general told Martha that his real devotion was to King George III and not to America?

"You, who know my heart, know that there is not a wish nearer to it than this is... Pity this cannot be accomplished without fixing on me that sad name, Rebel," the typeset letter declared. "I love my king. A soldier, a good man cannot but love him.'

Shortly after Martha's arrival at Valley Forge, Washington showed her the published letter so she could "see what obliging folks there were in the world." His sarcasm was as strong as his sense of honor and candor in this moment.

"It is no easy matter to decide whether the villainy, or artifice of these letters, is greatest," Washington declared.

Then the problem grew worse. Washington learned that this fake letter was not only circulating throughout New York City, where the British military had their headquarters, but it was also published in a newspaper there. Next, he discovered that extracts of this same letter had also been republished in the *Pennsylvania Ledger*. He soon learned that friends in Virginia had also seen it.

Next, Washington was awakened to even more terrible news. There was more than one letter. In fact, like a gunner firing cannon rounds, a New York newspaper editor with the surname of Rivington was publishing a new letter said to be from Washington to members of his family once a week. How long would this go on? Unlike the general public, the British military, and some of his officers, Washington instantly recognized these letters for what they were.

Forgeries. Washington knew these letters were fake.

"Not one word of which did I ever write. The enemy are governed by no principles that ought to actuate honest men—no wonder then that forgery should be amongst their other crimes," Washington fumed privately, though he kept mum publicly. A mysterious passage from the Martha letter provided a clue to the counterfeiter's intention.

"My attention is this moment called off to the discovery, or pretended discovery, of a plot. It is impossible to develop the mystery of it. No doubt it will make a good deal of noise in the country; and there are those who think it useful to have the minds of the people kept constantly on the fret by rumors of this sort. Thus much only I can find out with certainty, that it will be a fine field for a war of lies on both sides."

The war of lies was fought through these letters, a disinformation or propaganda campaign using paper and a printing press as weapons. The real question was this: who wrote these letters? Who was behind this plot of forgery, this "fake news," this new monster? Was this a propaganda tool of the British elite, or was this part of the internal cabal to remove Washington as Commander-in-Chief? Who had the motive, proximity, and skill to make these letters credible? How would Washington respond? Was this the first time that he had faced false reports against his personal character in newspapers? *War of Lies will* answers these and other questions that have lingered for more than 247 years.

While Washington absorbed the shock of these forged letters in February 1778 at Valley Forge and wondered who wrote them, a stranger's letter to him brought a fresh reminder of an old prophecy proclaimed about him when he was twenty-two years-old. This letter from London also revealed that the political awakening to tyranny was taking place on both shores of the Atlantic.

"As the great principles of truth and justice, however, they may for a time be obstructed by tyrants and bad men, yet sacred history teaches us that the Great Ruler of the universe has and will in due time vindicate his own honor by punishing in such a manner those who have abused the power they have been entrusted with . . ." Peter Labilliere wrote Washington from London on November 4, 1777. Even though they were unacquainted, Labilliere explained that patriotism had compelled him to write Washington.

"After a most serious and impartial examination and study of the American cause, and of the proceedings of the Congress, I found myself called upon by the same principles . . . in defense of their just and glorious cause of universal liberty," he explained.

A retired British soldier, Labilliere had been awakened to speak on the issue of civil rights in 1768 after British soldiers had fired into a crowd of protesters in London. The incident had turned Labilliere into a pamphleteer on topics sympathetic with America's cause.

Calling himself "A Christian patriot and citizen of the world," Labilliere was known for his French Protestant beliefs. "In the meantime, our prayers will not be wanting that by wisdom and strength you may become the glorious deliverers from tyranny, oppression, and cruelty."

After Labilliere ended his letter but before he mailed it, he came across a sermon published decades earlier, in 1755, that directly referred to George Washington. Labilliere added a postscript on his letter. "P.S. I am happy in being able to send you a note which I found lately marked at the bottom of a sermon entitled *Religion and Patriotism: The Constituents of a Good Soldier.* [This document] contains a note from a sermon preached in Virginia 1755, in which is a remarkable passage relating to Washington."

Though he didn't fight in the French and Indian War in America with Washington, Labilliere knew of Washington's miraculous battlefield experience that had made him a hero in America and England. A published sermon by Presbyterian minister Samuel Davies had prophesized about George Washington.

Davies had preached a sermon on August 17, 1755, to volunteer soldiers in Hanover County, Virginia. This group was raised after the disastrous Battle of Monongahela on July 9, 1755. A minister associated with the spiritual revival in America known as the Great Awakening, Davies had spoken from 2 Samuel 10:12: "Be of good courage, and let us play the men, for our people and for the cities of our God, and the Lord do that which seemeth to him good."

Labilliere had copied Davies's prophetic footnote in his postscript to Washington: "As a remarkable instance of this I may point out to the public that heroic youth Col. Washington, whom I cannot but hope Providence has hitherto preserved in so signal a manner, for some important service to his country."

How was Washington's life preserved? What had happened to him in 1755 that had led a minister to predict that Washington's life had been saved so he could perform a great service to his nation in the future?

Labilliere's letter brought up one of the most significant episodes of Washington's life. This prophetic word referred to the battle that had planted the seeds of George Washington's own awakening to tyranny and to his God-given purpose in life.

Unbeknownst to Washington, as he contemplated the forged letters at Valley Forge and read Davies's prediction, key events from the French and Indian War had caused him to cross paths, much earlier in life, with the families of the several suspects behind these *War of Lies* letters.

Likewise, the battles he had faced in his youth had also introduced him to propaganda in newspapers, which is especially dangerous during a time of war.

Were the allegations in the news true? Was George Washington not the hero that many thought he was? Or was he the victim of character assassination?

2 JOIN OR DIE

Wanting to expose liars and spreaders of false information, a Boston entrepreneur announced an upstart enterprise, a new form of social media so "that people everywhere may better understand the circumstances of public affairs, both abroad and at home, which may not only direct their thoughts at all times but at some times also to assist their businesses and negotiations."

Why did this businessman seek to publish news? With the diagnostic skills of a physician and the conscience of a clergyman, too often he'd seen the danger of misinformation as it sickened society. He hoped "that something may be done towards the curing, or at least the charming of that spirit of lying, which prevails."

Because "there are many false reports, maliciously made, and spread among us," he pledged to expose the name of anyone who was maliciously spreading a "false report." Doing so was a villainous crime in this man's view.

Promising to publish what he had "reason to believe is true" he assured his audience that he would rely only on the "best fountains of information." If he published anything that turned out to be a significant mistake, he promised to correct it in the next edition.

How long would a correction take? One month. Unless a "glut of occurrences happen, oftener," this social media was to be published monthly. Why would it take thirty days to publish news or issue corrections?

Because the year was 1690. A Boston book printer named Benjamin Harris published the first newspaper in Britain's American colonies on September 25, 1690. Called *Public Occurrences Both Foreign and Domestic,* this newspaper was four pages in length, with the first three pages featuring columns of news. The fourth page was blank so readers could make comments and pass them along to family members or friends, the colonial form of social media.

Public Occurrences Both Foreign and Domestic made good on its promise in 1690 as the first British American newspaper. The publisher understood the universal struggle between discerning fact from fiction. True to his Puritan culture, Harris also promised that "memorable occurrences of Divine Providence may not be neglected or forgotten, as too often are."

This concerned Bostonian shared news affecting his seven thousand neighbors. This news included an epidemic spreading throughout the countryside as well as concerns about crime. He revealed his anti-French bias by chastising the French in Canada for their treatment of prisoners: "whom they used in a manner too barbarous for any *English* to approve."

This aspiring news mogul, however, made a fatal mistake. Because he published tawdry news about the king of France and a daughter-in-law, Boston's Puritan authorities shut down his publication. They would not allow him to publish again unless he received a government license for printing his newspaper. Not wanting the government to control his publication, Harris refused. Hence, the colonies' first newspaper was also Harris's last.

With this truncated start, when did newspaper publishing first become a successful business? Postmaster John Campbell received a license in 1704 from Boston's colonial government to publish a newsletter. After hearing people talk about the happenings in their families and neighborhoods at his post office, he published their stories as the *Boston News-letter*, which became the city's long-standing newspaper. Instead of reserving a blank page for people to make comments, this four-page paper featured three pages of news with advertisements on the fourth page, which turned newspaper publishing into a commodity.

The escalation of conflict with the French and the rise of colonial newspaper publishing came together through a young newsmaker who captured the hearts of colonists and Londoners. When George Washington reported on the nefarious activities of French musketeers out west, this dashing, confident young military hero caused a sensation throughout all of the colonies, that is, until his enemies called him an assassin.

Why did he rise to fame at the age of twenty-two? And which now-famous newspaper publisher helped to elevate young George into a household name?

The invasion on the border had to end. "Mr. Washington, the

ambassador," the *Boston Gazette* began in its report on March 5, 1754, "is returned" from his nine-hundred-mile journey from the western territory of Ohio (now a part of present-day Pennsylvania) to Williamsburg, Virginia. Virginia's Royal Governor Robert Dinwiddie had sent twenty-two-year-old Major George Washington on a diplomatic expedition to discover if Frenchmen were building forts in English territory and violating their treaty. Dinwiddie ordered Washington to deliver cease-and-desist letters to commanders of every French fort.

What had Washington discovered? His mission had confirmed the worst fears of the king of England, King George II.

"It is undoubtedly affirmed for truth, that the French have settled and fixed several forts near the Ohio tract, especially one upon (a) French River," the *Boston Gazette* continued of Washington's discovery. Just as the English sought to expand their colonial territory to the west, so the French also sought to extend their territory to the south from Canada. Their paths crossed in land named after the Iroquois word for great river, O-Y-O, or Ohio.

During this dangerous mission, Washington had come across three French forts at the intersection of three rivers—the Ohio, Allegheny, and Monongahela. The commanders of the first two forts had rejected Dinwiddie's letter. Despite their hostility, Washington had observed their posts' size, the number of men they housed, and their defensive capabilities.

"Mr. Washington was received in a polite genteel manner by the commandant of the fort," the *Boston Gazette* explained of his reception at the last fort. This fort was the largest, boasting five hundred men and twelve cannon. After reading Dinwiddie's letter, the French commander revealed that his orders to build and defend these forts came from France's king. The commandant "added, that he had expected an army to be sent for 12 months past by the English, and that they were prepared for them." The *Boston Gazette* reported this ominous news that France was expecting to go to war against England. The question was this: Were the English ready and willing to go to war, too?

Why did Governor Dinwiddie choose Washington for this important mission? After all, Washington was part of the middle class, known as the mid-gentry, and not the upper class. Though he was at least six feet in stature, if not taller, Washington knew that he wasn't a standout for his education. He didn't have a status-making degree from the College of William and Mary, Virginia's university for those with higher social pedigrees.

Nor did he come from a wealthy family, such as the Randolphs, with connections to royalty. Virginia Attorney General Peyton Randolph and his brother John Randolph could brag that their ancestor, Sir Thomas Randolph, had been an advisor to Queen Elizabeth. Little did Washington know, but one member of the Randolph family would emerge as a suspect in the *War of Lies'* forgeries years later.

The stigma he carried over not having as high a social status as the Randolphs and other families in part stemmed from a childhood tragedy. If his father, Augustine Washington, had not died when George was eleven years old, George might have had the same educational opportunity as his half-brother Lawrence, who was fourteen years older. Like their father, Lawrence had been educated at a respectable school in England before returning to the colonies. Instead, George had to study at home, under the influence of his mother, Mary Ball Washington, who was loving and overbearing at the same time.

Without a formal education and a high social ranking, how did Washington stand out to Dinwiddie? Taking pride in his best assets, he leveraged two important qualifications: his experience as a land surveyor and his good manners.

As a youth, Washington had used a quill pen to copy of all of the social rules in the must-have book for up-and-coming modern-day gentlemen, *110 Rules of Civility and Decent Behavior in Company and Conversation,* which were originally developed by French priests. An English priest, Francis Hawkins, had translated the rules into English in 1640. Beyond practicing good handwriting, duplicating these guidelines deepened Washington's understanding of how to behave in social situations. The first rule provided a foundation for how to treat others: "Every action done in company ought to be with some sign of respect to those that are present."

While in the presence of someone of higher social rank, such as Governor Dinwiddie or Attorney General Randolph, Washington made sure that they spoke to him first and not the other way around. Likewise, he also extended courtesy to those of lesser social rank. Washington's good manners and polite behavior would be his best passport in delivering letters to hostile Frenchmen on the Ohio frontier. If need be, Washington's manners just might save his life.

How did George become a surveyor with six years of experience by age twenty-two? When he was fifteen, he moved in with his brother Lawrence and his wife, Ann Fairfax Washington, at their Potomac River home, called Mount Vernon. Lawrence taught him the precision of hunting, the art of horseback riding, the finesse of fencing, and the joy of dancing. Waking up to the crowing of the rooster and slumbering under the music of crickets at Mount Vernon had given the young George much happiness.

Mount Vernon had also expanded his social network by giving him a chance to know Lawrence's father-in-law, Colonel William Fairfax. Impressed by his manners and work ethic, the colonel asked George to survey his extensive land holdings. At age sixteen, Washington took on the respectable trade of surveying.

For six years, George developed important skills that would prove valuable in the years to come. He learned how to prepare for long journeys, arrange for supplies, and live off the land. With stamina to ride a horse for long periods of time, he also developed and honed the mathematical skills needed to calculate and measure terrain.

While Washington's good manners and surveying skills stood out to Governor Dinwiddie, why would Washington risk his life to find out if the French were building fortifications on England's claims? He had personal, financial, and patriotic reasons for accepting this duty. Lawrence was a shareholder in the Ohio Company of Virginia, the land speculation business that had bought land from the king and had sold it to settlers in the Ohio River territory.

Loyal to King George II, Washington saw the opportunity as a stepping stone to what he most wanted, to follow in his brother's footsteps and receive an officer's commission in the Royal Army. While serving as the military adjutant and training officer for Virginia, Lawrence had received a brevet officer's commission in the regular British army from King George II.

Success in Dinwiddie's mission could bring a commission to Major Washington, who was part of the Virginia militia but not the Royal Army. Despite his lack of social status, George knew he had what it took to be an excellent officer and diplomat.

Washington may not have realized it, but when the *Boston Gazette, Pennsylvania Gazette,* and *London's Gentleman's Magazine* reported on his first Ohio mission, he became a newsmaker and a reporter at the same time.

After returning to Williamsburg on his first mission in early 1754, Washington had given his journal to Governor Dinwiddie, who had needed an opportunity to boost his own sagging popularity. A year earlier in 1753, Dinwiddie had enforced a fee for new land grants in Virginia. Though approved by the Board of War, this tax had incensed the upper class and the House of Burgesses, Virginia's legislative body. They had sent Attorney General Randolph to London to plead with King George II's Privy Council to overturn the tax. Randolph's cousin, Thomas Jefferson, would reflect decades later that Dinwiddie and the crown's overuse of taxing power was done "without the sanctions of any law."

Dinwiddie quickly arranged to print Washington's journal as a pamphlet to widely spread the news of the French fortifications in British territory. This news would also distract from the fallout of the tax.

On May 14, 1754, the *Boston Gazette* published Washington's journal in installments to its six hundred subscribers to relay what had happened on his first Ohio mission. Boasting a motto of "Containing the freshest advices foreign and domestic," the *Boston Gazette,* like other newspapers, could not afford to hire staff reporters. Instead they relied on citizens sending them information. Washington's journal proved to be a goldmine of concerning information to fill newspaper columns.

"And they told me that it was their absolute design to take possession of the Ohio," Washington wrote in his journal. "And by G--, they would do it," he added, quoting the French commander while being careful not to spell out God's name lest he be accused of using the Lord's name in vain. After all, the *110 Rules of Civility* taught gentlemen to only use words of respect when speaking of God.

As other newspapers published his journal, readers throughout the colonies soon discovered Washington's day-by-day account of his mission, which spanned from October 1753 until mid-January of 1754. Not only did he break the news of emerging French fortifications, but he also provided rich details of the roadless Ohio territory, its native tribes, and its natural resources. Washington's journal revealed his good manners as he interacted with the indigenous people and Frenchmen. With each new installment, the colonists from New England to Georgia learned that they were in danger of losing their western territory. At the same time, they became more and more smitten with Washington.

In June 1754, people in England were also introduced to Major Washington in *Gentleman's Magazine*, which had reprinted a part of his journal. English readers discovered Washington's Lancelot-like athleticism, evidenced when he guided a raft on an icy river.

"In this distress, the major put out his setting pole, that , if possible the ice might pass clear of his raft, but the rapidity of the stream drove it with such violence against the pole, that being unwilling to quit it, he was jerked into ten feet of water. He fortunately saved himself by catching hold of one of the raft logs."

Readers on both sides of the Atlantic were developing a fondness—and even an infatuation—for George Washington in his dual role of reporter and newsmaker.

Among those readers in London were two brothers, John and James Rivington, who were about ten years older than Washington. As English as English can be, they ran their deceased father's publishing business at a shop long known by its white signboards of *Rivington* or *Bible and Crown* at St. Paul's Churchyard in London. John and James often advertised their new publications in the *Gentleman's Magazine*.

A month before publishing Washington's journal, *Gentleman's Magazine* featured an advertisement from the Rivington brothers for a publication of sermons by the Archbishop of Oxford. Like other editors, the Rivingtons understood that *Gentleman's Magazine* raised their status as advertisers and elevated the reputations of the men featured in the magazine's news stories about England and America. One of the Rivington brothers would soon become so smitten with America that he would make a life-altering decision and would play a significant role years later in the Revolution's *War of Lies*.

While readers' fingers became stained with ink in 1754 as they read about his exploits, Washington returned to the Ohio territory for a new mission. This journey would lead to an unusual test of his good manners and result in the most sensational news yet about him.

Governor Dinwiddie next sent Washington and other militiamen to support Englishmen who were constructing a new English fort at the Monongahela River. Arriving in mid-April in 1754 with a party of nearly one-hundred-sixty men and supplies, Washington learned the devastating news that the French had already captured this post. Many of the English survivors joined Washington, as the editor of the

Pennsylvania Gazette reported on May 9, 1754.

"Friday last an express arrived here from Major Washington, with advice that Mr. Ward, ensign of Captain Trent's company, was compelled to surrender his small fort in the forks of the Monongahela to the French, on the 17th past (April)," the editor relayed—with one technical error. By this time, Washington had received a promotion to the rank of lieutenant colonel in Virginia's militia. While this promotion was honorable and well-deserved, he still didn't have the regular British army commission that he wanted.

What stood out the most about this article were repetition and a new icon. First, the editor used the word *join* or *joined* three times. "Mr. Ward having but 44 men and no cannon to make a proper defense was obliged to surrender and they had accordingly *joined* Major Washington," the *Pennsylvania Gazette's* editor reported, noting that the French outnumbered the English with a fleet of three-hundred and sixty canoes, a thousand men, and eighteen pieces of artillery.

"The Indian chiefs, however, have dispatched messages to Pennsylvania and Virginia, desiring that the English would not be discouraged, but send out their warriors to *join* them and drive the French out of the country before they fortify, otherwise the trade will be lost, and to their great grief an eternal separation between the Indians and their brethren the English," the *Pennsylvania Gazette's* editor continued.

He purposefully used the word *join* a third time to describe French reinforcements. More than four hundred Frenchmen and six hundred of their native allies had come from a lake "to join them." Then the article switched from facts to opinion, which revealed the writer's purpose.

"The confidence in the French of this undertaking seems well grounded," he wrote. Then he pointed out the lack of cohesion in the colonies. "In the present disunited state of the British colonies and the extreme difficulties of bringing so many different governments and assemblies to agree in any speedy and effectual measures for our common defense and security, while our enemies have the very great distinction of being under one direction with one council and one purse."

The editor reminded his readers that the great distance between England from its colonies allowed the French Canadians to "presume that they may with impunity violate the most solemn treaties subsisting between the two crowns, kill, seize, and imprison our traders, and confiscate their efforts at pleasure (as they have done for several years past) murder and scalp our farmers, with their wives and children, and take easy possession of such parts of British territory as they find most convenient for them."

His conclusion was dire: if the French Canadians were allowed to persist, it "must end in the destruction of the British interest" in America. This news article turned editorial was followed by a second stand-out item, which had long lasting effects: a now-famous image.

Except for the reusable, engraved masthead, rarely did publishers include pictures in their papers. Why? Because it took too much time to whittle an image into a woodcut or etch a sketch for each edition. This crisis, however, was so concerning to the *Gazette's* editor that he'd taken time to carve a picture into a block of wood and set into his frame in between the typeset.

The image was of a snake divided into eight pieces, with the initials of the other colonies on each piece. New England, which represented the northernmost colonies, was the head, while South Carolina was the tail. In between were New York, New Jersey, Pennsylvania, Maryland, Virginia, and North Carolina. This woodcut included a slogan about the current crisis: *Join or Die*. The writer of this article and his supporting visual statement clearly conveyed that the colonists were going to have to join together to fight the French or lose their status as Britain's American colonies.

Who wrote this article and designed the first political visual cartoon ever printed in an American newspaper? Who concluded that this news from Colonel Washington, the suave and heroic newsmaker, was vitally important to everyone in the colonies, not just to those living in the West? Who was the brains behind this radical idea of bringing the colonies together under one government in the name of national security?

The author was the celebrated publisher, Benjamin Franklin. Little did the forty-eight-year-old Franklin realize that not only had he created America's first political cartoon, but he had also elevated the young military diplomat into colonial-style stardom. Franklin had turned George Washington into a media darling, the chivalrous knight fighting for English rights against England's centuries-old nemesis, the French.

Although he showed his patriotism in this join-or-die political statement, Franklin adhered to a higher principle, one tattooed on his heart. Franklin first and foremost was a passionate proponent of freedom of speech and its cousin, freedom of the press. The reason? Censorship had nearly cost him his family.

3 ASSASSINATION

Years earlier, at the age of sixteen, Benjamin and his older brother, James Franklin, had operated a Boston newspaper's printing press. They didn't mind the tedious toil of setting blocks of type by picking capital letters from the press drawer's upper case and choosing the smaller letters from the drawer's lower case. Their noses had gotten used to the fishy, sometimes nutty, smell of linseed oil mixed with soot to create oily ink.

James and Ben's hands were continuously stained by balls of wool, which resembled little handheld mops, called ink beaters. They willingly dipped the beaters into the ink and slathered it onto a rectangular frame holding rows of typeset blocks. They'd gotten used to the smelliest part of the job: cleaning the ink beaters every night with urine. They also eagerly accepted the repetitive motion of pulling the wooden lever as it pressed paper over the inked typeset to create a newspaper sheet. The Franklin brothers didn't mind this labor because James had a greater purpose to accomplish. To these awakened Bostonians, it was time to speak truth to power.

Frustrated at the hypocrisy of the government and clergy, James and a group of talented writers had started an anti-establishment rag called the *New England Courant* in 1721.

Instead of publishing news, and without receiving permission from the government, the *Courant* printed weekly essays on a variety of topics designed to stimulate discussion among Boston residents. Stimulate it did. Those who approved of the *Courant* referred to its writers as the Free Thinkers. Those who disapproved called them the Hell First Club and believed they were guilty of wicked libel.

In July 1722, Benjamin experienced horror when the British government arrested James and put him into jail. This left the teenage Benjamin in charge. What should he do? While his brother languished in a prison cell, Benjamin published one of his finest works on the July 9, 1722 edition of the *New England Courant's* front page. Its key passage resonates even today.

"Without freedom of thought there can be no such thing as wisdom and no such thing as public liberty without freedom of speech," Benjamin boldly wrote, using a false identity as a woman named Silence Dogood to avoid being thrown in jail like his brother. "Whoever would overthrow the liberty of a nation, must begin by subduing freeness of speech, a thing terrible to public traitors."

Meanwhile the government published a resolution against James and the *New England Courant*. "Resolved, that no such weekly paper be hereafter printed or published without the same be first perused and allowed by the Secretary, as has been usual (for other papers)."

When James was released four weeks later, he responded by publishing excerpts from the Magna Carta, the 1215 British document that guaranteed Englishmen political liberties. The conflict between freedom of the press and the British authorities in Boston continued for several months, leading the Massachusetts General Court, which was the House of Representatives, to issue an edict.

Because the "tendency of the said paper to mock religion" and injure His Majesty's government, the House of Representatives censored James. "For the prevention of the like offense for the future, the committee humbly proposes that James Franklin, the printer and publisher thereof, be strictly forbidden by this Court to print or publish the *New England Courant*, or any pamphlet or paper of the like nature except it be first supervised by the Secretary of this Province." In addition to stripping him of freedom of the press and speech by requiring government approval for each newspaper he published, they fined him.

How did James Franklin respond? He got creative. Instead of publishing in his name, he listed Benjamin as the publisher. Proving himself to be an effective writer through his Silence Dogood essays, Benjamin continued to show his writing prowess. As time wore on, it was clear that Benjamin had a more appealing, lighter writing style and a more congenial personality than his brother, both of which traits endeared Ben to readers. Such skill, however, also resulted in jealousy from James.

Eventually Benjamin left his brother's paper and moved to Philadelphia. Believing that "every body's business is no body's business, and the business is done accordingly," Franklin humorously led colonial newspaper publishing into its golden age when he bought the *Pennsylvania Gazette* in 1729. Because Pennsylvania had been founded by Quakers, the colony had welcomed all people, regardless of their religious beliefs, including Jews, Catholics, Anglicans, Baptists and so on. The result was a more tolerant society that gave Franklin what he wanted – freedom of speech and of the press.

From news to literature to science and mathematics, Franklin held a wide view of his world. Knowing that some colonies didn't have newspapers or even a printing press, Franklin also published a magazine and *Poor Richard's Almanac* to reach readers in other colonies, especially those in the South. For years the people loved reading Franklin, and he loved educating and entertaining them.

With George Washington's discoveries of the French incursion into English territory in 1754, Franklin called his friends to action through his *join or die* snake woodcut. The image was tied to an important June meeting in Albany, New York. For months, Franklin had been working to implement a British government edict to bring the colonies together under a common government called the *Albany Plan of Union*. Colonel Washington's news had given him the justification he needed to advocate for a united front against the French. Franklin hoped that his *join or die* message and Washington's journal would motivate these separately-charted colonies to unite under one national government.

The book *110 Rules of Civility* had given Washington a lifelong code for evaluating the truth or falsehood of something. "Be not apt to relate news if you know not the truth thereof," rule 79 instructed. That advice works best when people speak the same language as their opponents. If not, the results can be disastrously false.

As George Washington and his followers discovered in the spring of 1754, sometimes the truth is complicated, especially during the fog of war.

Because he'd been assured that additional recruits from Virginia, South Carolina, and New York were marching to join him, Colonel Washington remained in the Ohio territory in May 1754. Camping in an area called the Great Meadows, the colonel and his men prepared to defend themselves.

As he'd done on his first mission, Washington pragmatically enlisted the help of Half King, an indigenous ally of the English. Half King was a village leader within the Iroquois Confederation, which was a compact among several tribes. The English called him Half King because he could present diplomatic gifts as part of the Iroquois confederation but he lacked the power to make treaties.

Why was Half King an ally of the English? The answer was less about a preference for the English and more about vengeance against the French. Half King carried a grudge against the French for breaking their treaties with his tribe and killing his father. His story showed that native tribes allied themselves with Europeans for different reasons. This war pit tribe against tribe as well as European nations against each other.

"Major (Colonel) Washington had intelligence from our friend the Half King, that a party of French were encamped this side of the fork," the *Boston Post Boy* newspaper reported on July 1, 1754.

For a few days, Washington and Half King led their men in a game of hide and seek with this group of thirty Frenchmen, who seemed to be following them while attempting to conceal their location and intentions. Finally, fearing the French would attack first, Washington marched forty men toward the French camp on May 28, 1754. When the Frenchmen saw his men, they fired and killed one of them. Washington's soldiers returned fire, killing seven or eight Frenchmen. The rest of the French ran for their lives.

"But the Half King" and his native allies lay in an "ambush to cut off [the French's] retreat, fell upon them and soon killed and scalped five of them," the *Boston Post Boy* chronicled. Among the dead was a Frenchman named Sir de Jumonville. The rest of the Frenchmen surrendered and begged the native fighters for quarter. At first Half King refused, wanting to kill all of the Frenchmen.

"Major (Colonel) Washington interposed between them and it was with great difficulty that he prevented" them from "doing any further mischief, the Half King insisting on scalping them all, as it was their way of fighting and he alleged that those people had killed, boiled and eat(en) his father," the *Boston Post Boy* detailed.

Washington found himself in the most awkward social circumstance of his young life. No manners book could prepare him for this situation. What should he do? He employed his best manners and talked to Half King. If he followed the *110 Rules of Civility,* he gave Half King the chance to speak first and showed empathy for the native leader's desire for revenge.

"However, Major (Colonel) Washington at length persuaded him to be happy with the scalps he had already got," the *Boston Post Boy* reported. Sparing the lives of the remaining Frenchmen, Washington sent them back to Virginia as prisoners. His good manners saved his life and theirs.

Londoners learned about the news weeks later when a letter that Washington wrote to his younger brother Jack about the incident appeared in the August 1754 edition of the *London Magazine*.

"I fortunately escaped without a wound, though the right wing where I stood was exposed to and received all the enemy's fire and was the part where the man was killed and the rest wounded," Washington had written to Jack.

Readers of the *London Magazine* also discovered that this young Colonel Washington had a cocky side. "I can with truth assure you, I heard bullets whistle and believe me there was something charming in the sound," he'd penned. This sensational phrase caught the attention of the king of England. "He would not say so, if he had been used to hear many," King George II quipped of Washington's bragging about the charming sound of bullets.

Washington had also made a bold declaration to Jack. "We expect every hour to be attacked by a superior force, but shall, if they stay one day longer, be prepared for them."

Little did he know, but Washington would soon find himself at the center of a breaking news story.

The next standout news suddenly changed Washington's fortunes and his public image as the darling of the press. He was accused of being an assassin.

"The third of this instant July, about 9 o'clock, we received intelligence that the French, having been reinforced with 700 recruits, had left Monongahela, and were in full march with 900 men to attack us," the *New York Mercury* printed of the latest news from Ohio. Captain James Maccay had brought Washington reinforcements from the Carolinas. Their combined force was about two-hundred fifty men. Washington and Maccay issued a joint report, which was printed in multiple newspapers.

After building a crude fortification called Fort Necessity for his men and about eighty of their native allies' families, Washington and Maccay were outnumbered more than three to one. Though they tried to defend themselves, heavy rain dampened their ammunition, making much of it unusable. Despite hours of having the upper hand, the French suddenly called for a parley. The signal puzzled

Washington, who thought it was a ruse or a deceit because the French were winning. The French called for parley again.

What was going on? Had his men killed a French officer? Concluding this was likely the case, Washington sent an officer over to the French side. In a back-and-forth negotiation through a translator, Washington agreed to surrender in exchange for the Frenchmen that he had saved from Half King but had imprisoned five weeks earlier and had sent to Virginia. Had he allowed Half King to kill those men as Half King had wanted, the French might have killed him on the spot. The two sides signed the capitulation terms, which were written in final form in French.

Controversy about his surrender arose a few weeks later when the *New York Mercury* and other newspapers printed a translation of Washington's capitulation terms. "And as the English have now in their power an officer, two cadets and most of the prisoners made in the *assassination* of Sir de Jumonville, that they promise to send them back with a safe guard to the Fort Duquesne," the newspaper reported. Assassination was murder of a prominent person by a sudden or secret attack for political reasons. Assassinating a diplomat, who was presumed to be acting for the cause of peace, was considered a treacherous act contrary to the law of God and against the accepted laws of warfare.

The word *assassination* in this article, however, was fake news at worst, misleading at best. Yes, Half King and his men had killed Jumonville at the battle of Great Meadows. The term implied that Washington had assassinated Jumonville, whom the French claimed was a diplomat. If true, then Washington had violated the rules of warfare.

Washington's reputation was on the line. What should he do? Fully appreciating his dilemma requires understanding the role of the truth and standards for the press in his day. One person who understood this was Ben Franklin, especially after he faced colonial cancel culture.

4 COLONIAL CANCEL CULTURE

"**B**eing frequently censur'd and condemn'd by different persons for printing things which they say ought not to be printed, I have sometimes thought it might be necessary to make a standing apology for myself, and publish it once a year," Ben Franklin had publisshed decades earlier, on June 10, 1731, in the *Pennsylvania Gazette.*

Franklin, who was twenty-five-year-old at the time, had printed an advertisement from a captain seeking passengers for Barbados. At first, the advertisement had seemed as innocent as a carrier pigeon returning home. But the ad had concluded with a line discriminating against transporting the clergy, who need not apply. Worst of all, the announcement had compared preachers to loud birds.

Some readers were so infuriated that they vowed to stop buying the *Pennsylvania Gazette.* How did Franklin respond to their censorship, the colonial form of cancel culture? He published an essay called *Apology for Printers.*

"Men are very angry with me on this occasion," he wrote, showing his fear about losing customers. "That if they were printers they would not have done such a thing on any consideration; that it could proceed from nothing but my abundant malice against religion and the clergy: They therefore declare they will not take any more of my papers, nor have any farther dealings with me; but will hinder me of all the custom they can. All this is very hard!"

Denying him custom meant that they were socially ostracizing him. Despite his anxiety, he took the occasion to present a rational argument. Little did he know that his response would be as relevant in the 21th century as in the 18th century. "I request all who are angry with me on the account of printing things they don't like, calmly to consider these following particulars," Franklin wrote with the skill of the best attorney in town.

"That the opinions of men are almost as various as their faces; an observation general enough to become a common proverb, so many men so many minds." He'd then written a set of ethics that would shape the guardians of freedom of the press in America for centuries.

"That the business of printing has chiefly to do with men's' opinions; most things that are printed tending to promote some, or oppose others," he'd explained, noting that other professions and trades, such as carpenters and shoemakers, sold their products to everyone, people of all persuasions, without risk of offending them or "suffering the least censure or ill-will." When it came to commerce, a person's political opinion shouldn't matter as long as he had enough shillings to pay for the product.

Franklin's colonial common sense could apply to any generation. "That it is as unreasonable in any one man or set of men to expect to be pleas'd with everything that is printed, as to think that nobody ought to be pleas'd but themselves."

"Printers are educated in the belief, that when men differ in opinion, both sides ought equally to have the advantage of being heard by the public," he wrote, believing that truth and evidence would win in the end. "That when truth and error have fair play, the former is always an overmatch for the latter."

"Hence, they cheerfully serve all contending writers that pay them well, without regarding on which side they are of the question in dispute." As a printer and publisher, Franklin was not the arbiter of truth. His printing presses were neutral.

"Being thus continually employ'd in serving all parties, printers naturally acquire a vast unconcernedness as to the right or wrong opinions contain'd in what they print; regarding it only as the matter of their daily labor," he explained, noting that this practice led to publishing controversial ideas that may be hostile to some.

"They print things full of spleen and animosity, with the utmost calmness and indifference, and without the least ill-will to the persons reflected on; who nevertheless unjustly think the printer as much their enemy as the author, and join both together in their resentment."

Franklin's view on freedom of speech and debate set publishing standards for testing and proving truth. "That it is unreasonable to imagine printers approve of everything they print, and to censure them on any particular thing accordingly; since in the way of their business they print such great variety of things opposite and contradictory."

He knew what would happen if publishers printed only items that reflected their opinion.

"It is likewise as unreasonable what some assert, that printers ought not to print anything but what they approve. . . an end would thereby be put to free writing, and the world would afterwards have nothing to read but what happen'd to be the opinions of printers."

Freedom of speech would end and the world would only know one point of view: the view of those controlling publications. "That if all printers were determin'd not to print anything till they were sure it would offend nobody, there would be very little printed."

Franklin was good friends with members of the clergy and didn't intend to offend them by publishing the captain's advertisement. Previously, he had avoided publishing items that would promote vice or immorality or would "do real injury to any person, how much soever I have been solicited, and tempted with offers of great pay."

Remembering his brother's stint in jail for publishing essays that questioned the government, he'd often avoided offending either the church or the state in his essays.

"I consider the variety of humors among men, and despair of pleasing everybody; yet I shall not therefore leave off printing. I shall continue my business. I shall not burn my press and melt my letters."

Soon, another printer in South Carolina published Franklin's essay as a defense for something controversial that he'd printed. Franklin's common-sense approach helped his readers sort fact from fiction, to let truth win the day.

After being accused of being an assassin in 1754, Washington had to channel his inner Franklin and promote the truth in the newspapers without being self-promoting.

Within a couple of weeks, an officer in Washington's regiment came to his public defense by asking newspapers to publish a letter he wrote. Following rule number 50 in the *110 Rules of Civility*, "Be not hasty to believe flying reports to the disparagement of any," this unnamed officer stepped forward to defend Washington.

"As the articles of capitulation and as the English mention in your Philadelphia newspapers, are censored and thereby seem to reflect dishonor on Colonel Washington, who is a brave and worthy gentleman, as well as all the corps then present," the Virginia officer defended Washington in a letter to the *Pennsylvania Gazette*, published on August 22.

Taking issue with the term *assassination*, the officer explained that they had relied on a man named Jacob Van Braam as their translator.

Van Braam had been a lieutenant in the Dutch military and had recently come to the American colonies. He was recruited to join Washington's men.

"We were obliged to take the sense of them from his mouth (Van Braam's words); it rained so hard that he could not give us a written translation of them," the officer wrote, explaining that they had very little candlelight available to read anything in writing and relied on oral communication.

"Every officer there is ready to declare, that there was no such word as assassination mentioned; the terms expressed were, the death of Jumonville. If it had been mentioned, we would by all means have had it altered, as the French during the course of the interview seemed very condescending and desirous to bring it to a conclusion," the officer wrote to combat the intense public scrutiny. Noting that those who were criticizing them didn't understand their dire situation, he specifically defended Washington's predicament as a leader.

"Let any of those brave gentlemen, who fight so many successful campaigns over a bottle (of wine), imagine himself at the head of 300 men, whose lives in a great measure he is answerable for, laboring under all the disadvantages above-mentioned, and environed with four times his number of an active enemy, and would he not be glad to accept of worse terms than Colonel Washington did?" he wrote, claiming the surrender terms were well-conducted and citing that the French were instructed to pay their native friends with "our scalps and spoils."

"They call it an assassination; for my part, I call it a brave little action, and after hearing the whole, I doubt not but you will be in my opinion," the gentleman concluded.

With help from an intermediary, a relieved Washington began a habit of letting others come to his defense in the press. Such was an honorable approach, but would it always work?

Though he didn't defend himself in the newspapers, Washington privately conveyed his opinion about the *assassination* controversy.

"That we were willfully, or ignorantly, deceived by our interpreter in regard to the word *assassination*, I do aver, and will to my dying moment; so will every officer that was present," he privately reflected, writing in an unpublished document that their Dutch interpreter didn't understand enough English to properly catch the tone and meaning of certain words.

"But, whatever his motives were for so doing, certain it is, he called it the *death*, or the *loss*, of the (Mon)sieur Jumonville. So, we received and so we understood it, until, to our great surprise and mortification, we found it otherwise in a literal translation."

Reflecting on the events at Great Meadow, Washington didn't believe that Jumonville was a diplomat or that the motives of his party were honorable.

"And instead of coming as an ambassador, publicly, and in an open manner, they came secretly, and . . . they encamped, and remained hid for whole days together, and that, no more than five miles from us: From thence they sent spies to reconnoiter our camp," Washington had defensively written in his journal. "Besides . . . an ambassador has no need of spies, his character being always sacred."

Washington had conducted himself differently when he'd been an ambassador months earlier on his first mission. He hadn't hidden his presence but had openly approached the French forts when he delivered the cease-and-desist letters for Governor Dinwiddie. He believed that Jumonville and his men had been following them with the goal of attacking or killing them to launch a war.

"And seeing their intention was so good, why did they tarry two days, at five miles distance from us, without acquainting me with the summons, or, at least, with something that related to the embassy?"

Washington had also relied on the judgment of his native allies, who had more experience with the French in this region.

"It was the opinion of the Half King in this case, that their intentions were evil, and that it was a pure pretense; that they never intended to come to us but as enemies; and if we had been such fools as to let them go, they (Half King's men) would never help us any more to take other Frenchmen."

In other words, the French had engaged in propaganda or a disinformation campaign by claiming that Jumonville was a diplomat and accusing Washington of assassination. Washington relied on others to defend him publicly while privately documenting his side of the story. While this misinformation crisis passed, a new one was brewing.

Washington had lost his journal. As part of the capitulation terms, the French had seized everything, including his diary. Little did he know that in the years ahead, his journal would become the source of more deceit and the subject of 18th-century-style fake news.

Newspapers also published the response of government officials to the growing crisis in Ohio. *The New York Mercury* printed a speech by Horatio Sharpe, the royal governor of Maryland, to the general assembly. Sharpe's conclusion was emotional.

"The designs of the French must now be evident to everyone: they have openly, in violation of all treaties, invaded His Majesty's territories, and committed the most violent acts of hostility, by attacking and entirely defeating the Virginian troops under Colonel Washington," Sharpe declared in a call to arms.

While Washington suffered the humiliation of being called an assassin and Sharpe called for war, Benjamin Franklin and representatives from seven colonies met in Albany, New York, to discuss Franklin's plan to unite the colonies under a single central British government.

Franklin proposed a grand council made of representatives from the colonial governments. The British government would appoint a president general. With the power of taxation, the grand council would regulate the relationship between the colonies and native tribes as well as solve disputes between the colonies over territory and other issues. Though the Albany Congress adopted this plan on July 10, 1754, colonial governors and their assemblies rejected it.

The time for a united government for Britain's American colonies had not yet come.

As part of his capitulation to the French in 1754, Washington agreed to stay away from Ohio for one year. He did just that. However, when Washington returned to Ohio a year later, he would also meet, for the first time, two of the suspects in the Revolutionary War's *War of Lies*. And another false report that emerged in 1755 was enough to break his mother's heart.

.

5 WHEN FALSE NEWS IS DEADLY

T he news in July 1755 was false. How did Washington know? The truth was as obvious as the warmth of his breath. He was not dead. He was still alive.

"As I have heard since my arrival at this place, a circumstantial account of my death and dying speech, I take this early opportunity of contradicting the first, and of assuring you that I have not yet composed the latter," Washington urgently wrote from the crude, pathetic post known as Fort Cumberland, Maryland, to his brother Jack on July 18, 1755. Cumberland was named for one of King George II's sons, William Augustus, who was the Duke of Cumberland.

After the worst battle he'd ever witnessed, Colonel Washington had arrived at Fort Cumberland only to see shock on the sunburned faces of the regular British Redcoats when they realized that he was alive. Though they'd concluded that he'd died in the enemy attack near Ohio's Monongahela River, he knew that their intent wasn't malicious. Their assumption was understandable. After all their commander, General Edward Braddock, had also died, as had most of the officers. Sir Peter Halkett, the Scottish baronet and former member of Parliament who led the 44th Regiment was shot dead on the spot. Colonel Washington was the only aid-de-camp to Braddock who wasn't killed or wounded.

After Braddock's injury, Washington had stepped in to issue the general's orders to complete the retreat. As a result, he was one of the last to leave the battle and make the one-hundred twenty-mile journey back to Fort Cumberland.

With his name on the killed-in-action list, Washington feared that the survivors who'd already left Fort Cumberland to travel back to Virginia would deliver the false report of his death to his family. Hence, he speedily wrote separate letters to his mother and brother to assure them that he was alive.

"As I doubt not but you have heard of our defeat, and perhaps have had it represented in a worse light (if possible) than it deserves," he wrote delicately and diplomatically to his mother.

Seeing Washington walk into Fort Cumberland wasn't just shocking to his fellow soldiers. It was also miraculous. How did Washington survive? After all, the repeated fire of muskets in the forest created a cloud of smoke that hovered under the canopy of trees. This prevented the soldiers from being able to see both their fellow soldiers and the enemy, who hid behind the trees with their bellies on the ground and fired.

"But by the all-powerful dispensation of Providence, I have been protected beyond all human probability and expectation for I had four bullets through my coat, and two horses shot under me, and yet although death was leveling my companions on every side of me, escaped unhurt," Washington explained with awe to Jack the mystery of his preservation seemingly at the hands of angels. With so many bullet holes in his coat, he, too, was astonished that he hadn't been injured or killed.

In this near-death experience, Washington showed his sincere respect for God by crediting *Providence* for his survival. In contrast to the modern definition of good luck, in the 1700s, ministers defined *Providence* as God's presence among his people. Likewise, the *110 Rules of Civility* had taught that: "When you speak of God or his attributes, let it be seriously and with reverence." In Washington's world, *Providence* was a respectful way of invoking and celebrating God's divine intervention.

Washington also gave his mother a few details of the battle. "I have taken this earliest opportunity to give you some account of the engagement, as it happened within seven miles of the French fort on Wednesday the 9th Inst (July 9)."

In response to the construction of French forts in the Ohio River valley, King George II and the Duke of Cumberland had sent General Braddock with regiments of regular British soldiers to the colonies. Along with militia from Virginia, this combined English force of regulars and militia left Fort Cumberland in late May 1755 to march to France's Fort Duquesne. The advance parties literally cleared paths and built the roads on their route. Sometimes the hills were so steep and the paths so rough that they had trouble hauling their wagons, which carried supplies, cannon, and the sick. This included Washington for several days.

On their final advance toward Fort Duquesne on July 9, Braddock ordered his men to march with their British flags flying while the band played the Grenadiers' March. Such an ear and eye-catching spectacle was typical of European warfare, but not common among the area's native tribes, who fought from behind trees.

Hearing the rhythmic music and marching and seeing the red and buff uniforms of the English, the nearby French troops and their native allies fanned out in a crescent shape among the trees on both sides of the route and prepared an ambush. Colonel Thomas Gage led Sir Peter Hackett's regiment, the 44th, in the English procession. General Braddock was next with the 48th Regiment. As an aid-de-camp to Braddock, Washington accompanied him. Behind them were the soldiers from Virginia. As the advance regiment approached, the natives fired single shots at particular officers.

"We were attacked by a party of French and Indians, whose number, I am persuaded, did not exceed three hundred men; while ours consisted of about one thousand three hundred well-armed troops, chiefly regular soldiers, who were struck with such a panic that they behaved with more cowardice than it is possible to conceive," Washington angrily revealed to his mother about his brothers-in-arms, the Redcoats.

Gage ordered his men to maintain their rows and return fire, which was a signal to the French and natives to ambush them. Letting out a war cry, they fired at Braddock's soldiers from the forest. They continued to fire at specific officers, especially Washington, who stood out because of his tall height. Though the officers tried to rally the soldiers, the 44th and 48th regiments broke and retreated. The Virginians continued to fight, often taking positions behind trees, for three hours. In the midst of the fire, Washington had successfully moved the mortally-wounded General Braddock to a wagon, which carried him across the knee-deep river.

"I was the only person then left to distribute the general's orders, which I was scarcely able to do, as I was not half recovered from a violent illness, that had confined me to my bed and a wagon for above ten days," Washington wrote, referring to his recent bout with dysentery, an infection of the intestines that causes diarrhea.

During a pause in the action while the enemy scalped some of the wounded, Washington organized some of the fleeing troops into a rear guard. He brought wagons and medical supplies to remove the wounded. While assuring his family of his survival, he also fumed about the regular regiments, who failed to support the Virginia militia and instead fled in a panic.

"In short, the dastardly behavior of those they call regulars exposed all others that were inclined to do their duty to almost certain death; and at last, in despite of all the efforts of the officers to the contrary, they broke, and ran as sheep pursued by dogs; and it was impossible to rally them," he wrote with disdain.

Washington had also experienced snubbing and snobbery against him by the British officers before the battle. Refusing to recognize his rank as a lieutenant colonel, they had tried to place him under the authority of English officers in the regular army of lower rank than Washington's. To avoid being under the command of a junior officer in the British regular army, Washington had kept his self-respect intact by serving as an unpaid volunteer aid-de-camp for Braddock.

Whatever frustrations he may have had before the battle with his fellow officers from England, their behavior and abandonment left a seed of distrust against the British in his heart that only grew stronger with time.

After such a devastating loss, Washington longed not for his stern mother's home but for sturdy Mount Vernon, where his brother Jack lived. "We have been most scandalously beaten by a trifling body of men; but fatigue and want of time will prevent me from giving you any of the details till I have the happiness of seeing you at Mount Vernon; which I now most ardently wish for," he wrote to Jack, hinting that he needed a few days to regain his strength before traveling home. No doubt relief washed over him when he arrived at Mount Vernon on July 26, 1755.

The *Pennsylvania Gazette* published an article about the Battle of Monongahela River and Braddock's death along with the fate of his other two aide-de-camps. "The general had five horses killed under him and at last received a wound through his right arm and into his lungs of which he died the 13th instant; Secretary Shirley was shot through the head; Captain Morris wounded."

Because Washington had intercepted the erroneous military report of his death, the *Pennsylvania Gazette* reported the truth of his status while also praising his valor on July 31. "Mr. Washington had two horses shot under him and his clothes shot through in several places, behaving the whole time with the greatest courage and resolution."

Washington was not alone in his awakening to the cowardice of the British regulars.

The fallout from Braddock's defeat was discussed in London.

Contempt and accusations of corruption poured from the pens of Englishmen reeling from the resounding loss. Many were angry that the regiments had abandoned their duty to the Americans.

A prestigious publication of record published this story in London: "The Virginians who formed the rear still stood unbroken, and continued the engagement on very unequal terms near three hours, but were then compelled to retire." The *Gentleman's Magazine* praised the American fighters while also blaming the British regulars. "The European troops, whose cowardice has thus injured their country and (are) the same that ran away."

Likewise, private letters sent to Dublin, Ireland, from London were published in the *Pennsylvania Gazette* on October 30, 1755. The letters declared that "the regiments on foot commanded by Colonel Dunbar and Sir Peter Halkett being struck with a panic refused to fight, and laid down their arms, by which 62 of their officers, who fought bravely with the Americans, are killed or wounded." The author of this letter faulted the British soldiers. "Had these private men of the above regiment done their duty, victory would have been on our side."

Still others pointed to corruption as a reason for the failure. A report from London printed in the *Boston Evening Post* in December 1755 revealed that the crown rewarded Governor Dinwiddie in Virginia by sending the troops there, rather than where they were more needed. "That our land forces were sent to Virginia instead of Pennsylvania to their inseparable disadvantage, merely to answer the lucrative use of a friend to the ministry, to whose share the remittances would then fall at the rate of two and a half per cent profit."

This report believed that Braddock should have landed his troops in New York or Philadelphia and attacked France's Niagara fort instead. The assertion implied that someone in the British government was paying Governor Dinwiddie a political and financial favor by sending Braddock to Virginia. Though corruption may have played a role, General Braddock and his bosses failed to understand that the Potomac River was too narrow to carry troops by boat from Virginia into Maryland. They under-estimated the difficulty of clearing paths and building roads.

Braddock had been advised to be aware of being surprised and to listen to the Americans, who knew the territory and had allies with certain native tribes. "Your courage is undoubted, but accidents may happen; and they will be forgiven. What you were expected above all to guard against is a surprise and to keep in with the Americans, who will prove your best instructors in the important expedition you are engaged in," an anonymous source revealed his advice to Braddock.

The fallout from Braddock's defeat was a widespread war. "This unfortunate and unexpected change of our affairs will deeply affect every one of his Majesties colonies," the lieutenant governor of Pennsylvania declared in a speech to the general assembly. Benjamin Franklin published this speech alongside the account of Braddock's loss and Washington's miraculous preservation in the *Pennsylvania Gazette*.

Washington's near-death experience gave him a bond with those who'd also survived. Another officer who was wounded was thirty-six-year-old Lt. Colonel Thomas Gage, who led the 44th Regiment. Also shot in the chest was another British regular soldier, Horatio Gates. Both Gage and Gates had what Washington desired, a regular commission. Both men would later influence Washington's life in ways he couldn't possibly imagine in 1755. He had no idea he'd become a commanding officer over Gates and an enemy combatant to Gage.

"Sir Peter Halkett was killed in the field," Washington reported to his mother, Mary Ball Washington, of the aristocrat with a haughty history and questionable loyalty. This was possibly the first member of Parliament that Washington had ever met.

Though Halkett was a prestigious Scottish baronet who had lived in a castle, he had a notorious history—as did his regiment. Led by Colonel John Lee, the 44th Regiment was raised in 1741. When Prince Charles Edward Stuart landed in Scotland in 1745 and claimed the British throne for his father, an armed conflict broke out known as the Jacobite Rebellion. John Lee was conspicuously absent when this conflict erupted. This forced Halkett, a lieutenant at the time, to lead the 44th in Lee's place against the Jacobites at the Battle of Prestonpans in October 1745.

The battle was a swift victory for Stuart. Halkett and fifteen of his soldiers surrendered. The Jacobites freed them. In exchange, Halkett and the 44th Regiment did not participate in the British government's remaining battles with the Jacobites. Suspecting Halkett of treason, King George II and his son, the Duke of Cumberland, fired Halkett. Though the king later rehired him, he and others viewed him and his regiment with cowardice and incompetence.

Colonel John Lee was under similar suspicion for a time, though he was later promoted to a general. His son Charles Lee joined his father's old regiment under Halkett's leadership. General John Lee died before the conflict in Ohio broke out.

When the Duke of Cumberland chose the 44th Regiment to serve under Braddock, Captain Charles Lee was enjoying the spa resort town of Bath, England. "I fancy you have heard that our regiment is order'd to Virginia," he wrote to his sister, cancelling his visit to see her. He wrote his will and traveled to Cork, Ireland, where the 44th led by Halkett departed for Alexandria, Virginia.

In Washington's view, Charles Lee was one of "the sheep pursued by dogs" when he fled the battlefield with the 44th in Ohio. He was likely at Fort Cumberland when Washington arrived after Braddock's defeat. From the start of their relationship, the two were destined to be rivals.

News of Washington's miraculous preservation soon caught the attention of many colonists. Some wondered publicly if Washington's life had been preserved for a special task. His survival inspired many Virginians to sign up to fight, including Captain Overton's Independent Company of Volunteers in Hanover County, Virginia. They gathered on August 17, 1755, to hear from a minister who'd been part of the spiritual revival that had swept the colonies in the 1740s called the Great Awakening.

The Reverend Samuel Davies was a Presbyterian minister who'd recently traveled throughout England and Scotland to raise money to train ministers at a new college in New Jersey, which was later called Princeton. He'd returned to his ministry in Hanover County, Virginia, at the same time that Braddock had landed in Alexandria with this troops.

Davies spoke to Overton's company and pointed out the heroism of Colonel Washington, whom Providence had preserved for important service to his country. During this era, publishing sermons was common but ministers only published the sermons they considered to be their best. Fond of this one, Davies published this sermon with the footnote about Washington's miraculous survival and distributed it throughout the colonies and England in 1755. This sermon, along with newspaper articles, spread Washington's name and fame on both sides of the Atlantic Ocean. Washington's near-death experience elevated him to hero's status and erased any doubts the alleged assassination story may have created. Washington was more than a newsmaker. He was a media darling and a well-deserved war hero.

Within three months of returning to the comforts of Mount Vernon, Washington received urgent news that required him to leave again. "By an express just arrived (in Williamsburg) from Fort Cumberland," the *Pennsylvania Gazette* informed the public on October 30, 1755, that the enemy had "lately appeared in that neighborhood, and have killed and captured upwards of 20 families."

Governor Dinwiddie convinced Virginia's House of Burgesses to fund money for raising recruits to go to Ohio to fight. The House of Burgesses also gave Colonel Washington a new mission. The *Pennsylvania Gazette* reported that Washington would "take upon him the command of such of the recruits already raised, in order to go in pursuit of them [the French]."

Defeating the French now required Washington to mount his horse and ride to several places to recruit regiments of soldiers. For the first time, people in other colonies had the chance to meet their hero. His arrivals in Philadelphia, New York, and Boston were so significant that each made the newspapers in the winter of 1756.

The *Pennsylvania Gazette* reported on February 12: "Last week Colonel Washington arrived here from Virginia." A few days later on February 16, the *New York Mercury* reported that upwards of one hundred recruits had arrived along with Washington: "Last night Colonel Washington arrived here (New York) from Philadelphia."

"Colonel Washington, of and from Virginia . . . left this city (New York) for Boston on Friday last, there, 'tis thought to consult with General Shirley, measures proper to be taken with several tribes . . . particularly the Cherokees, some hundreds of whom, from the back parts of the two Carolinas, it is reported, have assured the Western governments of their coming in, and firmly adhering to the Indians of the English in opposition to the French."

Washington also lobbied Governor Shirley for a commission in the Royal Army. Though he didn't give Washington this honor, Shirley issued an order that officers in the Virginia militia would outrank officers of lower rank in the British army.

Recruiting wasn't easy. "You may, with almost equal success, attempt to raise the dead to life again, as the force of this country,"

Washington wrote sarcastically to his brother Jack about the challenges of convincing men to fight. Little did he know at the time, but by dutifully recruiting men from New York, Pennsylvania, and Massachusetts, he developed knowledge of these colonies and a kinship with the men he recruited. Such ties of brotherhood were strengthened over time.

Parliament officially declared war in May of 1756. In North America, the conflict was called the French and Indian War, while in Europe it was called the Seven Years' War. More Virginians rallied to Washington's heroism. The prominent Randolph family stepped forward. Though he'd failed to convince the king's Privy Council to repeal the tax issued by Dinwiddie, Virginia Attorney General Peyton Randolph had returned from London to Williamsburg. There he raised three hundred reservists called the associators.

"Some public spirited gentlemen have done me the honor to fix upon me as their leader, till we can come to the place where you command; when we shall be very glad to follow such orders, as you shall think most conducive to the public good," Peyton Randolph wrote to Washington on May 3, 1756. Not every member of the Randolph family would prove as loyal to Washington in the decades to come. One would become a named suspect in the Revolution's *War of Lies*.

Within a year of his recruiting efforts, Washington came face to face with false news that once again threatened his public image. As he soon discovered, the most convincing misleading news is a report that mixes truth with fiction, leaving people confused about what to believe.

The terms of his surrender after the Battle of Fort Necessity in 1754 had forced Washington to turn his journal over to the French. Three years later in 1757, the French commander of Fort Duquesne published Washington's journal in French. When Washington saw the English translation of the French version of his English journal, he instantly recognized that part of it was a forgery. At least some of the diary entries published under his name were fabricated.

Washington was traveling when he received a request from historian William Smith of Philadelphia to respond to the French publication of his journal. "In regard to the journal . . . rough minutes of occurrences I certainly took, and find them as certainly and strangely metamorphosed," Washington defended.

He made general observations about this translation of his journal, writing that "some parts (were) left out, which I remember were entered, and many things added that never were thought of; the names of men and things egregiously miscalled; and the whole of what I saw Englished is very incorrect and nonsensical."

Unlike the false report of his death at Fort Cumberland, this was maliciously fake, a forgery. Up until this point in Washington's life, false news was largely the result of inaccurate information. The delay of weeks before news from the frontier could arrive in places such as Philadelphia led to simple mistakes, such as calling Washington a major when he'd been promoted to a colonel. His commitment to linger at the Battle of Monongahela to care for the wounded and dead resulted in the Redcoats' erroneous assumption that he'd died.

In contrast, by publishing his journal and removing or adding passages in 1757, the French committed a malicious act, a form of war propaganda. This was a direct attempt to tarnish an English hero's chivalrous, shining public image. Great Britain's enemy was deliberately falsifying Washington's words.

Did Washington tell the public that his journal was a forgery? No. In this letter, he didn't have time to go into great detail or "point out such errors as might conduce to your use, my advantage, and the public satisfaction; but now it is out of my power."

This was one of several occasions where Washington chose not to directly and publicly refute false information about him in the newspapers. Without time to let it bother him, Washington put his faith in his fellow English subjects. Relying on his character and reputation, he believed that they would see the publication for what he believed it was: rubbish from their enemy. He seemed to be putting his faith in civility rule "50: "Be not hasty to believe flying reports to the disparagement of any." What mattered most to him was the big picture. He had a war to win for his country and king.

Deciding to reorganize their forces in America in 1758, the British military gave the command to General John Forbes. Colonel Washington and his Virginia regiment served under Forbes along with Colonel William Byrd's regiment. Forbes planned and organized the effort that culminated in an expedition to Fort Duquesne in 1758. Once again, the newspapers chronicled Colonel Washington's role in these events.

"Since our last we have had several imperfect accounts of a skirmish between a party of our army, and another of the French, near Loyal Hanna, from which the best account we can at present give is as follows," the *Pennsylvania Gazette* reported on November 30, 1758. Loyal Hanna was roughly forty miles east of Fort Duquesne. "That on the 12th instant, Colonel Washington being out with a scouting party, fell in with a number of the enemy, about three miles from our camp, who he attacked, killed one, (and) took three prisoners."

One piece of good news that came out of this incident was that one of the prisoners, Mr. Johnson of Pennsylvania, knew a lot about the French at Fort Duquesne. If enough pressure was put on him, he just might tell them everything. Best of all, they didn't need a translator. Johnson spoke English.

Warning him not to give "false intelligence," an interrogator said that he'd "forfeited his life by being found in arms against his king and country; the only way left to save it, and make atonement, was, to give as full information of the condition of Ft. Duquesne and of the enemy as he could; which being found to be true, his life should be spared."

Johnson complied, revealing that many of the French Canadians and their native allies had left Fort Duquesne. "The French were very scarce of provisions as well as weak in men." The sight of nearby horse carcasses was a sign that the French were short on food and had resorted to eating horses. "Whole skins and bones were afterwards found by some of our men." Convinced that Johnson was telling the truth, Forbes, Washington, and Byrd led their combined force of six thousand men to seize Fort Duquesne. Building a road, in late November of 1758, Washington's forces led the advance and approached the fort, which the French abandoned and burned. This allowed the British to easily make it their own.

"Pittsburgh, formerly Fort Duquesne," the letter published by the *New York Mercury* began. "I have the pleasure to write this letter upon the spot where Fort Duquesne once stood, while the British flag flies over the debris of its bastions in triumph," an unnamed member of the British forces wrote.

These victorious Englishmen renamed the fort to Pittsburgh after William Pitt, the leader of the House of Commons. This spot on the banks of the Ohio River was "the finest and most fertile country of America." With the French retreating, the war had turned in Britain's favor, at least in North America. The war would continue in Europe until 1763.

The victory was bittersweet for Washington. After all that he had sacrificed by risking his life numerous times in Ohio, the British military still withheld the one honor he felt he most deserved: a commission in the regular Royal Army.

Washington resigned his commission in the Virginia militia at the end of 1758. Recently elected to the House of Burgesses, he married Martha Custis, a wealthy widow with two children, on January 6, 1759. Together they lived at Mount Vernon, which he'd inherited from his brother Lawrence, who'd died in 1752. Washington took on a new occupation as a farmer. By this time, his life in one way or another had intersected with key people—Thomas Gage, Horatio Gates, Charles Lee and members of the Randolph and Rivington families—who later opposed him in various ways during the American Revolution. One or more of them would play a part in the theatrics of the *War of Lies*.

Except for occasional mentions in the newspaper as a member of the House of Burgesses or in advertisements he placed to sell real estate, Washington never envisioned that he'd ever play the role of newsmaker again, much less newsmaker-in-chief. How wrong he was. Five years before the American Revolution began, one chief with the insight of a prophet made an astonishing prediction.

6 FINAL AWAKENINGS

In October 1770, Colonel Washington returned to the Ohio River territory to survey land with Dr. James Craik and a group of men on a nine-week mission. They traveled through the mountainous frontier and settled for a time on the bank of a river at abandoned wigwams. They made this their base camp as they fished, hunted, and explored the region. As if the wind could speak, soon others learned of their presence.

One day, a trader and a group from the Kanawha tribe halted a short distance from the camp. Sent by the Kanawha to speak with Washington's group, the trader served as an interpreter and explained that he was assisting warriors led by a grand sachem who had learned of Washington's return to the area.

"The chief was a very great man among the northwestern tribes, and the same who commanded the Indians on the fall of Braddock . . . That hearing of the visit of Colonel Washington to the western country, this chief had set out on a mission, the object of which himself would make known."

When the chief arrived in camp, the men immediately noticed his lofty, dignified and imposing stature. Though he wasn't Elijah or Isaiah, he had the bearing of a prophet. Within a few minutes, the sachem "pointed out the hero of the Monongahela, from among the group, although (fifteen) years had elapsed since he had seen him, and then only in the tumult and fury of battle."

While the men greeted each other, the chief treated Washington with unusual reverence. Washington placed the chief at his side for a meal or feast together, but the sachem refused to eat. This both amazed and worried Washington's men. Finally, when they gathered around a council fire, the grand sachem addressed Washington with words along these lines.

"I am a chief and the ruler over many tribes. My influence extends to the waters of the great lakes and to the far blue mountains. I have travelled a long and weary path that I might see the young warrior of the great battle."

The seasoned chief recalled July 9, 1755, when British blood mixed with the streams of their forests and he observed Washington among the officers of General Braddock's army.

"I called to my young men and said, mark yon tall and daring warrior? He is not of the redcoat tribe — lie hath an Indian's wisdom, and his warriors fight as we do — himself is alone exposed."

The sachem recalled the decision he made in that moment. "Quick, let your aim be certain, and he dies. Our rifles were leveled, rifles which, but for him, knew not how to miss — 'was all in vain, a power mightier far than we, shielded him from harm.'"

Like Samuel anointing King David, the sachem made an astounding prediction. "He cannot die in battle. I am old, and soon shall be gathered to the great council fire of my fathers, in the land of shades, but ere I go, there is something, bids me speak, in the voice of prophecy."

"Listen! The Great Spirit protects that man, and guides his destinies — he will become the chief of nations, and a people yet unborn, will hail him as the founder of a mighty empire," the sachem concluded of his prophetic oracle.

The moment made a deep impression on the men who'd accompanied Washington on that journey, especially on Dr. James Craik, who embraced the sachem's prophecy.

"Yes, I do believe, a Great Spirit protects that man — and that one day or other, honored and beloved, he will be the chief of our nation, as he is now our general, our father, and our friend. Never mind the enemy, they cannot kill him, and while he lives, our cause will never die," Craik declared years later during the Revolutionary War.

★ ★ ★ ★ ★

While the *join or die* image maker didn't receive a prophetic oracle like Washington, Ben Franklin nonetheless experienced a final seminal jolt in 1774 that awakened him from his cognitive dissonance and turned him fully into a patriot. He found himself in the role of making news instead of publishing news when he endured a personal attack by the elite who had previously welcomed him as a luminary.

Franklin had moved to England in 1757 as a representative of Pennsylvania to help settle disputes about the colony's charter. He also became postmaster for Britain's North American colonies. Among the happiest years of his life, his time in London had allowed him to build a network of scientists and engineers who planned, plotted, and designed new technologies to build canals and other improvements.

Franklin had also attended King George III's coronation in 1760 only to watch the new king's policies tickle and then torture his American colonies over time into a state of awakening against tyranny. In 1768, Franklin had dined with two Englishmen whom he called "friends of America." Both men would later rival George Washington and become suspects in the Revolution's *War of Lies* against him.

On Christmas Day 1773, Franklin found himself in the role of newsmaker, and not in a good way. Because his actions had led to an inconclusive duel between two other men, he needed to stand up, tell the truth, and clear the air before one of them killed the other.

"Finding that two gentlemen have been unfortunately engaged in a duel, about a transaction and its circumstances of which both of them are totally ignorant and innocent, I think it incumbent on me to declare (for the prevention of farther mischief, as far as such a declaration may contribute to prevent it) that I alone am the person who obtained and transmitted to Boston the letters in question."

The controversy had arisen in Massachusetts, which had become a hotbed of protest against King George III over the years. Wanting to refill his empty coffers because of the wars of the 1750s, the new king had tried many ways to bring in revenue.

The colonists were accustomed to transitory duties that covered the costs of transporting goods from England to their respective colonies, but they were not accustomed to paying any kind of additional tax on imports or exports that went directly into the king's coffers. They had funded their own towns and colonial legislatures through property taxes, which is why landowners voted and other groups did not vote.

Hence, when King George had tried taxing his American colonists in various ways, such as by taxing sugar and other imported goods or by requiring taxes on almost all paper transactions through the Stamp Act, the American colonists pushed back. Their protests ranged from peacefully signing petitions to hanging effigies representing tax collectors.

Though George Washington had protested by supporting resolutions in Virginia's House of Burgesses against the British government, Franklin's childhood hometown of Boston had endured much abuse from British authorities.

The Boston Massacre had taken place in 1770, when British

Redcoats fired upon a mob and killed five colonists. The conflict had escalated from there, becoming a tug of war between the Royal Governor Thomas Hutchinson in Boston and the Massachusetts General Court, the colony's legislative body. Tension with Hutchinson came to a head in June 1773, when Samuel Adams, the Boston Gazette's publisher, printed excerpts of a letter from Hutchinson proving that he wanted to rein in Bostonians' liberties rather than uphold them.

"There must be an abridgement of English liberties, you wish to see further restraint of liberty in the colony," Hutchinson had written in a 1769 letter to another official, which Adams had published in the Boston Gazette on June 28, 1773. How had Adams acquired these letters? That was the question on the minds of Parliament for weeks.

Someone assumed that Hutchinson's letters had been stolen from the estate of a recently-deceased correspondent of Hutchinson. The conflict had escalated, leading to a duel between two men associated with the deceased man who had written Hutchinson. These men accused each other of possessing Hutchinson's 1769 letters and revealing them to colonists such as Samuel Adams.

When Benjamin Franklin, who'd been living in England off and on since 1757, learned of the duel over Hutchinson's letters, he felt obliged to confess enough to stop further violence. Franklin knew that neither of the gentlemen could have communicated the letters to Samuel Adams for publication in his newspaper because neither one of them had ever possessed the letters.

"Mr. W. could not communicate them, because they were never in his possession; and, for the same reason, they could not be taken from him by Mr. T. They were not of the nature of private letters between friends. They were written by public officers to persons in public station, on public affairs, and intended to procure public measures. They were therefore handed to other public persons who might be influenced by them to produce those measures," he wrote, declaring that the letters concerned public affairs and implying that he had seen them through his role as postmaster.

As the public agent for Massachusetts to Parliament, Franklin believed that the leaders in Boston needed to know Hutchinson's true position. Franklin knew that Governor Hutchinson was saying one thing in public and something else in private. Though Franklin didn't ask Samuel Adams or others to publish Hutchinson's letters, he sent them to Adams so Boston's local leaders could read them and respond.

"Their tendency (Hutchinson's letters) was to incense the Mother

Country against her colonies, and, by the steps recommended, to widen the breach, which they effected."

The conflict soon grew much worse. Reacting to Parliament's new tax on tea, a disguised mob dumped three-hundred forty-two chests of tea into Boston Harbor on December 16, 1773. When news of the Boston Tea Party reached England on January 20, 1774, the king and Parliament were outraged. Even though Franklin was in England during the tea party, British leaders smeared him, blaming him for the mob's actions in Boston.

Members of the King's Privy Council, which is the king's private council that includes cabinet and Parliament members, ordered Franklin to an unofficial hearing in January 1774. What was Franklin to do?

Accompanied by two attorneys and wearing a formal velvet suit, Franklin arrived at London's Cockpit Tavern on January 29, 1774. Here he received an epic English tongue lashing. Franklin endured the most humiliating experience of his life, what might be considered in modern times to be a "communist struggle session."

Thirty-five members of the Privy Council attended, including the Prime Minister, Lord Frederick North, and Lord Sandwich John Montagu, who would soon oversee the British Navy. Members of the public crowded into the packed Cockpit Tavern to watch this oral wrestling match.

Solicitor General Alexander Wedderburn rose and spoke against Franklin on behalf of Royal Governor Thomas Hutchinson for more than an hour. He accused Franklin of many things, including trying to "fix a stigma on the Governor (Hutchinson)."

Wedderburn's diatribe accused Franklin of being dishonest and losing his reputation as a man of truth. "He has forfeited all the respect of societies and of men. Into what companies will he hereafter go with an unembarrassed face or the honest intrepidity of virtue?"

Wedderburn accused Franklin of theft. "Nothing then will acquit Dr. Franklin of the charge of obtaining them [the letters] by fraudulent or corrupt means, for the most malignant of purposes; unless he stole them from the person who stole them." Worse, Wedderburn accused Franklin of being a spy.

"My Lords, Dr. Franklin's mind may have been so possessed with the idea of a Great American Republic, that he may easily slide into the language of the minister of a foreign independent state. A foreign ambassador when residing here, just before the breaking out of a war, or upon particular occasions, may bribe a villain to steal or betray any state papers; he is under the command of another state, and is not amenable to the laws of the country where he resides."

How did Franklin respond to these and other harangues? He was silent. This longtime man of letters and renowned literary great sat stock still. All he could do was absorb the multiple blows. Franklin left the Cockpit Tavern a different man. Gone was the Englishman, the scientist devoted to his king. Replacing him was an independent American. Franklin became a fully-devoted patriot that day. Leaving England, he returned to America. He soon took his seat at the Continental Congress, where he would meet George Washington, the man who'd inspired his *Join or Die* political icon.

George Washington was also seeing the bitter effect the tea tax was having on those around him. But unlike others, Washington was fully awake to the British tyranny by 1774. Starting with the nightmarish jolt of his fellow English soldiers abandoning him on the battlefield in 1755 followed by pricks of the needling policies of King George III, Washington had been ahead of others. He saw the conflict with a sober eye before many of his friends and family.

"That I differ very widely from you, in respect to the mode of obtaining a repeal of the acts so much, and so justly complained of, I shall not hesitate to acknowledge," Washington wrote to a friend, Bryan Fairfax, about the tea tax.

While Fairfax still had faith in the intentions of the king and his Privy Council, Washington was dubious. The haughty behavior of many of the British officers and soldiers toward him and his fellow Virginians in the 1750s had planted a seed of doubt that had only grown over the years, especially after King George III took the throne in 1760. The words of British authority figures, including the king and members of Parliament, were often pretentious. Their narratives said one thing but their actions often contradicted their words. Their behavior betrayed their true intentions. By 1774, Washington was fully awake to the tyranny facing the colonists.

"But as I see nothing on the one hand, to induce a belief that the Parliament would embrace a favorable opportunity of repealing acts which they go on with great rapidity to pass, in order to enforce their tyrannical system," he continued. He believed "that government is pursuing a regular plan at the expense of law and justice, to overthrow our (English) Constitutional rights and liberties."

He didn't expect any redress based on how the king and Parliament had responded on other similar conflicts. The pattern was clear. The British crown responded to each new conflict with increased authoritarianism. They were determined to govern as totalitarians and oppress liberty. This conflict wasn't about tea. It wasn't about taxes. It was about human rights, the colonists's ability to govern themselves.

"For, Sir, what is it we are contending against? Is it against paying the duty of 3d. pr lb. on tea because (it is) burthensome? No, it is the right only, we have all along disputed, and to this end we have already petitioned his Majesty in as humble, and dutiful a manner as subjects could do; nay more, we applied to the House of Lords, and House of Commons in their different legislative capacities setting forth that, as Englishmen, we could not be deprived of this essential, and valuable part of our Constitution."

Washington used his pen to prod his friend to awaken to the true nature of tyranny. When the time was right, he would stand and serve in any way he could.

Little did either George Washington or Ben Franklin know, but Lord Sandwich would soon launch a double-decker propaganda campaign against the colonies. Washington became a prime target in this information war, but who were the suspects that fired words at him?

Part Two

General Washington, Fake News, & the Revolution

"Be not apt to relate news if you know not the truth thereof."

#79 of 110 Rules of Civility and Good Behavior,
Francis Hawkins, 1640

7 SUSPECTS

As George Washington managed the burdens of an ill clad, hungry army in need of training at their encampment at Valley Forge, Pennsylvania, in the winter of 1778, one name frequently surfaced in his mind, especially when the subject of France came up: that of Benjamin Franklin.

By this time, Benjamin Franklin was the Continental Congress's top diplomat to France. His mission was to turn the French King into an ally of the United States. Official French recognition—along with French money, men, and supplies—would reverse the fortunes of war in America's favor. While he waited and wooed the king like a patient suitor, Franklin succeeded in other areas.

Relying on his celebrity as a scientist to receive introductions to key French figures, he used his beaver cap to attract their attention and dished out funny quips to keep it. Franklin used private French sources to acquire resources to aid the Continental Army in multiple ways, including hiring a drill instructor.

"I yesterday received the honor of yours from Portsmouth (New Hampshire) enclosing the copy of a letter from Franklin and Dean," General Washington had written in December 1777 to the Baron Von Steuben, a Prussian military officer recommended by Franklin for his military experience and zeal for the American cause. Washington hoped that Von Steuben would come to Valley Forge and train his men to hurl stones with the precision of David at the English Goliath.

Once he had settled in at the two-story stone house at Valley Forge in January 1778, the Commander-in-Chief had also told Congress that the mode of providing clothing to the troops was so inadequate that "it will be next to impossible to keep an army in the field" unless future efforts are more effective. At least a third of his men lacked shoes and many didn't have coats and blankets. Although Congress had requested that the states provide these necessities to their men, Washington doubted that enough of the states had the manufacturing capability to keep up with the demand. Before the war, colonists had relied on England to supply them with cloth. Now they had to rely on their own sheep to harvest enough wool to make cloth for coats. They lacked thread to sew proper durable uniforms.

"For my own part, (with all deference I speak it) I have little conception, that our extensive wants can be completely satisfied, in any other way, than by national, or governmental contracts, between Congress and the Court of France."

Clearly, Washington had many weighty issues to contemplate at Valley Forge. After all, General Horatio Gates's recent victory at Saratoga had led to an attempted coup to oust him as Commander-in-Chief. Holding a long strategic view of winning independence, Washington knew that ultimate victory wasn't solely about battlefield glory but it was also about preserving the troops' good health through provisions of clothing, blankets, and food and preserving their training through the military discipline that Von Steuben could offer.

Also troubling Washington at Valley Forge were the pesky forged letters that deserved to be called the *War of Lies*. Would revelations about the published forgeries at the valley cause a volcanic-like eruption from Washington, one heard from New England to Georgia? Or would he keep his feelings private?

"I have seen a letter published in a hand-bill at New York, and extracts of it republished in the Philadelphia paper, said to be from me to Mrs. Washington," Washington hotly but privately conveyed in a letter to his friend, Richard Henry Lee, on February 15, 1778. Washington let out some steam while writing one of dozens of letters on military business that week.

The circulating handbill was not the only problem. The *Pennsylvania Ledger*, a Tory newspaper, had also published the same "letter to Martha" in Philadelphia on Christmas Eve, December 24, 1777. Readers in both Philadelphia and New York discovered many eyebrow-raising, tantalizing sentiments. The most shocking statement suggested Martha believed that Washington doubted her prudence and fidelity to him and the cause. "I have the highest opinion of them both," the forged letter assured.

After salaciously declaring that the conflict between England and America would be a war of lies with plots surrounding him, the counterfeit Washington added, "But why should I tease you with tedious details of schemes and views which are perpetually varying?"

Then the news grew worse on February 14, 1778, when New York's *Royal Gazette* published a new letter said to be from George Washington to Lund Washington, his cousin overseeing Mount Vernon in his absence. Painting Washington as being very close to his cousin, this letter suggested that Washington had told Lund his private thoughts, such as: "For I will not conceal it from you, that, at this moment, I feel myself a very coward."

This letter damaged Washington by suggesting that he was a hypocrite.

"There cannot, in the nature of things, be a situation so truly irksome to an ingenuous mind, as the being perpetually obliged to act a part foreign to our true feelings; yet this, alas! As you know, is, and must be, my lot."

Instead of an honorable man, was Washington a glory seeker, more afraid of hanging as a traitor than anything else? Were his real sentiments about glory and not his duty to his new country? After all, the counterfeit letters declared: "I am not afraid to die, why should I? I am afraid only to die with infamy and disgrace."

Did America's Commander-in-Chief truly doubt they would be victorious? "But we have overshot our mark. We have grasped at things beyond our reach. It is impossible we should succeed, and I cannot with truth, say that I am sorry for it, because I am far from being sure that we deserve to succeed."

The newspaper editor in New York continued to publish one new counterfeit letter a week from Washington to Lund or from Washington to his stepson, Jackie Custis.

What would Washington do about these letters? Would he angrily and publicly refute them or would he let his reputation be his shield? After all, he'd relied upon this tactic when the French military had published his journal and accused him of assassination two decades earlier. For now, he would stay silent and trust the public to follow civility rule 79: "Be not apt to relate news if you know not the truth thereof."

If Washington didn't write the letters being published in the *Royal Gazette*, then who did? Four suspects deserve particular scrutiny in this history mystery.

★ ★ ★ ★ ★

The most obvious person who had both the motive and talent to write these letters was the ambitious, pretentious, and clever James

Rivington, the publisher of the *Royal Gazette*. Eight years older than Washington, Rivington had developed his writing and printing skills early in his life. When his father Charles Rivington died, James was only twenty years old. He and his older brother John ran the family printing business until 1756, when James left the business and went into a partnership with another London printer for four years.

Then James Rivington ventured to New York in 1760, the same year that King George III ascended to the British throne. Opening a bookshop in Hanover Square in New York, Rivington sold books, paper, ink, and stationary parchment. He also ran a printing press. Finally, he decided to expand his business in an ambitious, public way.

Rivington took out an advertisement in the *Boston Gazette* on March 22, 1773, to announce his new business. "Honored with encouragement from the finest personages in this country," he promised to publish news and information of interest every week in a new newspaper called *Rivington's New York Gazetteer*. He planned to publish Parliament's speeches, book reviews, natural science essays, and important events both foreign and domestic. "In short, every improvement that may contribute to the improvement, information, and entertainment of the public shall be constantly conveyed through the *New York Gazetteer*."

Rivington named his newspaper the *New York Gazetteer*, partially after the Italian coin, *gazetta*, which was the cost of the first European newspaper published in Venice in 1531. London printers began publishing gazettes in 1588. Etymologically, a gazette or gazetteer was a very European name for a newspaper. Gazettes were also an intellectual upgrade to the publicly posted one-sheet broadsides that had published sensational news and gossip for centuries. Before printing presses, the public relied on orators to gather in the town square to deliver the news. Now they eagerly stained their fingers on newspapers to keep up with both foreign and domestic occurrences. This created a culture of readers and learners.

Promising that "integrity and candor" would govern his conduct and that he would have an "open and uninfluenced" press, Rivington was among three dozen weekly newspaper publishers operating presses in the colonies prior to the revolution. By 1774, Rivington boasted three thousand subscribers throughout the colonies. Could he replace Ben Franklin in terms of publishing prowess and prominence? So Rivington hoped.

This entrepreneur faced a major obstacle. He'd started his business during a time of political escalation. Tensions between the colonists and King George III had been brewing for years over the issues of taxation, corruption, and other matters. To pay for the Seven Years' War that had left England in great debt, King George III had attempted to tax the colonists through numerous acts of Parliament.

One of the most oppressive decisions came after Bostonians dumped chests of tea into Boston Harbor in December 1773 to protest the tea tax. While reporting on Ben Franklin's inquisition-like before the Privy Council in January 1774 that took place in the wake of the protest, Rivington had published that the "situation in America is become more alarming than ever" and that "the fate of America" depended upon the Privy Council's recommendation to the king after the Boston Tea Party. Before being expelled from England, Franklin had petitioned King George III to remove the governor of Massachusetts because the "people of New England had no confidence in their governor."

The British lion roared back and charged at his American subjects. Not only did he remove Massachusetts's governor, but he also replaced him with a British general—not a civilian administrator. Then King George III went even farther by dissolving the colonial charter of Massachusetts. Boston was now under the dictatorial thumb of British General Thomas Gage, whose troops camped in the heart of Boston to police the people.

Gage's martial law led the colonists to a tipping point. They organized with other like-minded residents throughout the colonies by sending delegates, such as Washington and Franklin, to the first meeting of the Continental Congress in Philadelphia in 1774.

To his credit, Rivington printed submissions from colonists on both sides of the conflict. For example, in October 1774 while the Continental Congress held its first meeting, more than eighty residents in Rye, New York, asked Rivington to publish their emotional letter of loyalty to Britain: "Being much concerned with the unhappy situation of public affairs we think it our duty to our King and country to declare that we have not been concerned in any resolutions entered into or measures taken, with regard to the disputes at present subsisting with the mother country."

These Rye residents likewise opposed the Continental Congress. Signing their names to their petition, these loyalists ended with a final promise. "We also declare our great desire and full resolution to live and die peaceable subjects to our gracious Sovereign King George the Third, and his laws."

To show he was fair and balanced, Rivington also published a passionate letter from patriots in Newburgh. "Whereas . . . our troubles with the mother country continue to increase, and we are now convinced that we have no other alternative left but to repel force by force, or submit to be slaves," their statement began.

"Sensible that this is our deplorable situation, and in order to continue to link our chain of friendship still more firm, and to convince our friends and the friends of American liberty in general, we do hereby solemnly and sincerely swear on the Holy Evangelist that we will from hence, heartily agree, and consent to whatsoever our Continental and Provincial Congresses have, or may do, direct, ordain, and appoint for the preservation of our constitutional liberties," they wrote, signing their names to this petition.

By 1775, many of Rivington's readers, however, detected a bias from Rivington favoring the British crown in his newspaper. Most newspaper editors chose a side and used their newspapers to promote their views rather than try to present a neutral voice. Those who did paid a high price for being neutral. The editor of Connecticut's *Norwich Packet*, for example, was driven out of town and forced to take refuge in New York for using his newspaper to present both sides of the issue.

The *New York Journal* showed its preference for the patriots by taking Franklin's *Join or Die* slogan, updating it into the *Unite or Die* slogan, and including a snake picture on its masthead. Many colonists adopted new versions of this image for their flags and proclamations against the crown.

In contrast to patriot newspaper publishers, a week after publishing news from the Continental Congress in Philadelphia, Rivington boldly made his position clear by replacing the only picture in his newspaper, an image of a ship in the masthead, with a new one: a royal crest featuring the British lion. After that no one doubted his loyalist leanings, which made him vulnerable to violence.

"Last Thursday was hung up by some of the lower class of inhabitants, at New Brunswick (New Jersey), an effigy representing the person of Mr. Rivington, the printer at New York, merely for acting consistent with his profession as a free printer," Rivington published on April 20, 1775, the day after the first shots of the American Revolution were fired in Lexington and Concord, Massachusetts.

Rivington described the perpetrators as "the very dregs of the city" who were "flushed with the inebriating draughts, not of the juice of the vine, but of New England rum." They transferred his effigy from liberty "pole to pole" in New Jersey.

In a rare addition of another graphic beyond the masthead, Rivington also printed a woodcut depicting his face and body hanging in a tree. Defending his actions and beliefs, he boldly asserted "that his press has been open to publications from ALL PARTIES; and he defies his enemies to produce an instance to the contrary."

Rivington viewed his job as a type of public service. "But the moment he ventured to publish sentiments which were opposed to the dangerous views and designs of certain demagogues, he found himself held up as an enemy to this country, and the most unwearied pains taken to ruin him." In England he had grown up hearing "LIBERTY OF THE PRESS represented as the great security of freedom." He'd also heard similar sentiments in the American colonies.

With his politics overtaking him, Rivington unleashed his venomous opinion that the Sons of Liberty were seeking to "establish a most cruel tyranny, and the printer thinks that some very recent transactions will convince the good people of this city of the difference between being governed by a few factious individuals, and the GOOD OLD LAWS AND CONSTITUTION, under which we have so long been a happy people."

In a couple of days, news arrived in New York of the Battles of Lexington and Concord and the start of the war, which emboldened Rivington's local enemies. Within a month, a mob burned his house and office, destroying parts of his livelihood.

Was this a strong enough motive to lead Rivington to commit forgery by writing letters in Washington's name? Possibly. After losing his house, Rivington fled to a ship in the harbor and called upon the patriots' authorities to issue him a pardon. Would they allow him to return to New York? So he desperately hoped.

Another possible author of the *War of Lies* letters rode side-by-side with General Washington in the army at the start of the war. Named commander-in-chief of the Continental Army, Washington had traveled to Cambridge, Massachusetts, in July 1775 to resolve the standoff following Lexington and Concord. His mission was to turn the militia in the countryside into an army and eject General Gage and his British Redcoats from Boston. Joining him on this 300-mile journey from Philadelphia to Cambridge was General Charles Lee. They were a pair of opposites. Could this unlikely duo emerge as the saviors of

America? This was the hope of the Continental Congress, who knew both men.

Washington and Lee had different life experiences. Though born in the same month and year, February 1732, Lee was from Cheshire, England. His father was General John Lee and his maternal grandfather was a member of Parliament. Unlike Washington, Charles Lee had received an education at different schools, including a prestigious academy in Switzerland. Then he followed his father's footsteps and joined his father's regiment, the 44th Regiment that fled the Ohio battlefield in 1755.

Both men also nearly died in their twenties. Like Washington, Lee was also part of the mission that turned Fort Duquesne into Pittsburg in 1758. In a similar way and in the same war, Lee also had a near-death experience in the 1750s when he was nearly killed after a failed assault on Fort Ticonderoga.

Unlike Washington, Lee had displayed abusive, violent behavior, especially in the immediate aftermath of his injury. Lee's quarrel with his army surgeon became so heated that the physician attempted to assassinate him. Lee also lost two fingers dueling, which was a practice that Washington abhorred.

Hence, Charles Lee and George Washington differed greatly in style and temperament. While Washington was known for minding his manners, Lee was known for finding fault with his superior officers and disparaging others with his caustic tongue.

Unlike Washington, Lee's military career in the Royal Army continued for years after the French and Indian War. In contrast, Washington resigned his commission in the Virginia militia and retired to private life. As a result, Lee had more years of military experience than Washington. He was more deserving of commander-in-chief of the Continental Army, on paper at least.

Lee's military experience included receiving half-pay after the dissolution of his regiment. He went on missions with other military troops to far-away places such as Poland, Turkey, and Portugal, where he served under British General John Burgoyne as a lieutenant colonel. For his service, he received honorable mention for gallantry. Despite this, Lee became angry with the British top brass for refusing to promote him higher than lieutenant colonel and giving him only half pay. Eventually, Lee left England but remained on the British military's payroll.

Upon arriving in America in 1773, Lee purchased land in western Virginia and began consulting with patriot leaders. When the

Continental Congress met, he lobbied to become commander-in-chief. His popular pamphlets decrying the tyranny of the crown and showing how to organize a military colony in America won over many hearts. Yet, his rash temperament combined concerned some, as did his preference for dogs over people. He'd written to John Adams, "Consequently when once I can be convinced that men are as worthy objects as dogs I shall transfer my benevolence." Perhaps sensing that Lee's personality and skills were lacking, Congress overlooked Lee for the top job.

Instead, they named Washington as commander and gave Lee third-in-command status, with Artemis Ward earning the honor of second-in-command. They hoped the combination of Washington's temperament and Lee's experience would work well together to drive the British military from the heart of Boston. Congress was not alone. The arrival of General Washington and General Lee in Cambridge in 1775 was met with cheers and huzzahs.

"July 6. Last Sabbath came to town from Philadelphia, His Excellency, George Washington, Esq. appointed by the Continental Congress General and Commander in chief of the American forces . . . His Excellency was accompanied by the Honorable Charles Lee, Esq. and a number of other gentlemen," the *Maryland Journal* published on July 26, 1775, noting that Lee had been named a major general.

Was Lee jealous that Washington had received the position of Commander-in-Chief? With such a caustic personality and a penchant for duels, why wouldn't Lee have been jealous? However, he wasn't the only general close to Washington who was suspected of envy and political machinations.

8 MORE SUSPECTS

In addition to strategically sliding bishops around a checkered board and showing off his skills at developing military strategy, General Charles Lee had something in common with his friend, Horatio Gates, another suspect in the *War of Lies*. Both had met Benjamin Franklin in London at the same social occasion while they still served in the Royal Army.

"I dined yesterday with General Monckton, Major Gates, Colonel Lee, and other officers who have served in, and are friends of America," Benjamin Franklin had written to his son William from London in March 1768 about meeting Gates and Lee. Both were officers in the British Army at the time. Both shared an attachment for America. They'd also both played chess with Franklin after dinner, which Franklin later reflected to Gates, "May God give us soon a good peace, and bring you and I together again over a chessboard, where we may have battles without bloodshed."

Born in Essex, England, in 1728, Gates had begun his military career in the British Army at an early age. As a captain, he'd served with Colonel Washington during the fall of Braddock in 1755. Though Gates had also served with General Robert Monckton in a successful battle in the Caribbean, he'd become frustrated at not being able to advance in the British Army beyond the rank of major.

Four years after his dinner with Franklin, Gates sold his military commission. He moved to America with his family. In 1773, he bought a plantation in Berkeley County in Virginia's lower Shenandoah Valley called Traveler's Rest.

During the first two years of the war, Gates had every reason to be happy with Washington. The commanding general had given Gates something that the British Army had never done: the title of general.

Following the Battles of Lexington and Concord, Gates had paid a call on Washington at Mount Vernon in early May 1775. After Washington was appointed Commander-in-Chief the following month, he'd recommended to Congress that Gates become the first adjutant general of the Continental Army. Gates had served in this capacity as the army's chief administrative officer until Congress had promoted him to major general. Then Washington had given him a field command in May 1776 at Fort Ticonderoga in New York.

But had winning the Battle of Saratoga in October 1777 filled Gates with too much battlefield glory? Had he become so desirous of replacing Washington as Commander-in-Chief that he was willing to conspire with General Conway in a cabal to convince Congress to overthrow Washington? Was Gates so ambitious and devious and skilled as a writer that he forged letters in Washington's name to get what he wanted?

Another possible but lesser-known suspect behind Washington's counterfeit letters was John Randolph, Virginia's attorney general who was Thomas Jefferson's cousin. Randolph was a loyalist who fled Virginia. He had served under Lord Dunmore.

While Washington was in Cambridge in 1775, his distant cousin, Lund Washington, oversaw Mount Vernon in his absence. In early October, Cousin Lund wrote Washington about the threat that Virginia's Governor, Lord Dunmore, posed to Mount Vernon. Since the summer, Dunmore had taken refuge aboard the *HMS Fowe*. Sending raiding parties up and down the main rivers of Virginia, Dunmore had ordered his men to target the estates owned by rebels. Because of Washington's new status as commander of the Continental Army, some feared Dunmore would attack Mount Vernon and kidnap Washington's wife.

"'Tis true many people have made a stir about Mrs. Washington's continuing at Mt. Vernon but I cannot think her in any sort of danger," Lund assured Washington on October 5, 1775. While explaining the source of the rumors, he noted that Washington's brother Jack had been alarmed. "Mr. John Augustine Washington wrote to press her to leave Mount Vernon—she does not believe herself in danger, nor do I."

Lund concluded that if they attempted "to take her in the dead of night they would fail, for ten minutes' notice would be sufficient for her to get out of the way."

He believed that John Randolph the attorney general was with the loyalist governor and wouldn't let him harm Martha. "Lord Dunmore will hardly venture himself up this river. . . Surely her old acquaintance the attorney (who with his family are aboard his ship) would put him off doing an act of that kind."

John Randolph had owned a large estate in Williamsburg, Virginia. His brother Peyton had also served as attorney general in the 1750s. Generations of the Randolph family had long known Martha's family because Martha's great-grandfather had been a rector at Williamsburg's Bruton Parish Church.

John Randolph had also recently defended his honor in a newspaper. He'd denied accusing Patrick Henry, a known patriot, of robbing local merchants. After his feud with Henry became public and because the British crown paid his salary, Randolph realized that he could no longer stay in America. He put his house up for sale and fled Williamsburg with his wife and daughters.

"I am sorry the situation of our country should render it not eligible to you to remain longer in it," Thomas Jefferson had written to his cousin John on August 25, 1775.

Randolph's story revealed the civil-war-like nature of the American Revolution. In July 1775, John's son Edmund had joined George Washington as an aid on Jefferson's recommendation. In contrast to his father, Edmund shared the colonial politics of his father's brother Peyton. A patriot who served as the president of the first Continental Congress a year earlier, Peyton died of a sudden stroke in October 1775.

With so many patriot connections in his family, would the loyalist John Randolph convince Lord Dunmore to leave Martha and Mount Vernon alone? Lund believed Randolph would prevent Dunmore from harming both Martha and their farm. Nonetheless, Lund remained watchful.

"I have never advised her to stay nor indeed to go . . . you may depend I will be watchful and upon the least alarm persuade her to move," he told Washington.

Lund may have been incorrect about the whereabouts of Attorney General John Randolph. Concluding that Randolph was on his way to England or already there, Jefferson wrote his cousin John again on November 29, 1775, to tell him of his brother Peyton's death. Jefferson did not let his political differences with John prevent him from passing along critical family news.

"I am to give the you the melancholy intelligence of the death of our most worthy speaker," Jefferson wrote. Unlike Lund, Jefferson didn't think Randolph was with Dunmore.

"You will have heard before this reaches you that Lord Dunmore has commenced hostilities in Virginia. That people bore with everything till he attempted to burn the town of Hampton. They opposed and repelled him with considerable loss on his side and none on ours. It has raised our country into perfect frenzy."

Then Jefferson updated John Randolph on his son Edmund, who'd left Washington's service. "Edmund passed through this city (Philadelphia) on his way to Williamsburg to see whether his presence might be of service in settling his uncle's affairs. He was in perfect health, and will return again to the camp at Cambridge."

Little did Jefferson or Washington know at the time how John Randolph's exile to Britain would raise Washington's suspicion about his role in the forgeries. He wasn't the only loyalist with a motive to politically harm the patriots.

James Rivington received absolution from New York's provincial congress, returned to New York City, and resumed his newspaper publishing business. Despite the burning of his property and being hung in effigy, a courageous Rivington continued to publish submissions from both loyalists and patriots.

He showed his loyalist bias in how he presented and prioritized these submissions. On November 2, 1775, Rivington published a plan for reconciliation from England. The article took up most of the second page of his newspaper. After this long pro-crown article, Rivington printed a shorter article on the far-right column about news from the patriot side.

"An express just arrived from General Washington, camp at Cambridge, Oct. 24, 1775," the article began. "Enclosed information being of the highest importance, I thought it proper to transmit it to you with all dispatch, I am, sir, your obedient servant, George Washington, on service of the services of the united colonies." By using the phrase *united colonies*, Washington reinforced the Continental Congress's goal for unity of America. The name *United States* had not been born.

Under Washington's dispatch, Rivington printed an enclosure that Washington had received from a witness in Falmouth, Massachusetts. On October 17, 1775, a British ship with sixteen guns, a schooner, and an armed sloop had arrived at Falmouth. The next morning, the captain of this small fleet announced that he would save the town if the townspeople gave up all of their guns and ammunition.

When the people refused, the captain initiated his orders. Within five minutes, his ships had fired on several houses. They were instantly ablaze. "He continued firing till after dark the same day, which destroyed the largest part of the town." This British captain "was ordered to set fire on all the seaport towns between Boston and Halifax and ... he expected New York was to be burnt next."

Both sides knew how to start a fire. Publishing his New York newspaper proved short-lived for Rivington. A mob burned his property again in November. This time, instead of calling on the patriot authorities for help, Rivington sailed for England at the start of the New Year. If he wasn't a fully committed loyalist before the war, he had every reason to be an embittered loyalist after losing his livelihood and property in the autumn of 1775.

With all that he'd experienced in his short tenure as the publisher of the *New York Gazetteer*, Rivington certainly had a motive to use his skills as a writer and printer to invent letters from George Washington and publish them. Was Rivington the culprit? To judge, we must ask: Did he have enough knowledge about Washington to make up letters that were believable? If not, did he know someone who did?

As the New Year of 1776 approached, Lord Dunmore, with or without British Attorney General Randolph's influence, spared Mount Vernon while Martha courageously travelled to Cambridge to be with Washington. The Royal Governor of Virginia did not show the same courtesy for the shipping town of Norfolk. On January 1, 1776, Dunmore fired on the coast of Norfolk, Virginia. Buildings caught fire, which spread and burned the town.

Ten days later, an anonymous printer released a provocative but well-reasoned pamphlet called *Common Sense* in Philadelphia. The author presented a logical case that America should be a separate nation from England. It was time to part.

From his post at Cambridge, Massachusetts, on January 31, 1776, Washington shared his opinion of both *Common Sense* and the fiery tactics of the British in a letter he wrote to Lieutenant Colonel Joseph Reed, one of Washington's military secretaries.

Viewing the burning of towns as acts of war, Washington hoped they would motivate his countrymen against the British. That it "will have no other effect than to unite the whole country in one indissoluble band against a nation which seems to be lost to every sense of virtue, and those feelings which distinguish a civilized people from the most barbarous savage," Washington wrote Reed on January 31, 1776.

"A few more of such flaming arguments as were exhibited at Falmouth and Norfolk, added to the sound doctrine and unanswerable reasoning contained *Common Sense*, will not leave numbers at a loss to decide upon the propriety of a separation," he told Reed.

Author Thomas Paine couldn't print copies of his *Common Sense* fast enough. Colonists everywhere were reading it and considering its ideas. Likewise, by this time they were learning that King George III had rejected the Continental Congress's Olive Branch Petition and had declared war against them.

Despite this blow, Washington knew that the next step wouldn't be easy. Who was ready for independence?

9 INDEPENDENCE

Perhaps there is no better example of the transformation from a loyalist lionizing the British lion into a patriot longing for liberty than Phillis Wheatley. Though not as dramatic as blind Saul's conversion to Paul, Wheatley's switch to the patriot side can be seen in verses, not of scripture, but of sonnets. This former slave's letter to George Washington pricked his heart, not with the force of Cupid's dart but with the rhythmic flair of Calliope's lyre.

In February 1776, George Washington re-read a "letter and poem addressed to me by Mrs. or Miss Phillis Wheatley," as he wrote to Joseph Reed. Coming to America as a child, she was sold into slavery to the Wheatley family in 1761 and freed in 1775. Phillis had overcome many hardships but she also had an important distinction. Phillis was the first black American to become a published author.

The Wheatley family had intended to train her as a domestic servant, but when she took an interest in learning to write and read, they made a counter-cultural decision instead. They educated her in classic literature and the Bible. Phillis reminded the Wheatleys of their daughter who'd died as a child at age eight, which was around the same age as Phillis when she arrived in America.

As a young teen, Phillis began writing poems, from lyrical religious obituaries of Bostonians to verses praising King George III. But when the king's men fired their muskets at boys just blocks from Phillis's home on King Street, her loyalty to King George III disintegrated into grief. She poured out her feelings through her pen. When lines from her poem about the Boston Massacre and the recent death of eleven-year-old Christopher Snider that were published in newspapers in 1770, the Wheatleys sought to promote her genius to a wider audience. She went to England in 1773 and won over the heart of a financial patron, who published a collection of Wheatley's poems called: *Poems on Various Subjects, Religious and Moral.*

By 1775, Wheatley had returned to Boston, where her allegiance and politics had fully switched to the patriot side. Overflowing with a belief in freedom and liberty, she wrote a poem for George Washington and sent it to him. How did Washington, a slave-owner respond to an educated, former slave?

"I thank you most sincerely for your polite notice of me, in the elegant lines you enclosed; and however undeserving I may be of such encomium and panegyric, the style and manner exhibit a striking proof of your great poetical talents," he wrote Wheatley on February 28, 1776.

If he directly asked a newspaper editor to publish a poem that praised him, then it would be a mark of his vanity rather than giving "the world this new instance of [her] genius." Washington, however, directly invited Wheatley to come visit him. "If you should ever come to Cambridge, or near headquarters, I shall be happy to see a person so favored by the muses, and to whom nature has been so liberal and beneficent in her dispensations." He ended his letter to Wheatley the same way he did anyone else. "I am, with great respect, your obedient humble servant."

The fact that Washington wanted to send the poem to the newspapers showed that he understood both her talent and newspapers' influential power. His sense of manners competed with his desire to elevate Wheatley and her inspirational poem. Despite his fear of looking like he was promoting himself instead of her, Washington passed the poem along to Joseph Reed, who arranged to publish her work in newspapers.

When the *Pennsylvania Magazine* published Wheatley's poem on April 2, 1776, they noted her accomplishments: "The following letter and verses, were written by the famous Phillis Wheatley, the African Poetess, and presented to his Excellency Gen. Washington." The *Virginia Gazette* also published the poem.

In these verses, Wheatley depicted America as a female hero named Columbia. "Celestial choir! Enthron'd in realms of light, Columbia's scenes of glorious toils I write. While freedom's cause her anxious breast alarms, she flashes dreadful in refulgent arms."

Expressing her hope for America's freedom, she wrote "The land! Of freedom's heaven-defended race!" She defined race not by skin color but by a shared goal of liberty.

Phillis embodied the hopes of her countrymen and women. "Shall I to Washington their praise recite? Enough thou know'st them in the fields of fight. Thee, first in place and honors,—we demand. The grace and glory of thy martial band. Fam'd for thy valor, for thy virtues more, Hear every tongue thy guardian aid implore!"

The poem concluded with Columbia leading Washington and the army. "Proceed, great chief! With virtue on thy side, thy ev'ry action let the goddess guide. A crown, a mansion, and a throne that shine, with gold unfading, Washington! Be thine."

Publishing this poem had a two-fold result. The first result was promotional. Publishing her poem encouraged like-minded newspapers to promote the patriot cause and showcase her talent. The second result had an influential effect on Washington. Wheatley's poem challenged society's views on the intellectual capabilities of slaves and former slaves. His interaction with Wheatley was one of many incremental influences that slowly changed his views on slavery and enslaved persons, leading him to make a counter-cultural decision near the end of his life to free his slaves in his will.

Publishing Phillis's verses about liberty came at a time when the idea of *independency*, as Washington described it, was raging as a matter of common sense.

"My countrymen I know, from their form of government, and steady attachment heretofore to royalty, will come reluctantly into the idea of independency; but time, and persecution, brings many wonderful things to pass; and by private letters which I have lately received from Virginia, I find *Common Sense* is working a powerful change there in the minds of many men," Washington wrote again to Reed on April 1, 1776.

These words were a contrast to the lie attributed to Washington in his forged letter to Martha, which suggested the opposite opinion: "Pity this cannot be accomplished without fixing on me that sad name, Rebel. I love my king; you know I do: a soldier, a good man cannot but love him."

What did Washington really think about King George III and the loyalists in America? Long gone was the colonel who put his life on the line for his king in the war of the 1750s. Long gone was the man who fought alongside British regular soldiers and endured their superior attitudes against their American colonial counterparts. Long gone was the idealism of youth. Replacing them was pragmatism. The seeds of doubt and distrust planted inside Washington after his near-death experience on the battlefield in 1755 had grown into a fervent belief in honor and justice for the cause of independence and self-government.

In his letter to Reed, Washington observed that the loyalists in Boston had fled faster than the British troops in March 1776. "I believe I mentioned in my last to you that all those who took upon themselves the style and title of government's men, have shipped themselves off in the same hurry, but under greater disadvantages than the King's . . . troops have done."

So many had fled that there weren't enough local men to serve as pilots for guiding the military ships through the narrow rocky harbor and out to sea. "Seamen not being . . . had for the King's transports," Washington also wrote to Reed on April 1.

The next statement he made was so brash that he clearly hadn't shed all of his youthful cockiness, despite his good manners. Yet, these words showed how strongly he opposed the tyranny of the British Ministry. "One or two of them have committed what it would have been happy for mankind if more of them had done long ago—the act of suicide."

Clearly Washington held disdain for the likes of John Randolph and other loyalists, who seemed to view the king as part God. "By all accounts, a more miserable set of beings does not exist than these— taught to believe that the power of Great Britain was almost omnipotent." Washington's estimation of loyalist government officials, such as John Randolph, couldn't have been worse.

Washington's low opinion of loyalists now included his old friend and new opponent, British General Thomas Gage, who was one of his fellow survivors from the Battle of Monongahela River in 1755. The military governor implementing martial law in Massachusetts, Gage had overseen the British forces in Boston and all of North America— that is, until the Battle of Dorchester Heights had cost him his dictatorship.

General Washington had outfoxed his friend-turned-foe in the spring of 1776, when his men posted cannons, taken by Henry Knox from New York's Fort Ticonderoga, on Dorchester Heights. With these defenses placed on a high overlook position, Washington's army could target British supply ships coming in to Boston Harbor. How did Gage respond? He ordered an evacuation of Boston. Washington was disgusted at the contemptuous attitude of the loyalists who evacuated with the British military.

"When the order issued therefore for embarking the troops in

Boston, no electric shock—no sudden flash of lightning—in a word, not even the last trump(et), could have struck them with greater consternation," Washington wrote of Boston's heartless royal officials, who didn't seem remorseful over their conduct.

Charles Lee wrote Washington a flattering letter. "I most sincerely congratulate you, I congratulate the public on the great and glorious event—your possession of Boston—it will be a most bright page in the annals of America, and a most abominable black one in those of the beldam Britain," Lee wrote to Washington on April 5, 1776, without realizing that Washington tried to live by the *110 Rules of Civility's* rule number seventeen: "Be no flatterer."

Lee's effusion continued, as if he longed to hear the sentiment that he espoused. "My Dear General, crown yourself with glory and establish the liberties and luster of your country on a foundation more permanent than the capitol rock."

With ships flying out of Boston faster than rats fleeing the rising sun, where would the Redcoats go next?

From personal experience, Washington knew that British officers loved New York City, which was like a little London. Three years earlier, on May 27, 1773, Washington had attended an entertainment honoring General Gage at Hull's tavern in New York City. Rivington had reported on the "cheerfulness and harmony which presided at every table" of that event and noted that Gage had lived in New York for ten years.

Washington had been in New York to oversee his stepson, Jackie Custis, as he enrolled in King's College, which later became Columbia University. At that dinner honoring General Gage, Washington concluded that many British officers preferred New York to other places in the colonies because it was more cosmopolitan.

Because Rivington had published the news of Washington's attendance at Gage's dinner, he might have known that Washington was in town to oversee Jackie Custis's entrance to college. Custis was one of four children from Martha's marriage to her first husband, who died. If Rivington wrote the forged letters, he drew upon his knowledge of Washington's fatherly relationship to Jackie.

One of the forged letters was from Washington to Custis in which Washington discouraged hist stepson from being a soldier while also reinforcing his love for Custis's mother, Martha. "Yet, I love arms; I am married to my sword, as well as to your amiable mother; and herein is my witness, that I am in earnest when I say death alone shall divorce me from either," Washington's forged letter to Custis declared. "I am not so blindly devoted, however, to my profession, as not to see by how frail a tenure I hold the little reputation I have in it."

Two of the strongest clues about the forged letters were the dates of the letters and where they were alleged to have been written. The first false letter was dated June 12, 1776, and the last one was dated July 22, 1776, in New York.

After Boston's Battle of Dorchester Heights in May 1776, the Redcoats fled to Canada to regroup. Washington concluded that Gage's successor, General Howe, would seek to make New York his headquarters because of its strategic location as a port city. Likewise, New York's governor had promised to make New York City a haven for loyalists.

While Washington and his men went to New York, members of the Continental Congress prepared for their next meeting in Philadelphia. The topic on everyone's mind was simple: independence. Was it time to declare independence from England? Were the people ready for it? What did Washington believe?

The author of the forged letters portrayed the patriot Commander-in-Chief as a conflicted man who opposed independence and secretly sought reconciliation with his king.

"I do not really wish for independence. I hope there are few who do," Washington had allegedly written to Custis. "What you say on the subject of independency is perfectly judicious ... I have no reluctance to confess to you, that the measure (independence) is diametrically opposite to my judgment."

Would Americans believe that Washington really didn't want independence from England? Would they view him as a man who wasn't honest with himself or the public? Did he secretly desire reconciliation with the British, as he appeared to believe in this paragraph?

"For I have not yet despaired of an honorable reconciliation; and whilst I can entertain but a hope of that, both interest and inclination lead me to prefer it to everything else upon earth," he supposedly declared.

In contrast, the real Washington wanted independence and a new government for America. In late May and early June 1776, Washington expressed his hope that Congress would declare independence to one of the other Jacks in his life, his brother Jack. He wrote him after learning that Virginians had gathered at the Virginia Convention in May 1776.

Authorizing new delegates to the Continental Congress on May 15, the Virginians voted to give their delegates permission to propose that Congress declare independence from England. The next day, they had a parade and launched fireworks. The Virginians were the first colonists to launch fireworks for independence. Washington was pleased. "I am very glad, to find that the Virginia Convention have passed so noble a vote, with so much unanimity," Washington wrote Jack between May 31 and June 4, 1776 after hearing the news.

Not only did Washington approve of the Virginia Convention's support for independence, but he also gave his brother advice as he and other Virginians met to write a new Constitution for the state of Virginia. "To form a new government, requires infinite care, and unbounded attention; for if the foundation is badly laid, the superstructure must be bad," he wrote Jack. "Every man should consider, that he is lending his aid to frame a constitution which is to render millions happy, or miserable, and that a matter of such moment cannot be the work of a day."

By the time he'd written Jack this letter, Washington had left New York for a temporary sojourn in Philadelphia to meet with the Continental Congress about the preparations to bolster and defend New York. In this authentic letter to Jack, he declared that "things have come to that pass now, as to convince us, that we have nothing more to expect from the justice of Great Britain—also, that she is capable of the most delusive arts." Those last words referred to the rumors that Britain was sending peace commissioners while also hiring foreign fighters from Germany. The king's actions were contradictory.

Believing that these peace negotiators were a pretense or an effort to fool the colonists into thinking that King George III wasn't going to war against them, Washington showed he didn't buy the tactic. "The idea was only to deceive, and throw us off our guard." Washington was worried that the ruse had worked and some members of the Continental Congress were "still feeding themselves upon the dainty food of reconciliation."

There was nothing dainty about what Washington, and all of New York, witnessed a month later.

"The colony of New York is said not only to be hearty, but zealous in the cause—I wish, and I hope it may be so, but . . . I will suspend my opinion till the arrival of the troops there," Washington had genuinely declared in 1775. Though he knew patriots lived in New York, he strongly believed that the Howe brothers would bring the British fleet to New York City. When this happened, he concluded that it would be hard for patriots living in Manhattan and Long Island to openly support the Continental Army.

For weeks in the spring of 1776, snippets of news sailed into America's colonial ports. British ships carrying hundreds of soldiers had been sighted leaving places like Ireland, Scotland, and Amsterdam. Most were bound for Canada and then somewhere else in the colonies after that.

The sight of British ships was as ominous as it was frequent. On Saturday, June 29, 1776, hundreds of ships carrying thirty-two thousand British fighters arrived at Sandy Hook, New Jersey, across from New York's Staten Island. "The fleet from Halifax, we informed our readers in our last, was arrived at Sandy Hook (New Jersey) . . . we suppose it does not exceed 130 sail," the *Pennsylvania Evening Post* reported.

Led by the British brothers Admiral Richard Howe and General William Howe, this caravan of ships began to move between Staten Island and Long Island. "Monday (July 1) it came up into Yank's Bay below the narrows."

Each day the sight of more British ships made news. "Tuesday several ships came to at the Watering Place (Staten Island) -- Wednesday more followed -- and by Thursday noon the whole fleet was at anchor in a line from Kill van Kull to Simonson's ferry on the Eastside of Staten Island."

The fleet included forty battleships and three hundred support vessels, according to the reports at the time. With hundreds of vessels filling the three-mile long and thousand-foot-wide Kill van Kull strait, no wonder the newspaper described the sight of Redcoats as a "swarm of locusts escaped from a bottomless pit."

The final ship met with some interference. "The *Asia* brought up the rear of the fleet, and in the narrows was fired at from a small battery on Long Island, which complement was returned by about forty 24 pounders, one of which was lodged in the wall of the house of Mr. Bennet, but did no hurt to the family."

On the same day that the entire British fleet lined Staten Island's strait of Kill van Kull, the Continental Congress made even bigger news. They issued the Declaration of Independence on July 4, 1776.

The *Pennsylvania Evening Post* published the entire document two days later on the front page of their Saturday edition. The length of each issue of this newspaper was shorter than most newspapers, but it was printed more often at three days a week instead of once a week. This frequency gave the *Pennsylvania Evening Post* an advantage, making it one of the first newspapers to publish the Declaration of Independence.

Their headline was larger than usual and put the news this way: "In Congress, July 4, 1776. A Declaration by the Representatives of the United States of America in General Congress assembled."

"We hold these truths to be self-evident, that all men are created equal; that they are endowed by their creator with certain unalienable rights; that among them are life, liberty and the pursuit of happiness."

Under the belief that government derived its "just powers from the consent of the governed," the Declaration cited twenty-seven bullet points of how the king of England had become a tyrant.

"The history of the present King of Great Britain is a history of repeated injuries and usurpations, all having in direct object the establishment of an absolute tyranny over these states. To prove this, let facts be submitted to a candid world."

Among the many abuses, "he has dissolved representative houses repeatedly . . . obstructed the administration of justice, by refusing his assent to laws for establishing judiciary powers."

"He has made judges dependent on his will alone . . . He has kept among us, in times of peace, standing armies, without the consent of our legislators."

Referring to martial law, the Declaration pointed out that: "He has affected to render the military independent of and superior to the civil power."

Without the consent of the people, the king had allowed laws for "cutting off our trade with all parts of the world . . . Depriving us, in many cases of the benefits of trial by jury . . . (and) taking away our charters."

As the residents of Falmouth and Norfolk could testify: "He has plundered our seas, ravaged our coasts, burnt our towns, and destroyed the lives of our people."

Not knowing that the British and their hired German fighters had already arrived in New York, the Declaration proclaimed, "He is, at this time, transporting large armies of foreign mercenaries to complete the works of death."

Proving that a nation could be born in a day, this document not only declared independence but it also declared that the colonies were no longer colonies but states. In all capital letters, the Declaration proclaimed: "We, therefore, the representatives of the UNITED STATES OF AMERICA, in General Congress assembled, appealing to the Supreme judge of the world for the rectitude of our intentions, do, in the name, and by authority of the good people of their colonies, solemnly publish and declare, that these United Colonies are, and of right ought to be, FREE AND INDEPENDENT STATES."

The date July 4, 1776, marked the first use of the phrase *United States of America*, which makes July 4 the origin and birth of this country. Gone were Britain's American colonies. Replacing them were independent states united together. Gone was allegiance to royalty. Replacing it was representation. Gone was *God Save the King*. Replacing it was long live the people. A new nation under a new philosophy was born.

As free and independent states, the Americans dissolved all political connections between them and the British crown. As free and independent states, the Declaration asserted that they had the power to levy war and conclude peace. As free and independent states they could contract alliances, establish commerce, and do everything else a nation might do.

What did this newspaper editor print next, immediately after the Declaration of Independence? Did he publish an analysis of the Declaration by journalists or a reaction from local residents? A set of interviews with the author, Thomas Jefferson? An interview with the humorous retired newspaper editor, Benjamin Franklin, who predicted that if they didn't hang together, they'd all hang separately?

No. Instead, immediately after printing the Declaration of Independence, this grand document that became a beacon to the world, the next article in the *Pennsylvania Evening Post* was this advertisement: "A few hog heads and barrels of Jamaica sugar, of the best quality to be sold by David Sproat."

This sales pitch was followed by ads from an upholsterer, who sold custom furniture, and a tailor named Amelia Taylor, who specialized in "children's robes, jams, frogs, vails, tunics, gentlemen shirts, and all kinds of needlework in the very neatest manner."

What better way to follow the Declaration of Independence than by publishing examples of people who were pursuing happiness through making a living?

How long did it take for George Washington to receive the Declaration of Independence?

Washington couldn't have been happier to announce the Declaration of Independence in his General Orders five days later on July 9.

"The Honorable the Continental Congress, impelled by the dictates of duty, policy and necessity, having been pleased to dissolve the connection which subsisted between this country, and Great Britain, and to declare the United Colonies of North America, free and independent STATES."

Not only that, but Washington was so pleased with the Declaration that he also decided his men should hear it right away. "The several brigades are to be drawn up this evening on their respective parades, at six o'clock, when the declaration of Congress, shewing the grounds and reasons of this measure, is to be read with an audible voice."

In contrast to the lies that would be spread about him later, a thrilled Washington believed the Declaration of Independence would motivate his troops. He knew they needed a boost after the arrival of British troops. The sight of the "red sea" had intimidated them.

"The general hopes this important event will serve as a fresh incentive to every officer and soldier to act with fidelity and courage, as knowing that now the peace and safety of his country depends (under God) solely on the success of our arms: And that he is now in the service of a state, possessed of sufficient power to reward his merit, and advance him to the highest honors of a free country," Washington ordered his troops on July 9.

"The brigade majors are to receive, at the adjutant general's office, several of the declarations to be delivered to the brigadiers general, and the colonels of regiments."

Also included in his general orders was the encouraging news that Congress had approved the inclusion of chaplains in the Continental Army. "The Honorable Continental Congress having been pleased to allow a chaplain to each regiment, with the pay of thirty-three dollars and one third month."

Understanding that some of his men would die in battle, General Washington attended to the spiritual and emotional needs of his soldiers by bringing chaplains into the corps. "The colonels or commanding officers of each regiment are directed to procure chaplains accordingly; persons of good characters and exemplary lives."

Washington wanted all officers and soldiers to respect the chaplains and "attend carefully upon religious exercises: The blessing and protection of Heaven are at all times necessary but especially so in times of public distress and danger."

He also wove faith into the cause. "The General hopes and trusts, that every officer, and man, will endeavor so to live, and act, as becomes a Christian soldier defending the dearest rights and liberties of his country."

The beheading that happened later that night was quite a contrast to Washington's instructions on proper behavior for soldiers.

The most raucous show on Broadway in 1776 took place that night. No, it wasn't a performance of *Romeo and Juliet* or *Julius Caesar*. Many of Washington's troops were so thrilled at the Declaration of Independence that they got carried away in a frenzy. On the Bowling Green, at the south end of the street known as Broadway, was a large, gilded lead statue of King George III. Mounted on a horse, the king was dressed like a Roman emperor.

"Last night, the statue of George the Third was tumbled down and beheaded—the troops having long had an inclination so to do, thought this time of publishing a Declaration of Independence, to be a favorable opportunity—for which they received the check in this day's orders." So one of Washington's soldiers, who was an assistant to Washington's military secretary, recorded the theatrics of July 9 in his diary.

This check wasn't a monetary payment or a ticket to the performance on New York's Broadway. Rather it was a rebuke for their lack of order and mob-like behavior. The next day on July 10, Washington issued these General Orders.

"Though the General doubts not the persons, who pulled down and mutilated the statue in the Broadway, last night, were actuated by zeal in the public cause; yet it has so much the appearance of riot and want (lack) of order, in the army, that he disapproves the manner, and directs that in future these things shall be avoided by the soldiery, and left to be executed by proper authority."

The news of melting His Royal Highness made its way to London, as the *St. James Chronicle and Evening Post* later reported, noting that the Declaration of Independence was "received with loud huzzas, and the utmost demonstrations of joy."

Reporting that "the sons of freedom laid prostrate (King George III's statue) in the dirt," this British article pointed out that the monument's lead "is to be run into bullets to assimilate with the brains of our infatuated adversaries, who to gain a pepper corn, have lost an Empire."

Missing from this British report, of course, was news about Washington's orders and his disapproval of mob tactics. They would soon learn that the Commander-in-Chief of the Continental Army found an unusual way to stand up to Lord Howe.

10 MANNERS & FODDER

On July 13, 1776, British Lieutenant Philip Brown brought a letter from Lord Howe to General Washington under a flag of truce to signal an invitation for a conference. He gave the letter to Washington's officers, Colonel Joseph Reed, Colonel Henry Knox, and Reed's assistant Samuel Webb. When the officers realized that Lord Howe had addressed General Washington as "George Washington, Esquire" and not as General Washington, the officers refused to open the letter. Instead they ordered Brown to anchor his boat until they received instructions on what to do. One of them rowed back to the tip of Manhattan Island, a short distance away, and told Washington about the letter.

In both England and America, esquire was a name given to a commoner who had obtained the social status of a gentleman. Esquire was not the appropriate title for the general of a legitimate army. Reed told Brown that there was no such person as Mr. Washington, Esquire, in the Continental Army. A letter intended for a general should be addressed to a general, not a civilian. Washington agreed.

"I immediately convened such of the general officers as were not upon other duty who agreed in opinion that I ought not to receive any letter directed to me as a private gentleman," Washington wrote to the president of the Continental Congress about the incident.

"The officer expressed great concern, said it was a letter rather of a civil than military nature." The timing of the Declaration of Independence had interfered in Howe's plans to offer pardons. "Lord Howe regretted he had not arrived sooner."

As Brown began to row away with the unopened letter, he stopped and called out to ask how Mr. Washington preferred to be addressed. "Colonel Reed answered his station was well known and that certainly they could be at no loss how to direct to him," Reed's assistant recorded.

Washington's military title of *general* was widely known. By not properly addressing Washington as a general, Howe showed that he didn't view the Continental Army, Congress, or Washington's leadership as valid.

While he wouldn't risk someone's life over a "punctilio" or for the sake of manners, the Commander-in-Chief nonetheless asked his officers for their opinion. Shouldn't the British treat him as a commanding general? Or was he making too much of this? They all agreed with his demand to be addressed as a general, not as a private person. If General Howe wasn't ready to call Washington a general, then he wasn't ready to recognize the independence of the United States or negotiate a peace treaty.

"I deemed it a duty to my country and my appointment to insist upon that respect which in any other than a public view, I would willingly have waived. Nor do I doubt but from the supposed nature of the message and the anxiety expressed they will either repeat their flag (of temporary truce) or fall upon some mode to communicate the import and consequence of it," Washington defended.

Was he about to worsen the war because the British didn't mind their manners to his satisfaction? So it seemed on the surface. But Washington was a farmer and he knew how to use a plough. He rightfully sensed that this controversy over manners would enable him to dig beneath the surface and discover the mettle of the enemy's mindset. What was in Howe's letter? Washington suspected that it had to do with the king naming Howe as a peace commissioner. How Howe approached peace would prove or disprove the necessity of war.

Washington believed that reports declaring the British intended to negotiate peace were an attempt to "to distract, divide, and create as much confusion as possible." He was worried that these reports would prove false and blindly lead people astray.

This commander had concluded that the time for peace could only occur when the British acknowledged America's new government. "No man can wish the restoration of peace more fervently than I do; but I hope, whenever made, it will be upon such terms as will reflect honor upon the councils, and wisdom of America," Washington had written.

How did Howe respond to Washington's refusal of the letter? On the morning of July 20, Howe sent one of his aid-de-camps, Colonel James Paterson, to discuss the matter. Under a flag of truce but without blindfolding Paterson, Colonel Reed and his assistant escorted this chatty and sociable officer to Colonel Knox's quarters in Manhattan, where a uniformed General Washington waited with his body guards.

Reed took notes of what transpired. "After usual compliments in which as well as through the whole conversation Colonel Paterson addressed General Washington by the title of Excellency. The colonel entered upon the business by saying that General Howe much regretted the difficulties which had arisen respecting the address of the letters to General Washington."

Paterson reminded Washington that he had accepted General Howe's letter in August 1775 that was addressed to him as esquire. Washington explained that the soldier on duty had accepted and opened that letter without knowing of Washington's objections. He had no choice but to respond, lest he risk his soldiers' lives.

"That Lord Howe and General Howe did not mean to derogate from the respect or rank of General Washington—that they held his person and character in the highest esteem," Paterson backtracked about the Howe brothers and then handed Washington the same letter, which was still addressed to him as a private citizen. Washington declined it again.

"That a letter directed to a person in a public character should have some description or indication of it otherwise it would appear a mere private letter. . . . That he should absolutely decline any letter directed to him as a private person when it related to his public station," Washington pointed out to Paterson.

"The goodness and benevolence of the king had induced him to appoint Lord Howe and General Howe his commissioners to accommodate this unhappy dispute," Colonel Paterson explained of the King's benevolent intentions for peace and a lasting union between Great Britain and America.

"That those who had committed no fault wanted no pardon: that we were only defending what we deemed our indisputable rights," Washington replied politely but pointedly. He observed that Lord Howe and General Howe were only offering Americans pardons, not recognizing their rights.

His logic reflected the new Declaration of Independence. Because the Americans were only asking for their natural rights, those derived from their Creator and part of English law, they were not violating any law.

Realizing that they couldn't solve this skirmish over etiquette, Washington diplomatically expressed his hope that they could find a way to communicate with each other through proper military protocol. Believing this was still an open question, Paterson left.

How did Howe respond? "This interview was more polite than interesting; however, it induced me to change my superscription for the attainment of an end so desirable," Howe wrote to the British foreign minister. The next time he sent Washington a letter, Howe addressed Washington as a general.

Washington had won this war over literal words. For their part, after receiving his memorandum about the meeting, Congress decided to make his memo public. Washington's meeting with Paterson was printed in several newspapers on both sides of the Atlantic. This quarrel over manners, however, led to an unforeseen consequence. It gave fodder to the person forging Washington's letters.

★ ★ ★ ★ ★

Newspaper reports about Washington and his penchant for politeness gave the *War of Lies* counterfeiter material for making his forgeries appear authentic. The culprit who forged the letter from Washington to John Parke Custis, wrote this false but believable statement:

"I will not endure anything mean or sordid either in your principles, or your manners; having determined, if it were left with me, to be as strict and rigorous in these particulars, as were the knights of old, when a candidate was to be invested with the orders of chivalry."

The lies continued in another false letter, suggesting that Washington's top priority for the United States was reconciliation and not independence.

"We must, at last, agree and be friends; for we cannot live without them, and they will not without us: and a bystander might well be puzzled to find out, why as good terms cannot be given and taken now, as when we shall have well-nigh ruined each other by the mutual madness of cutting one another's throats."

This forged letter made it seem that Washington frequently said things he didn't mean. "How often it is my lot to find it my indispensable duty to act a part contrary to both my own sentiments and inclinations." Though Washington had told Paterson that he who'd committed no fault needed no pardon, the forged letters implied the opposite: "How peculiarly hard then is our fortune to be deemed traitors to so good a king! But I am not without hopes, that even he will yet see cause to do me justice; posterity, I am sure, will."

The forged letters indicated that Washington was willing to

negotiate peace at all costs and didn't expect the war to continue: "Suffice it that I say, what I have often before told you, that, as far as I have the control of them, all our preparations of war, aim only at peace. Neither do I, at this moment, see the least likelihood of there being any considerable military operations this season; and, if not in this season, certainly in no other."

In reality, Washington anticipated the opposite would take place. "We expect a very bloody summer of it at New York and Canada," Washington had actually written to his brother between May 31 to June 4, 1776. Just as he did after his near-death experience decades earlier, the real Washington looked to God for protection and comfort. "However, it is to be hoped that if our cause is just, as I do most religiously believe it to be, the same Providence which has in many instances appeared for us, will still go on to afford its aid."

Washington was fortunate that these forgeries, which were dated in 1776, were not published until 1777. The counterfeit letters were written sometime during this time period.

Much like a playwright or a novelist, the *War of Lies* counterfeiter had the ability to pretend that he was Washington. Had the general suppressed his opposition when he was a member of the first Continental Congress, as one of the forged letters declared? Was this how he ended up in a position contrary to his conscience? "Unused to the many arts and devices, by which designing men carry their points, I unwillingly listened to my own apprehensions, when early in the first Congress, I thought I saw a tendency to measures which I never could approve of, I reasoned myself."

Was Congress relying on a general who thought their cause was unreachable? "At length, however, when a continental army came to be voted for, my fears returned with redoubled force; for then, for the first time, I clearly saw our aims reached farther than we cared to avow."

What was General Washington's real reaction to being named Commander-in-Chief? He took a sober view of the opportunity, his capabilities, and what would happen to his reputation if he failed.

"I am now embarked on a tempestuous ocean from whence,

perhaps, no friendly harbor is to be found," Washington had revealed to a Virginia friend shortly after the Continental Congress named him to his post in 1775. Washington's ambition did not match General Lee's.

"It is an honor I by no means aspired to—It is an honor I wished to avoid," Washington had penned, explaining that he didn't want to leave his peaceful life as a family man at Mount Vernon. He'd also held "a thorough conviction of my own incapacity and want of experience in the conduct of so momentous a concern."

Despite his misgivings, he was a seasoned enough politician after spending time in the House of Burgesses to understand the politics behind John Adams of Massachusetts nominating a man from Virginia for the post. The most practical way to unite the colonies was to name a leader from the largest Southern colony, Virginia, to command the army fighting in Northern colonies. Aware of the politics, he felt he had no choice but to accept the nomination.

"May God grant therefore that my acceptance of it may be attended with some good to the common cause and without injury (from want of knowledge) to my own reputation."

Washington's insecurities over his lack of experience as a general were understandable. Never before holding the rank of general, he looked to justice and virtues as justification for accepting the role.

"I can answer but for three things, a firm belief of the justice of our cause—close attention in the prosecution of it—and the strictest integrity."

What he lacked in experience, he made up for in character and conviction. He was a true believer in the principles undergirding the patriots. "If these cannot supply the places of ability and experience, the cause will suffer, and more than probable my character along with it, as reputation derives its principal support from success."

Notice that he didn't believe he was committing treason. Washington didn't express a fear of dying in a hangman's noose at the hands of the Redcoats.

Wanting his friend to know that he wasn't seeking personal glory or led by vain ambition, he added: "I shall not be deprived therefore of a comfort in the worst event if I retain a consciousness of having acted to the best of my judgment."

That "worst event" took place in New York in 1776 as green summer leaves tossed and turned into swirly orange and red autumn breezes. How the newspapers reported on both Washington and the Battle of Long Island reveal the challenges of gathering accurate information during the fog of war.

Journalism has often served as the first draft of history. Newspapers in 1776 proved just that. Lacking the resources to pay for correspondents in the field, newspaper editors relied on eye witnesses to send them letters about the happenings in New York. Occasionally, a dispatch explained why, not just who, what or how, something had taken place. A newspaper publisher had to trust his source's integrity and accuracy.

A council member in a New York town sent a letter to General Howe. He was convinced that "this city and province is the only spot in America for carrying on the war with affect against the rebels." He praised New York's location and natural resources, which would supply the Redcoats with food. "It (Long Island) is 130 miles long, is very fertile, abounding in wheat and every other kind of corn, innumerable black cattle, sheep, hogs etc."

Noting that Long Island, especially Suffolk County, was highly populous, the author suggested that the British would encounter little resistance to controlling New York City and Long Island. Why? In his opinion, New Yorkers were "all good and loyal subjects, of which they have lately given proof, and only wait to be assisted by the King's troops."

Often the essence of a news report was correct, but without a camera's eye to see the big picture, the details were sometimes marked by errors. Because of this, journalism serves as a rough—but not always a final—draft of history.

"By sundry letters from New York we are informed, that a body of about 10,000 British troops had landed on Long Island last Thursday (Aug. 22) that on Friday their advanced party was attacked by Colonel Hand's regiment of riflemen, and beat them back with some loss," the *Virginia Gazette* reported two weeks later. Was this disinformation? Perhaps, but the fog of war—or any breaking news story—leads to errors. The difference between publishing disinformation and making mistakes is intent. No matter the era, integrity is important.

In this article, the date was correct but the number of British soldiers was mistaken. Under General Howe's direction, British ships transported twenty-two thousand troops, twice as many as initially reported, from Staten Island to Long Island's Gravesend Bay on August 22, 1776. The total number of available Continental soldiers to defend Manhattan and Long Island was about ten thousand.

"That a reinforcement of 6,000 men had been sent by General Washington to Long Island to annoy the enemy," the *Virginia Gazette* also reported. On August 23, Washington toured the Continental fortification on Long Island where General Putnam was in command. Washington ordered Putnam to defend Gowanus Heights near Jamaica Pass.

"Extract of a letter from General Sullivan to General Washington at New York, dated Long Island, August 23, 1776," the *Virginia Gazette* reported. "This afternoon the enemy formed and attempted to pass the road by Bedford; a smart fire between them and the riflemen ensued. The officer sent off for a reinforcement, which I ordered immediately."

Dividing their soldiers into columns, British soldiers marched over land and blocked the Continental troops on the south and east. Howe ordered ten thousand men to march overnight. This mobile red sea reached Jamaica Pass on August 26.

The battle of Long Island, also known as the battle of Brooklyn Heights, took place the next day on August 27. With the British crushing Putnam's left flank and threatening his center and right, Putnam and his men retreated to Brooklyn Heights. "In the skirmishes which have been for the several days past, the enemy has lost upwards of 1,000 men, and we not much more than 500." The numbers were inflated estimates in this first draft of what happened. Subsequent drafts more accurately concluded that three hundred Americans were killed while sixty-three British soldiers died.

The *Virginia Gazette* published an extract of a letter from New York about what happened after losing this battle. "In a council of war held yesterday, it was determined that our lines on Long Island were not tenable and therefore the council concluded to evacuate them."

The news report also gave snippets of what took place next. "Saturday's post brings us the agreeable intelligence of General Washington having affected a safe retreat for the army out of Long Island, in spite of the great numbers in that commanded by Howe."

Giving an explanation for how they slipped away from the British forces, the newspaper continued: "The retreat was conducted with the greatest secrecy, and by 6 o'clock in the morning we had everything embarked."

The *Virginia Gazette* also praised Washington's conduct in overseeing this evacuation. "There never was a man that behaved better upon the occasion than General Washington; he was on horseback the whole night, and never left the ferry stairs till he had seen the whole of his troops embarked."

Despite ordering the retreat, Washington was praised for being the last to leave Long Island for Manhattan. "The manner in which our retreat was performed reflects the highest credit upon our commander-in-chief and the officers in general."

Washington also received help from Providence. A fog concealed his army's retreat while another act of nature stalled the British. "We learn from New York that on Thursday evening there was a most violent storm of thunder and lightning."

This news report ended the story on a cliffhanger with Washington's troops in Manhattan expecting Howe's men to follow them there. "That the enemy ships only waited for a fair wind to move up to the city of New York where an attack was hourly expected, and our troops in high spirits waiting with impatience for it."

The fallout on Long Island was as brutal as it was swift, as another newspaper soon reported of the British occupation there. "They have opened the courts of justice upon Long Island, in which Mr. Ludlow presides as chief judge," according to the *Pennsylvania Gazette* on September 25.

The seizure of Long Island had devastating consequences for many New Yorkers. "They have confiscated several estates, and condemned one man to perpetual confinement, to linger out his life in chains, and to be fed on bread and water."

The patriot who submitted this article to the *Pennsylvania Gazette* gave his opinion. He believed that the British bullying would backfire. "I think such acts of oppression will turn to our advantage; they carry a high hand, and, flushed with the success which nature and not their own strength has given them, they think in a little time to sweep off our army and be in possession of America."

In contrast, loyalists found acceptance by the British. One well-known New York loyalist named Oliver De Lancey joined the British on Staten Island. "Old Oliver De Lancey is a colonel," the *Pennsylvania Gazette* published. Delancey's name would later appear in the counterfeit letters. This newspaper also reported on the death of another prominent New Yorker. "Your poor friend Woodhull is killed. This intelligence was got from a person who has been among them sometime, and I think maybe depended on."

General Nathaniel Woodhull had led a New York militia. After being captured in the aftermath of the Battle of Long Island, he was allegedly tortured. The British wounded him with bayonets and denied him medical assistance. Dying of injuries a few weeks later, Nathaniel Woodhull's grisly death later motivated his cousin, Abraham Woodhull, to become a spy for Washington. This, of course, was not reported in the gazettes.

One historic event was noted by newspapers. On September 6, the Americans embarked on a secret mission by employing a new covert underwater ship called the *Turtle,* which was invented by David Bushnell of Connecticut. Although this submersible ship, or submarine, made history when its pilot navigated underwater, he failed to attach an underwater bomb to Howe's flagship the *Eagle.* Had the bomb been successful, this one action would have changed the trajectory of the war and possibly have sent the Redcoats back to Canada.

With this failure weighing on them, the Continental generals held a war council three days later on September 9 and voted to evacuate New York against Washington's wishes, though he obeyed their directive. Little did anyone realize at the time, but this decision set the stage that launched the *War of Lies* against Washington.

11 FORT LEE

Twins proved to be pivotal as George Washington's men battled the British military in New York in the fall of 1776. At the top end of Manhattan, Washington's men had constructed Fort Washington. Across the Hudson River to the west in New Jersey, they'd built Fort Lee, named after General Charles Lee, who was now second only to the Commander-in-Chief in military power. The strategy behind these double defenses was to use cannons to stop British ships from freely sailing through the Hudson.

Like the mistaken identity of twins in Shakespeare's *Comedy of Errors*, Fort Lee would later play a farcical role in the counterfeit scheme, specifically in how Howe's men supposedly found the forged letters. What happened next was more akin to a Shakespearean drama than a comedy.

The Red Sea seemed to part again, but this time in favor of the Redcoats led by a British pharaoh on September 15, when Lord Howe arrived with more than four thousand British soldiers at Kip's Bay on the east side of Manhattan. Mrs. Robert Murray, who was married to a loyalist, invited some of the officers in for tea. A secret patriot who was far from a loyal Caesar's wife, she stalled them long enough to allow the Continental Army to escape further up Manhattan.

One American officer, who was not full of tea and crumpets from the Manhattan hostess, was particularly hopeful of victory at Harlem Heights. "The enemy, from their different maneuvers in great preparations, intend soon to strike a decisive blow," the *Pennsylvania Gazette* published an extract of his letter dated September 14 in New York. "Their plan is to outflank and hem us in, but I think they will be disappointed, for the heights above Harlem and Kingsbridge are strongly manned and fortified."

He was correct. Washington camped with the main body of his army at Harlem Heights. On September 16, his men launched a counterattack, which halted three battalions of British light infantry, giving the patriots a much-needed victory.

Weeks later, Washington's focus shifted to nearby White Plains after General Howe arrived there with fourteen thousand men. More than half of them were Hessians, or German soldiers hired by Britain to fight with their regular soldiers. The Battle of White Plains took place on October 28. Overwhelmed by the number of British and Hessian forces, Washington's men couldn't win and retreated once again.

This loss forced General Washington to return his focus to Fort Washington and Fort Lee. Despite failing at White Plains, hopes remained high for victory at these twin forts, especially as rumors flew that many Hessians wanted to defect to America. On November 8, a soldier penned a letter, which the *Virginia Gazette* published. "Our garrison at Fort Washington are in high spirits, and go a Hessian-hunting every day."

Mistakenly identifying the intentions of the Hessians, the Americans soon realized that most of the Hessians were staying put as Howe's hirelings. Because the Continental Army had nearly three thousand soldiers at Fort Washington, Nathanael Greene convinced Washington that they could hold this garrison. He was wrong. Instead, the British and Hessians attacked Fort Washington on three sides. Unlike their retreat from Long Island, this time the Americans were forced to surrender.

Colonel Paterson, the aid-de-camp who'd met with Washington in July 1776 about Howe's letter addressed to Mr. Washington and not to General Washington, played a key role in Fort Washington's surrender. *The Connecticut Journal* printed the summons that Paterson sent to Fort Washington's commander on November 16, 1776.

"The garrison must immediately surrender prisoners-of-war, and give up all their arms, ammunitions, and stores of every kind, and send two field officers to headquarters as hostages; in so doing the General (Howe) is pleased to allow the garrison to keep possession of their baggage and the officers to have their swords," Patterson wrote in his role as the British adjutant general.

The Continentals gave up two thousand eight hundred men on November 16 at Fort Washington. Anguished but forced to be practical, General Washington had no choice but to evacuate Fort Lee and fully retreat with his remaining troops into New Jersey. Four days later, British General Cornwallis and his men easily captured Fort Lee. By prohibiting the Hessians from pursuing the Continental forces, Cornwallis enabled Washington and his men to live to fight another day.

"You have no doubt heard all the particulars of our retreat from Fort Lee to Hackensack, from Hackensack to Acquackanonk and from thence to this place," the *Pennsylvania Journal* published of a letter from a soldier in New Jersey. "We lost some of our large mortars, part of our cannon in stores at Fort Lee as well as at Hackensack."

Despite the sacrifice of men and artillery, this unnamed soldier wasn't ready to give up the cause. "I hope these losses will rouse the virtue of America; if she does not exert herself now, she deserves not the independence she has declared." He wanted the retreat from New York and their remnant of an army to arouse patriotism across the states.

"I have still hopes of success—I heard a great man say many months ago, that America would not purchase her freedom at so cheap a rate as was imagined—nor is it proper she should, what cost us a little, we not value enough."

Reaching Trenton, New Jersey, on December 2, Washington's dwindling army crossed the Delaware River and camped across from Trenton in Pennsylvania. Little did he know at the time that an aspiring Shakespeare was crafting a ridiculous tale that took place at Fort Lee.

The counterfeiter used Fort Lee's evacuation to explain where he had acquired Washington's forged letters. In the preface that went along with the forged correspondence, the author named Oliver De Lancey, whose name had been in newspapers. De Lancey was an American-born loyalist who recruited New Yorkers to fight for the British under General Howe. According to the counterfeit letter writer, a soldier serving under De Lancey supposedly encountered General Washington's personal African valet or body guard at the captured Fort Lee.

"Among the prisoners at Fort Lee, I employed a mulatto fellow, whom I thought I recollected, and who confirmed my conjectures by gazing very earnestly at me... He was Billy, and the old servant (slave) of General Washington," the preface to the forged letters explained.

The soldier in De Lancey's service claimed that Billy had been carrying a small suitcase owned by Washington. Within the suitcase were several copies of letters from Washington to family members, such as his brother Jack, his stepson Jackie, his caretaker at Mount Vernon, Lund Washington, and of course, one letter to his wife.

Why would Washington have copies of letters he'd already mailed? Was this a red flag that these were forgeries? No. A common practice in this era was making two copies of a letter. Often people would write a letter, make a copy of it in a letter book, and mail the original. In this way, they could use their letter book to keep track of their communication and refer back to their letters when responding. This filing system was a common practice.

De Lancey's aide "asked him a great many questions, as you may suppose; but found very little satisfaction in his answers. At last, however, he told me that he had a small portmanteau of his master's; of which, when he found that he must be put into confinement, he entreated my care."

A portmanteau was a small trunk. The writer noted that it "contained only a few stockings and shirts; and I could see nothing worth my care, except an almanac." Tucked within this almanac was "a journal, or diary of his proceedings since his first coming to New York: there were also two letters from his lady (Martha), one from Mr. Custis (her son Jackie), and some pretty long ones from a Mr. Lund Washington (overseer at Mount Vernon)."

Not only did this supposed almanac include letters that Washington had received, but they also included copies of Washington's response. "And in the same bundle with them, the first draughts, or foul copies, of answers to them. I read these with avidity; and being highly entertained with them, have shown them to several of my friends, who all agree with me, that he is a very different character from what they had supposed him."

The writer gave his opinion about Washington. "I never knew a man so much to be pitied. If I remember right, you have seen, and have some knowledge of him; but it is impossible you could form so just an estimate as these letters will give you," the letters' true author wrote, promising that these letters from Washington were not a case of mistaken identity but were one of a kind.

Employing the marketing strategy of exclusivity to encourage people to read the letters, the writer added: "They contain also, as you will find, a deal of information, not to be had anywhere else. I assure myself, therefore, you will thank me for the trouble I have taken in copying them for your perusal."

While the identity of this writer was unknown, he clearly knew enough about the fall of Fort Washington and Fort Lee—either from newspapers, personal experience, or eyewitnesses—to use it as the backstory for how he acquired Washington's correspondence. Who would learn about these letters first? The British subjects in London or the Americans in the United States? The answer to that question gives a few more clues about the sham correspondence.

General Washington privately sized up the dire situation that he and his army faced in an authentic letter he wrote on December 18, 1776, to his younger brother Samuel from his camp near the falls of Trenton, New Jersey. This was not a letter to share with the press.

After their loss at White Plains and their retreat to Hackensack, their affairs "took an adverse turn," the downcast Washington wrote, explaining that their retreat and the enemy's movements "pushed us from place to place till we were obliged to cross the Delaware (into Pennsylvania)." Compared to the ten to twelve thousand soldiers in Howe's army, Washington's army was a remnant of "less than 3,000 men fit for duty owing to the dissolution of our force by short enlistments."

Many of his men had signed agreements to fight for a short period of time. Hundreds of the three thousand he had left were under contracts that would expire at the end of the year on December 31, 1776. The fact that these agreements were short-term was a cursed policy in Washington's view because the army could not survive without longer-term commitments.

At least one soldier's enlistment had been shortened, temporarily, for another reason. Serving in the Sixth Massachusetts Regiment was a minute man from Framingham, Massachusetts, named Peter Salem, called Salem Poor. At the Battle of Bunker Hill, Poor had taken out Major John Pitcairn, the British officer thought to have ordered the first shots of the American Revolution at Lexington on April 19, 1775. Poor's heroism had accomplished more than striking a blow at the British. His example had fired up change in the Continental Army.

Poor was a black patriot, a former slave who'd trained as a minute man in Framingham and had defended Concord immediately after the Battle of Lexington. Washington had been pressured by men in South Carolina to exclude African Americans from serving in the army.

Citing Poor's heroism and skills, it is believed that Poor's commander touted his service as a reason to open the ranks to African Americans. In this way, Poor's example helped to convince Washington and others to allow black soldiers to serve.

Now Washington had to do something to motivate all of his men to stay and re-enlist. After retreating from New York, he desperately needed a win. With great vulnerability, he told Samuel that "between you and me I think our affairs are in a very bad way." The reason? His men from New York, New Jersey, and Pennsylvania would soon leave him. He was also disheartened to find so many loyalists among New Jersey's residents. "In short, the conduct of the Jersey, has been most infamous—Instead of turning out to defend their country and affording aid to our army, they are making their submissions as fast as they can."

He believed that his army might have made a stand at Hackensack if the locals had been more supportive. "In a word, my dear Sir, if every nerve is not strained to recruit the new army with all possible expedition, I think the game is pretty near up."

During the evacuation from New York into New Jersey, Washington's forces were divided into two groups, with Washington leading one column and General Charles Lee leading the other column. Lee led about seven thousand soldiers, a number which would soon dwindle to three thousand as their enlistments expired.

When Washington sent Lee instructions to join him, Lee stalled for two weeks before marching his men to meet up with the rest of the Continental Army. Why? One reason was that Lee claimed he saw an opportunity to close in on a British flank from Morristown. On the night of December 11, Lee and about a dozen guards inexplicably made his headquarters four miles away from his army at White's Tavern in Basking Ridge.

When a British loyalist got wind of Lee's position, he sought out the British army, which sent a couple dozen soldiers and officers to the tavern. Finding Lee in his night clothes while writing at his desk in the early morning of December 12, they captured him. One of Lee's men escaped, while others died or were captured.

Jacob Francis, a black patriot who served in the 16th Continental Regiment, reported that "General Lee was taken in or about Basking Ridge. I heard the guns firing." The imprisonment of his next in command was another blow to General Washington. After Lee's capture, Lee's army did what Lee had been slow to do—join up with Washington's army.

"You can form no idea of the perplexity of my situation. No man, I believe, ever had a greater choice of difficulties and less means to extricate himself from them," Washington continued to Samuel.

Despite these gloomy words and his dismal situation, Washington chose optimism. "However, under a full persuasion of the justice of our cause I cannot entertain an idea that it will finally sink though it may remain for some time under a cloud."

Washington knew he had to do something. How could he keep his remnant alive to fight another campaign in 1777? Would a surprise attack give him and America what they needed, a reason to continue the revolution? A newspaper editor soon published the answers to these questions.

Thomas Greene in New Haven, Connecticut, had already started printing his January 1, 1777, issue of *The Connecticut Journal* when he received an express letter from New Jersey. This newspaper publisher was far from green when it came to his craft. A descendant of a line of colonial printers, Greene had thirteen years of publishing experience at the time he received this express. By this point, he knew how to assess the value of a report.

Filled with relief at finally receiving good news and a desire to immediately notify his readers, he removed a portion of one of his articles on page two. He then typeset a new block quoting an extract from the letter he'd received, but left the other article dangling and incomplete. This new story was so important, Greene was willing to leave another article incomplete so he could get the news from Trenton to his readers.

"That early on the 26th of December General Washington with about 3,000 men crossed the Delaware, and at 8 in the morning engaged the enemy at Trenton, who were about 1,600 in number, and in about 35 minutes routed the whole, taking 919 prisoners, exclusive of killed and wounded," Greene joyfully published.

Washington's men had attacked the British position at Trenton, which was held by Hessians. Expecting them to have been drinking and enjoying the Christmas holiday, Washington tapped the element of surprise and caught them off guard and inebriated. The article then listed the number of officers and soldiers captured by rank along with the types of artillery and ammunition that they captured.

Greene added an explanation for interrupting the article with this insert. "We had printed off a number of papers before the above came to hand." Receiving a letter from an officer in the American army in Newtown, Pennsylvania, Greene published additional details eight days later.

"I have the pleasure of giving you an account of an advantageous victory obtained over the Hessians yesterday," this officer explained of why Washington had attacked. "Something was necessary to check the progress of the enemy; it was therefore resolved by his Excellency to attack the Hessian Army at Trenton; for which purpose everything was in readiness."

Giving additional details, this officer provided another first draft of this historic event. "And on Christmas night we marched down to the river with upwards of 2,000 men and 12 pieces of artillery, at M. Conkey's Ferry, Delaware River, and at half after 3 began our march to Trenton."

Emotions followed facts. "A colder or icier season I've never felt. Rain and hail, with high winds -- but no difficulties were too much for our worthy commander to surmount at this important crisis," he wrote of his personal experience while praising Washington.

The officers had divided their men into columns and began their attack at eight in the morning. "His Excellency commanded in person, and in about three quarters of an hour they surrendered." Only four Americans died and eight were wounded. "We intended the attack should have been before daylight but the fatigue of marching and trouble of crossing the Delaware detained us."

The Hessians had been preparing for a retreat but took their time because "the extremity of the weather made them conclude we were not coming (as they had information) and so all . . . thought themselves quite secure."

The officer exalted his fellow soldiers and General Washington. "Too much praise cannot be given to our brave troops, his Excellency was pleased at their undoubted courage; not a soul was found cowardly skulking, but was fierce for the battle."

Washington would soon use another newspaper to recruit an important member to his military family.

With the loss of New York behind him and after the success of crossing the Delaware River, Washington was ready to tap the press to his advantage. He needed to leverage the power of newspapers to both communicate with the public and get the attention of a particular soldier. The third page of *The Pennsylvania Evening Post* featured several items related to the Continental Army on January 25, 1777. Issuing a declaration of thanks, General Washington had publicly lauded the contributions of the Pennsylvania militia, as the *Evening Post* published. Likewise, General Horatio Gates had issued general orders to the leaders of the companies in Philadelphia to "be diligent in preventing their men firing off their arms in and about the streets." Following this, was a very specific, unusual advertisement targeted at only one particular person, who was ultimately under Gates's command.

"Captain Alexander Hamilton, of the New-York company of artillery, by applying to the printer of this paper, may hear of something to his advantage." At the time, Washington was in winter camp in Morristown, New Jersey, while Hamilton was in Pennsylvania. What did Hamilton discover when he came to the local newspaper office? He found further information waiting for him. Washington had written Hamilton a letter on January 20 that contained an offer of employment. Recognizing Washington's offer as a possible big break, Captain Hamilton followed the letter's directions.

Who was Alexander Hamilton at this time? Born to unmarried parents on the British island, Nevis, in the Caribbean, he'd fought societal stereotypes against illegitimate children. Hungry to learn, he'd read and studied numerous books. Members of his community were so impressed with his intelligence and gumption, that they had given him financial support and had sent him to America to get an education.

Hamilton's first big break came with a set-back, when he was denied admission to the College of New Jersey (Princeton University). Picking himself up, he pursued King's College in New York. Because King's had already started its school year in May, Hamilton began his studies there in the autumn of 1773 as a special student.

How did Hamilton first learn of George Washington? Among nine students who were new to King's College that year, he may have first learned of Washington through one of his classmates, John Parke or "Jackie" Custis, who was Washington's stepson.

Custis and Hamilton weren't destined to be classmates for long. Joining the college's president, Myles Cooper, on a journey south in late September, Custis returned to Mount Vernon to be with his family after his sister's sudden death. When Custis decided to marry his fiancée, Washington wrote a letter in December 1773 to Cooper to withdraw him from school. Despite their brief overlap, Hamilton and Jackie were likely aware of each other.

Hamilton soon faced some obstacles. Because King's College was originally chartered to honor King George II and supported by the Church of England, many of its students were loyalists. Hamilton along with John Jay, a graduate, were among the few exceptions.

Despite these differences, Hamilton didn't hide his politics. As a student he'd written logical and passionate pamphlets supporting the patriot cause. When war came to New York in the summer of 1776, Hamilton left school and served as a captain of an artillery unit. How did Hamilton come to Washington's attention?

Though it's unclear exactly what sparked the idea in Washington to put an ad in that newspaper asking for Hamilton's services, what may have first caught Washington's attention was how Hamilton faced adversity during a difficult time in his unit in April 1776. When several men in his company were court martialed for mutiny, Captain Hamilton's leadership skills may have stood out, such as his resolution and excellent writing capabilities. After answering the newspaper ad in January 1777, Hamilton learned that Washington wanted him to become one of his military aides. Accepting this as the best opportunity of his military career, Hamilton was all in.

The news was made official on March 1, 1777, in Washington's General Orders: "Alexander Hamilton Esquire is appointed Aide-De-Camp to the Commander in Chief; and is to be respected and obeyed as such." While hundreds of Washington's letters were soon written in Hamilton's handwriting, Hamilton would later prove pivotal in quelling internal military fake news and put his life on the line at Valley Forge.

Washington would need trusted aides to have his back in the disinformation war brewing in the coffee houses of London, where the *War of Lies* in his name was launched.

12 RIVETING RIVINGTON & THE RUSE

"**I**n the press, and speedily will be published, letters from General Washington to sundry of his friends in the year 1776," English printer John Bew boldly revealed in an announcement in London's *Public Advertiser*, on May 24, 1777. The news soon filled the coffee houses of London, where men gathered to drink coffee and tea and devour the gossip in the latest gazettes.

Five days later on May 29, 1777, Bew made good on his promise in an advertisement in London's *Evening Post,* which was the newspaper that he regularly printed. "This day were published letters from General Washington to several of his friends, in the year 1776, in which are set forth a farther and wider view of American politics than ever yet transpired or the public could be made acquainted with through any other channel," he published.

Unlike a feather-light, one-page handbill that was small enough to be easily passed around, Bew's eighty-page pamphlet required a stitched binding and cost more than usual. Hoping to make a killing by attacking Washington, the American Zeus, Bew sold this pamphlet for one and a half shillings.

Bew operated his printing press at building number 28 on Paternoster Row, which was the London street packed with publishing establishments and several coffee houses. At this time, coffee-houses were gathering places for men of all classes. Because they featured newspapers and other literature, they were often literary resorts of sorts. There, men temporarily escaped the smell of manure from the horse-drawn carriages on London's cobblestones for the fine aroma of coffee, including the latest roast.

As a result of Bew's latest tract, many Londoners at coffee houses throughout the city and elsewhere became acquainted with George Washington declaring a war of lies and proclaiming his torment over his love for his king while also finding himself forced to rebel against him. These juicy tidbits suggested that Washington was a conflicted man who viewed himself as a traitor trapped into fighting for a cause he didn't believe in.

Some publishers in London's literary world viewed this pamphlet with skepticism, perhaps out of jealousy that they hadn't published the information themselves, or perhaps out of knowledge that many lies were circulating in London about America. England's *Critical Review* wondered if Washington's letters in this pamphlet were forgeries. Their reason was not altruistic. Because they were skeptical of and condescending about Washington's education, they doubted he had the ability to write such eloquent prose.

"It is difficult to determine, their authenticity from any intrinsic evidence. They contain no facts of a private nature, and they discover not only sentiment, but a correctness of composition." They did include opinions about known events that were published in newspapers, such as Washington's meeting with British Colonel Paterson over Howe's failure to address Washington as a general.

The Monthly Review also questioned the authenticity of the letters, but thought they reflected well on Washington, at least from a loyalist's viewpoint. "We cannot look upon these letters, as genuine; but we must pronounce them well written: they would do great honor to General Washington, could his claim to them be indisputably established."

Who knew Bew? This provides another clue. The first printer of the forged letters had taken over the printing presses at 28 Paternoster Row from another printer in 1774. The three-story building included an impressive open space for the printing presses and respectable living quarters above. Known for publishing tracts, picture prints, and other ephemeral material, John Bew had no known connection to George Washington.

Yet he worked across the street and a block and a half away from two shops run by the Rivington family, 58 Paternoster Row, and another shop around the corner. Known as the Church of England's printer, John Rivington had taken over the family business from his father, Charles Rivington, who'd operated the Book and Crown on St. Paul's Courtyard. Because Bew had been the first to publish the news of Rivington's return to London, Bew certainly knew the answer to this question: What had Rivington been up to since leaving New York and returning to London?

★ ★ ★ ★ ★

Several months after Bew's pamphlet appeared on the tables of London's coffee houses, James Rivington returned to America. "The printer of this paper, being again happily arrived in this city, presents his most respectful compliments to the public in general, and to his former subscribers in particular," James Rivington joyfully declared in his new newspaper, *Rivington's New York Royal Gazette,* on October 4, 1777. With the word *royal* in his newspaper, he clearly showed where he placed his allegiance.

The British military occupation of New York gave Rivington the security he needed to return and resume publishing his newspaper. He wanted to make it clear that the robbery against him in 1775 had not changed his principles.

"When he first began to publish a weekly paper, he is conscious to himself that he set out with the most upright intentions," Rivington wrote about himself in an article while thanking his supporters. He confessed that when the rebellion began, he'd tried to be neutral "by printing such detached, pieces, and pamphlets as had a tendency to preserve peace, order and legal government, to keep up and strengthen our connection with the Mother Country."

This time, however, he would not pretend to be neutral. Why? Rivington had a new title as "Printer to the King's Most Excellent Majesty." He expressed his joy over this new role.

"Supremely happy will the printer be, if he can make his paper subservient to the intentions of government—the restoration of peace, order, and happiness through the continent." Though he was now on the King's payroll, he intended to write and print with veracity. "He assures them that truth, candor and decorum, shall ever preside over his press," he printed, promising both "quality and quantity, of intelligence and other literary matter in his paper."

He would not be like others who had "sacrificed their own reputations to the idol of American independency." Rivington believed that he could bring the rebels back to their senses through his newspaper "by recalling the infatuated multitude to the use of their reason and understanding and by convincing them how grossly they have been imposed upon by the misrepresentations and false glasses of their leaders in sedition and rebellion."

In other words, Rivington was now a propagandist for King George III in New York.

The evidence revealed that while he was in London, he'd gone shopping. For a man who'd lost his business and livelihood in 1775, he certainly didn't lack credit or money. As the King's printer, he had received a sizable sum that enabled him to bring numerous goodies back to America to sell. For several weeks in his newspaper in the autumn of 1777, he published an advertisement that took up most of the last page and announced all sorts of goods that he was selling at his store.

Need footwear? Go to Rivington's for gentlemen's shoes, silk stockings, and spectacles. Want luxury items? Rivington had telescopes, flutes, and violins to sell. Want bestselling books or the latest pamphlets? Rivington had it all, making his shop, a storefront facing New York's coffee house bridge, a luxury literary resort.

Was John Bew's May 1777 pamphlet of Washington's forged 1776 letters in his treasure trove? If it was, Rivington didn't advertise it to his New York readers, at least not yet. Perhaps he was waiting for the right time to reveal his most provocative item for sale, or maybe the war would end soon and he wouldn't need to advertise his silver bullet of propaganda.

At the same time he resumed publishing his newspaper in New York, Rivington couldn't have been more pleased with the progress of the war favoring England. He had good reasons to be happy. Washington's troops had recently lost the Battle of Brandywine on September 11, 1777, in Pennsylvania. This victory gave the British the ability to march to Philadelphia, where Congress met.

Rivington reported that on General Howe's march toward the American metropolis of Philadelphia, the British had stopped at a place called Valley Forge. "On the same day, September 21, we advanced with the (Royal) Army and baggage to the Valley Forge," Rivington published a report from a British soldier of his army's movements.

What Rivington didn't print or know was the fact that at the same time, Washington had sent Colonel Alexander Hamilton to retrieve or destroy the rebel supplies at a flour mill in Valley Forge. On September 18, Hamilton and six American dragoons left their camp. When they approached the flour mill, which was along the Schuylkill River, they had to descend a hill and cross a bridge over rapidly-flowing water from recent heavy rain. After they reached the mill, Hamilton took one of the flat-bottomed boats in case they needed to escape. Sure enough, two British soldiers arrived at the top of the hill and fired to announce their presence.

When more British soldiers arrived, Hamilton ordered his men to evacuate. He and four of his dragoons hopped into the boat while two others headed toward the bridge on horseback to divert attention away from the boat. The British fired twelve to fifteen shots, and Hamilton and his men tried to shoot back while fighting the fast, violent current of the water.

The two American men on horseback escaped, not knowing the fate of the men in the boat. One of them immediately wrote a letter about the incident and his fears that Hamilton and the others were lost and sent it to General Washington, who was with part of the army at Reading Furnace. The possibility of Hamilton's death deeply impacted Washington.

What happened to Hamilton? He and his men escaped, but not without injury. Ever quick-thinking, Hamilton kept his eye on the big picture and took initiative. "If Congress has not yet left Philadelphia, they ought to do it immediately without fail, for the enemy has the means of throwing a party this night into the city," Hamilton wrote in a quick dispatch to John Hancock, president of the Continental Congress, in Philadelphia. He explained that the British had fired on them in the boat "by which means I lost my horse. One man was killed and another wounded. The boats were abandoned and will fall into their hands. I did all I could to prevent this but to no purpose."

The minutes of the Continental Congress on this date explained that they were in recess when Hamilton's note arrived. "During the adjournment the president received a letter from Colonel Hamilton, one of General Washington's aids, which intimated the necessity of Congress removing immediately from Philadelphia; Whereupon, the members left the city." They fled to Lancaster, Pennsylvania.

When Hamilton arrived at Washington's headquarters, he didn't know that Washington had been told that he'd died. When Hamilton entered Washington's tent, Washington felt immense relief and joy at seeing Hamilton alive and well. Foremost on Hamilton's mind was his fear that the two men on horseback had died. Washington told him that the pair had escaped and were safe.

Rivington published the outcome of this incident from the point of view of a British soldier, who sent him a report of what happened at Valley Forge, "where we had taken a great quantity of flour, shovels, picks, nails, hatchets, soap, candles, horseshoes, etc. plenty of which articles were stored there for the use of the rebels."

The good news kept arriving at Rivington's shop, which he gleefully reported. "The Royal Army under the command of his Excellency Sir William Howe, Knight of the Bath, marched from their encampment" and seized Philadelphia on September 26, 1777.

"The happy prospect now opening to use from the great success with which it hath pleased God to bless his Majesty's arms," Rivington wrote with unfeigned joy. Even better news soon came to him from upstate New York.

"We have got a confirmation of the TOTAL ROUTE and DISPERSION of the REBEL ARMY on the 4th instant (Oct)," Rivington published of an early report of the Battle of Germantown on October 18, 1777, though he had to wait nearly a month for more information. "October 3rd, dawn of day under a very thick fog, General Washington with his whole force made an attack. The principal one was at Germantown."

After defeating Washington's troops at Brandywine and occupying Philadelphia, General Howe had sent nine thousand troops to camp nearby in Germantown, Pennsylvania. Why was Germantown significant to Howe? Despite his recent victories, he didn't control Philadelphia's water transport to the Atlantic Ocean, the Delaware River. Hence, he needed to prevent an assault on his position in Philadelphia. Sending a large contingent of men to Germantown protected Howe's supply route by land.

How did General Washington respond? Concluding that the British soldiers at Germantown were not well fortified, he decided that his men were skilled enough to attack. Math entered into his offensive strategy. Washington divided his men into four groups to attack the British on each of the four roads leading to Germantown. Would his plan prove better on paper than in reality?

Two columns failed to arrive in time. Led by General John Sullivan, the third column attacked the British at their center. At first his men caught the British soldiers by surprise. When the fourth column, led by Nathanael Greene, arrived later than expected, the battlefield was covered with gun smoke and fog. The result was friendly fire, where Greene's and Sullivan's men accidentally fired on each other thinking they were engaging the enemy.

By the time the two columns realized what had happened, the

British counter-attacked, which led the patriots to retreat. About five hundred British soldiers were killed or injured compared to one thousand Americans wounded or dead.

While Rivington described the battle as a total rout of the Continental Army, Washington's men had performed better than prior battles, despite their losses. Their skills were better, which gave Washington hope that with more training, his men could become a formidable force. The question was this: How could he give his men the training they needed to fight a European army?

In addition to reporting on Germantown, Rivington dispelled rumors that America would ally itself with France, which was King George III's greatest fear. A French frigate was sailing to Philadelphia with "notice from the French King, which is to be delivered to the French officers in the service of the Congress, on pain of death, immediately to return to France," Rivington published on October 25. Another report suggested that the King of France had also issued the same order for any French citizen aiding the American patriots.

Not only that, but a letter from Paris also reported "that the American deputies were preparing to return home, having found all their endeavors ineffectual with respect to establishing a union between France and America against Great Britain."

Sandwiched between this good news about Britain's victory in Germantown and the patriots' failure to make France an ally, Rivington published news that greatly concerned him. "Various reports have been propagated in this city since our last, relative to the situation of General Burgoyne's Army; some of them too ridiculous to justify a repetition," Rivington hinted on October 25 about rumors regarding the British army in upstate New York.

Giving his opinion, Rivington accused the rumors of being made up, a ruse. "It seems this news originated with and came from the rebels, who fabricated the story with a view to enlist men; and, to give an air of truth to it, at Elizabethtown (New Jersey) they caused guns to be fired, bonfires to be made, and every other demonstration of joy and triumph at the same time dealing out rum to the rebels, without measure."

If Rivington thought this was a ruse, then why did he publish it? Was he trying to dispel propaganda or did he truly have an eye and ear for real news? As the King's printer, he had to be careful to report information, even if true, that didn't favor the British.

A week later on Nov. 1, he asked for forgiveness for publishing the subterfuge about a British loss. "As no accounts, properly authenticated, of the situation of the northern Army, have yet been brought to the city, the printer entreats the public to excuse his inserting any of the reports that have been circulated, until he may be warranted by intelligence derived immediately from General Burgoyne."

Reading Rivington had become riveting for royalists. But would his decision to employ anonymous sources make it difficult to determine one very important thing: the truth?

13 ANONYMOUS SOURCES

Anonymous sources are as critical to a propaganda war as cannons are to an army and gunpowder is to a musket. As if sharpening the blade on his bayonet, James Rivington sought to allay his readers' fears that France would aid the Americans through sharp jabs from unnamed sources in the *Royal Gazette*.

Rivington first published a scathing opinion piece in October 1777 from an anonymous source who didn't believe that France would "attack this country (England) in support of the rebellious Americans, [for in doing so] she would engage in a war far more ruinous to herself than to us."

Why was this source so confident that France wouldn't get involved? Money. France was in debt. "The power of France, like the power of all other countries of this age, depends upon the sum she can annually apply to the war," this unnamed source pointed out. Starting a war with England would put King Louis XVI into greater debt, which would ruin his country. All the musketeers in the world couldn't save him from financial insolvency.

In that same newspaper under the heading "Foreign Intelligence," Rivington published a daring tidbit from an anonymous French source. "We are assured our court (France) will enter into no war, so long as our flag remains free from insult." Not only that, but the article stated that the French Admiralty had also ordered the capture of American merchant ships.

Still another source emphatically claimed that France would not enter the war. Rivington published an "extract of a letter from a person of distinction at Paris to his friend in London."

"Be assured, my dear Sir, that your apprehensions of an approaching rupture with France are groundless; at least, such an event is at a considerable distance." This was in part because one of King Louis XVI's advisers, who favored America, had been replaced by a duke who opposed the rebels. The combined force of these articles was sure to thwart the rumors that France was covertly aiding the Americans.

"As to assisting and supporting the Americans underhand[ly], and covering their trade both in Europe and the West India Islands, that cord had been strained till it was ready to break, and they have already got all the money of the Americans for arms, ammunition," this third source wrote, seeking to put down the possibility of a formal French-American alliance.

Still a fourth report from a gentleman in the know wrote in the sharpest of terms: "The present disposition of the French cabinet: the King (of France) is point blank for peace at all events."

Was there anyone in the French court who supported going to war against England? Yes, there was a very visible supporter, who loved extravagant hairstyles as much as the finest gowns money could buy. King Louis XVI's wife, Queen Marie Antoinette, who was originally from Austria, supported the American patriots. "Her Majesty is for war; which opinion, is it said, is highly agreeable to that of her brother the emperor." Her brother Joseph was the Holy Roman Emperor.

Not to worry. This anonymous source believed that King Louis XVI's position was against America. "In this divided interest it is at present the better opinion in Paris [that] the King will prevail; and when he takes a thing in his head, he is known, to be very positive."

Rivington ended this rhetorical campaign with a final fifth source, who took a stab at the failure of America's celebrity diplomat in France, Benjamin Franklin.

"Notwithstanding the many reports which have been raised relative to the consequence of Dr. Franklin in Paris," Rivington's final source pointed out. "He never once had a conference on business with any, even of the most inferior officers of the (French) cabinet."

To reinforce the report that Franklin was not making progress, Rivington's source claimed "that on the contrary, he is very little noticed, except by some of the least considerable of his countrymen at the English coffee houses (in France), and in general seems to have little to do."

This source's conclusion was simple. "France had never more reason to dread the power of England than at this time, or England more right to chastise that insidious and deceitful people."

The problem with anonymous sources is that they can be faked. How can readers know if a newspaper article is accurate if no one is willing to put their name next to their claims?

Perhaps this is why Rivington slipped in a tiny tart detail, which revealed some truth. "On Wednesday very large orders for military stores of all kinds necessary for another campaign, were delivered to the tower (in France), to be got ready with all expedition for America." Off the record, France was unofficially helping the United States.

If Rivington had consulted George Washington, the former hero against the French from decades earlier, he might have received further ammunition to douse this rumor of a French-US alliance.

General Washington had privately agreed with Rivington and expressed his deep doubts that Congress would be able to make France an ally. "For I profess myself to be of that class who never built sanguinely upon the assistance of France," he'd written in April 1777, to Richard Henry Lee, who was a member of the Continental Congress' secret committee to enlist France's assistance.

An angry Washington also fumed about the latest dirty trick by the British, who'd succeeded in lowering the value of Continental bills of credit. Washington had called it "low arts and dirty tricks" and a "diabolical scheme" from what was once a "virtuous people."

Why did he doubt that a French alliance would take place? First, he'd continued to believe that Britain would be able to thwart ships coming from France to America. Washington had known about the Continental Congress's secret plan to enlist France's help.

On April 18 and May 9, 1776, Washington had ordered General Artemis Ward to purchase the *Little Hannah* and *Jenny*, which were British vessels captured by the patriots. Congress's secret committee sought "to purchase a small fast sailing vessel" to cross the Atlantic. "It is a fast sailor we want as the principal object is to go and come safe. . . . You'll please to call this vessel *The Dispatch* and keep her in readiness to sail in a few hours after orders arrive from the committee for her to depart."

Following Washington's and the committee's directions, Ward had changed the *Little Hannah's* name to *The Dispatch*, and this ship sailed for Bordeaux, France in mid-July 1776. Carrying letters to purchase cannon, muskets, and ammunition from French merchants, *The Dispatch* was captured by a British warship off Delaware on July 22, 1776. Hence, Washington had long known that the first attempt to reach France had failed.

Not only had he doubted the ability of American merchant ships to slip past British ships in the Atlantic, but Washington also still held a measure of contempt for France. He'd not forgotten the foe he'd faced in the 1750s. Washington believed that France wouldn't take any meaningful steps to help the patriots "further than her winking at our supplies from thence for the benefits derived from our trade."

Despite this, several Frenchmen had arrived in Philadelphia to offer their assistance to the American cause in 1777. Some of them had given Washington advice that was as irritating as it was useless. "The plan drawn by the French general is of such a nature, that it is impracticable to carry it into execution this campaign," he shared with Richard Henry Lee. Tapping his diplomatic skills, he hadn't discarded the options presented by this unnamed French general. "It may however be kept in view, and the whole, or such parts of it adopted, as our circumstances upon a full consideration of the matter may hereafter admit of."

One of those French officers who'd received a command from Washington was rumored to be an anonymous newspaper source after the battle of Germantown.

Unlike Rivington, not every newspaper editor believed that anonymous sources were the best ways to discover the truth. A candid article appeared in *Dunlap's Maryland Gazette* after the Battles of Brandywine and Germantown. Newspaper publisher John Dunlap had printed broadsheets of the Declaration of Independence. Broadsheets or broadsides were large sheets of paper printed on one side. Dunlap published an editorial that critiqued anonymous sources.

"Perhaps nothing has a greater tendency to impose upon the public, and do injustice to mankind, than the frequent publications of extracts from anonymous writers, whose sole aim seem to be to please and flatter one particular corps in which they have some connections, and to detract from the merit of all others," Dunlap's editorialist wrote, deriding recent publications from his fellow American soldiers.

"I observe in your paper of the 2nd of October you have published an extract of a letter from a gentleman of distinction in Philadelphia, to his friend in Boston, dated September 15, 1777, respecting the Battle on Brandywine, which is perhaps as complete with misrepresentations as any yet published. As I was a spectator in the action, I shall point out some of them."

After detailing many of the mistakes in this previous anonymous letter, this author criticized the other soldier for failing to mention key units that served with distinction at Brandywine, such as "Lord Stirling's division and particularly Conway's brigade."

The writer referred to Lord Stirling, who was William Alexander, a New-York-born Scottish American who claimed lands in Scotland and the title of Lord Stirling. One of Washington's officers at the Battle of Long Island, General Stirling had been captured by the British but had stalled their advance long enough to allow other soldiers to escape. After Stirling returned in a prisoner exchange, Washington gave him command in the 1777 campaign.

The other gentleman was Brigadier General Thomas Conway, who moved from Ireland to France as a child and later joined the French Army, serving in an Irish unit. Recruited by Silas Dean in France to serve as an English-speaking French officer in America, Conway arrived in 1777, received a brigade to command, and performed admirably at Germantown.

"Perhaps the late battle at Germantown has finally convinced the world, that those principal commanders do not want skill or the troops efficient bravery, to do what no other troops have done since the war commenced," the soldier wrote, detailing a number of egregious mistakes in the previous publication by the other soldier. What made him even more furious was that the other soldier hid behind anonymity.

"Whenever this gentleman shall think proper to support the facts contained in his letter, and a fix his name to the performance, he shall then see the evidence to prove his mistakes, with my name a fixed to the answers; until that time, I shall pass by the name of CANDIDUS."

The irony, of course, was that an anonymous author named Candidus was critical of anonymous sources. Who was Candidus? Some believe it was an aide to General Conway or Conway himself. Not long after Brandywine and without consulting Washington, Conway asked Congress for a promotion. A positive newspaper article about this Frenchman and his men aided his case for promotion. Conway's loyalty to Washington, however, would soon come into question as he sought to become chummy with General Horatio Gates, who led the Continental Army in New York.

Anonymous sources would continue to supply newspaper editors, whether patriot or loyalist, throughout the war. The most reliable news in the fall of 1777, however, for James Rivington came on-the-record, from the named sources of General Burgoyne and General Gates.

"The following is published from good authority, articles of convention between Lieutenant General Burgoyne and Major General Gates," Rivington printed on November 8, 1777 of the British general's surrender after the Battle of Saratoga.

Rivington's initial report of this patriot victory celebration was not a ruse. Burgoyne's surrender to Gates took place in New York after two battles, one at Saratoga followed by a defeat at Bemis Heights several days later.

Burgoyne and his troops had entered New York from Canada. Quickly and easily capturing Fort Ticonderoga, Burgoyne had attacked General Gates's army on September 19, 1777, at Freeman's Farm in Saratoga, New York. Benedict Arnold, one of Gates's officers, had gained permission from a reluctant Gates to aid Daniel Morgan's riflemen, who were top notch sharpshooters. Morgan's men had taken out a number of British soldiers and had significantly weakened Burgoyne.

Taking his time and expecting reinforcements, Burgoyne waited two weeks before attacking Gates's army at Bemis Heights. While Gates had ordered Arnold to stay in his quarters, Arnold had defied him and led a counter attack that had forced the British to retreat. Though Arnold was seriously wounded, he emerged as a hero. Unable to fight the waves of patriot militia joining Gates, Burgoyne had surrendered to Gates ten days later on October 17.

"The troops under Lt. General Burgoyne to march out of their camp with the honors of war and the artillery of the entrenchments, to the verge of the river where the old Fort stood, where the arms and artillery are to be left," Rivington published on November 8 of the surrender terms. He assured his loyalist readers that Burgoyne would be safe. "A free passage is to be granted to the army under Lt. General Burgoyne to Great Britain on condition of not serving again in Northern America during the present contest."

One key component was missing from the articles of surrender. Burgoyne had not signed Gates's document, as was custom. To his credit, Rivington published this information. "To prevent any doubts that might arise from Lieutenant General Burgoyne's name not being mentioned in the above entry, Major General Gates hereby declares that he is understood to be comprehended in it as fully as if his name had been specifically mentioned. Signed Horatio Gates, M. G."

While the surrender of General Burgoyne to General Gates was a major victory published in newspapers, the initial fallout would unleash a war within, an internal war inside the Continental army, while turning Rivington's ruse about the French alliance on its head.

Was the next news about Gates true? Was he disobeying an order from Washington and conspiring with another officer to take Washington's job?

14 BATTLING THE WAR WITHIN

Unlike his commanding officer, General Horatio Gates occasionally forgot to mind his manners. What was his faux pas? He notified the Continental Congress of his victory over General John Burgoyne at the Battle of Saratoga in New York in 1777 before he alerted General Washington. As a result, he insulted his Commander-in-Chief. Was his breach of decorum on purpose to kowtow to Congress or was it a mistake in the fog of war?

Pushing aside the affront, Washington met with his war council of officers to discuss the immediate threat in Pennsylvania. He desperately needed additional troops to prevent the British military in Philadelphia from gaining full control of the Delaware River. The Continental Army had already lost the nation's capital, but if they could keep access to the Delaware River, they could control supply lines. With General Burgoyne and his troops captured as prisoners of war, the officers concluded that Gates no longer required as many soldiers in New York.

The Commander-in-Chief needed someone to relay to Gates the war council's decision to relocate some troops. Conscious that he'd lost more than he'd gained, Washington also knew he couldn't just send anyone to the victorious Gates. He needed someone who was exceptionally polite, well-spoken, firm, and able to see the big picture of winning independence and taking initiative. He also needed someone who'd served under Gates. Who could he entrust with this mission?

"It having been judged expedient by the members of a council of war held yesterday, that one of the gentlemen of my family should be sent to General Gates in order to lay before him the state of this army and the situation of the enemy," Washington wrote to Alexander Hamilton from his headquarters of Whitpain Township, Pennsylvania, northwest of Philadelphia, on October 30, 1777, "I have thought it proper to appoint you that duty." Washington then ordered Hamilton to immediately depart for Albany to find Gates.

"What you are chiefly to attend to is to point out in the clearest and fullest manner to General Gates the absolute necessity that there is for his detaching a very considerable part of the army at present under his command to the reinforcement of this." Washington explained that the war council had chosen which of Gates's troops should come to Pennsylvania.

Though he didn't quite achieve Paul-Revere-like speed, Hamilton nonetheless arrived in Albany, New York, within six days, a respectable amount of time. He soon had both good and bad news to share.

"I arrived here yesterday at noon and waited upon General Gates immediately on the business of my mission; but was sorry to find his ideas did not correspond with yours for drawing off the number of troops you directed," Hamilton wrote General Washington on November 6 of the resistance Gates had given him.

"I used every argument in my power to convince him of the propriety of the measure, but he was inflexible in the opinion that two brigades at least of Continental troops should remain in and near this place," Hamilton relayed, detecting a lack of logic coming from Gates. This young colonel was as incredulous as he was mystified by their conversation. Why would Gates defy General Washington and the war council? After all, Gates had participated in such war councils as adjutant general when both he and Washington were at Cambridge in 1775.

"The force of these reasons did by no means strike me, and I did everything in my power to show they were unsubstantial . . . I found myself infinitely embarrassed and was at a loss how to act," Hamilton continued, realizing it was hard to oppose Gates after his recent success that had "raised him into the highest importance. General Gates has won the entire confidence of the Eastern States."

Hamilton proved why Washington had sent him. Unlike some of his military aides, he understood the politics of what was happening.

"General Gates has influence and interest elsewhere; he might use it, if he pleased, to discredit the measure there also," he wrote, referring to the Continental Congress and those members who were basking in the glory of Gates and Saratoga. "On the whole it appeared to me dangerous to insist on sending more troops from hence while

General Gates appeared so warmly opposed to it."

Despite his forthrightness, so strong was his disappointment that Hamilton felt he'd failed Washington.

"I am afraid what I have done may not meet with your approbation as not being perhaps fully warranted by your instructions; but I ventured to do what I thought right, hoping that at least the goodness of my intention will excuse the error of my judgment."

Determined not to give up, Hamilton took his time before returning to Pennsylvania. A few days later, he tried again to convince Gates and thought he made some headway only to "find everything has been neglected, and deranged" by one of Gates's officers who wanted to lead an expedition against the British headquarters. To Hamilton, attacking New York City, which was overflowing with Redcoats, seemed a futile choice as long as the Delaware River could still be protected. By this time Hamilton was furious.

"Not the least attention has been paid to my order in your name for a detachment of 1,000 men from the troops hitherto stationed at this post. Everything is sacrificed to the whim of taking New York," he reported to Washington on November 10. Realizing what he was up against, Hamilton tried another tack.

"The plan I before laid having been totally deranged, a new one has become necessary." Just as Washington had surveyed and gathered information about the French forts in the 1750s, so Hamilton used his time in Albany to gather intelligence over what the Northern Army's needs were.

"My opinion is that the only present use for troops in this quarter is to protect the country from the depredations of little plundering parties and for carrying on the works necessary for the defense of the river. Nothing more ought to be thought of," he told Washington. "'Tis only wasting time and misapplying men to employ them in a farcical parade against New York."

For his part, Gates put his opinion about both the demand and Hamilton in writing to Washington.

"After sending upwards of five thousand men to the succor of the Southern Army, I hoped a further draught from this department would have been unnecessary," Gates bluntly wrote Washington on November 7. "But Colonel Hamilton acquaints me, it was the unanimous opinion of a council of war."

He explained that he needed more men to defend upstate New York than what would be left if he agreed to send the men south. "With the greatest deference to the opinion of the Council of War, Colonel Hamilton, after presenting me with Your Excellency's Letter, verbally demanded, that almost the whole of the troops now in this department, should be ordered to proceed directly," Gates complained about Hamilton.

"I told the colonel that your Excellency's orders should be obeyed, but that if my opinion was to be taken upon the subject, I was entirely averse to more than one brigade being sent from hence."

Hidden behind his angst against Hamilton was ambition. If General Gates gave in, he knew he could never possess Canada with the number of men he had left. A victory north of the border would bring more honor and glory to Gates, but what good would it do if Pennsylvania was lost in the process?

"Although it is customary and even absolutely necessary to direct implicit obedience to be paid to the verbal orders of aides de camp, in action to delegate that dictatorial power to one aide de camp sent to an army 300 miles distant," was too much, in Gates's view. Because these words questioned Washington's judgment, Gates decided to mind his manners. He reconsidered this passage and ultimately omitted the last sentence in his final draft to his Commander-in-Chief.

With his eagle eye surveying the big picture, Hamilton took a risk by taking initiative before he left Albany. Employing his excellent composition skills, Hamilton wrote General Gates a letter.

"Since my arrival in this quarter, I have been endeavoring to collect the best idea I could of the state of things in New York in order the better to form a judgment of the probable reinforcement gone to General Howe," Hamilton wrote Gates on November 13.

Calculating the enemy's movements in New York, Hamilton concluded that six to seven thousand Redcoats had left New York to reinforce General Howe in Pennsylvania. "If so, the number gone and going to General Washington is far inferior—5,000 at the utmost."

What was going on with Gates? Why was he resisting Washington? After all, they had a common bond. Gates had been injured in the same battle as Washington's near-death experience in 1755. He had served Washington with ease as adjutant general in Cambridge in 1775. Was something else behind Gates's decision to question the war council's judgment and his rejection of Hamilton? Gates's actions and attitude toward Washington seemed to convey a selfish motive. While Gates balked, another general called him out.

"Such wicked duplicity of conduct, I shall always think it my duty to detect," Lord Stirling wrote with as much disgust as indignation in a letter to General Washington on November 3, 1777. "The enclosed was communicated (an) idea of the state of politics and parties in this country." General Gates's military aide had given Stirling military intelligence about a secret letter between General Gates and General Thomas Conway.

"Heaven has been determined to save your country; Or a weak general and bad counselors would have ruined it," General Conway had written to General Gates after his victory at Saratoga. Who was the weak general? Stirling concluded that Conway was referring to General Washington.

General Gates had ordered his aide-de-camp, James Wilkinson, to travel to York, Pennsylvania, to give the Continental Congress news about Burgoyne's surrender. Along the way, Wilkinson had stopped at Lord Stirling's position in Reading, Pennsylvania. While there Wilkinson had given Stirling's aide-de-camp a copy of Conway's letter to Gates.

How did Washington respond to this news that Conway thought he was a weak general?

Receiving Stirling's letter on November 4 at his camp at Whitemarsh, Washington took swift action the next day. Concealing his feelings, he wrote General Conway a short, concise letter, without any emotion or requests. He simply notified Conway that he'd obtained this information.

"Sir, a letter which I received last night, contained the following, paragraph. In a letter from General Conway to General Gates he says— 'Heaven has been determined to save your country; or a weak general and bad counselors would have ruined it.' I am Sir, your humble servant."

How did Conway respond? That same day, from the same encampment at Whitemarsh, Conway defended himself. Yet he did so in writing rather than riding a horse or walking over to Washington's headquarters and speaking to him in person. Declaring that he'd congratulated Gates and "spoke my mind freely, I found fault with several measures pursued in this army; but I will venture to say that in my whole letter the paragraph of which you are pleased to send me a copy cannot be found," Conway wrote Washington.

He particularly disavowed the offensive phrase attributed to him. "I believe I can attest that the expression 'weak General' has not slipped from my pen." Denial alone wasn't a strong enough defense. Going on the offense, Conway also told Washington what he thought of him: "My opinion of you Sir, without flattery or envy is as follows: you are a brave man, an honest man, a patriot, and a man of great sense. Your modesty is such, that although your advice in council is commonly sound and proper, you have often been influenced by men who were not equal to you in point of experience, knowledge, or judgment."

Pledging his word as an officer and a gentleman, the Irish Conway added, "I know, Sir, that several unfavorable hints have been given to you about me."

How did General Gates react to the news that Washington knew about this letter from Conway to him? He acted like a mouse caught in a trap.

"I shall not attempt to describe what, as a private gentleman, I cannot help feeling, on representing to my mind, the disagreeable situation, which confidential letters, when exposed to public inspection, may place an unsuspecting correspondent to," Gates wrote to Washington on December 8.

Realizing that he was on the verge of a severe rupture with his Commander-in-Chief, the one who'd given him the rank of general when the British military had denied him promotion any higher than a major, the loyal soldier in Gates stepped up. He asked Washington to help him "in tracing out the author of the infidelity, which put extracts from General Conway's letters to me, into your hands." Gates was unaware that his aide Wilkinson had passed the intelligence along to Lord Stirling.

"Those letters have been stealingly copied; but, which of them, when, or by whom, is to me, as yet, an unfathomable secret," Gates wrote, calling on Washington to find the wretch who had betrayed him. Then Gates increased the stakes. "The danger of my being betrayed to the enemy by the same traitor," Gates emphasized in a letter that asked Congress to investigate this crime of magnitude.

Was Gates's outrage genuine, or was he placating Washington to buy time as other actions in Congress threatened Washington's power?

Though they'd received a letter from General Conway offering his resignation on November 14, the Continental Congress instead assigned Conway to the newly-created position of inspector general and the rank of major general.

Not only did they promote Conway instead of reprimanding him, but the Board of War also named Gates as its president on November 27. This created a conflict of interest and technically made Gates Washington's civil superior. One member of Congress who supported this move was Washington's Virginia friend, Richard Henry Lee.

Was something more afoot? Were Congress's chess piece movements on the military board an attempt to take out Washington as Commander-in-Chief? Such was the worry among Washington's most loyal aides. These true-blue Continentals feared that Conway was creating a cabal against General Washington.

Of course, they also had to always keep their eyes on the primary enemy, who wore red.

In early December 1777, the British Redcoats had launched a failed surprise attack at the Continental Army's camp at Whitemarsh, which bordered the Schuylkill River northwest of Philadelphia. Why weren't they successful in attacking? Because a woman with the heart a dove had made a lion-like decision.

A Philadelphia Quaker, Lydia Darrah, had been forced to allow British officers to take over her home. In the middle of the night, this anti-war pacifist had pretended to be asleep. Then she'd crept down the hall and overheard the British officers discussing the attack as they'd met in her parlor. Later when they had knocked on her bedroom door to say they were leaving, she had waited a couple of minutes, forcing them to knock again. Through this stealthy maneuver, she'd convinced them that she had been asleep so they wouldn't suspect her next move.

Receiving a pass from Philadelphia's British guards to go to a flour mill outside of town the next day, she passed the mill and continued to Whitemarsh. There she alerted a few of Washington's guards of the plan she'd overheard. When the British soldiers arrived near the Whitemarsh encampment, the advanced Continental guards were armed and ready, stopping the surprise attack. Washington then decided to move to a safer position further west and chose Valley Forge, where they had to build their winter encampment from scratch.

With nonstop smoke from fires to keep them warm, Washington's men began building huts and shelters. Missing, of course, were their stores of candles, soap, shovels, nails, flour, and other supplies that the British military had taken from Valley Forge's flour mill after their skirmish with Alexander Hamilton the previous September.

However, one of Washington's stars had fallen. At least, he feared he'd fallen out of favor with his beloved commander. Like Conway, he'd been trained by the French military. Unlike Conway, he knew how to be a loyal friend to the Americans. Who was this patriot?

15 FRENCH ROAST

When a bold French officer tried to visit General Washington at his Valley Forge headquarters in December, he was shooed away as if he were a pesky Gallic rooster. The general was too busy with the details of building his winter camp to answer the Frenchman's call.

Burdened with the news he carried and worried that Washington's rejection signaled personal disapproval, this young Frenchman decided to write Washington a letter. Proclaiming that his respect and friendship was as true and candid as the best of patriots, this nobleman affirmed his ardent support for the cause and "enthusiastic wishes for the happiness and liberty of this country."

Was this gentleman the Irish-French general, Thomas Conway, seeking to make amends? No, this was the Marquis de Lafayette—Marie-Joseph Paul Yves Roch Gilbert du Motier de La Fayette. He was born in 1757 into one of France's wealthiest families. His father died in a military battle two years later, and his mother died when Lafayette was only eleven. Choosing a military career, Lafayette had become a captain and part of France's elite Black Musketeers when he was sixteen years old. His commission had ended when the French government, greatly in debt, cut spending.

Two years later in 1775, while Washington was trying to expel the British from Boston, Lafayette had attended a dinner with King George III's brother, the Duke of Gloucester. The duke had spoken despairingly about his brother's British subjects in America. To the duke, Americans were merely Yankee doodles lacking the sophistication of traveling to Italy and tasting exotic food like macaroni. The "Grand Tour" was a rite of passage for any well-bred Briton and macaroni was frequently on the tour's menu.

Lafayette openly disagreed with the duke's insults and snobbishness. The American ideas of self-rule and equality had enchanted Lafayette so much that he decided to become a patriot.

"My heart was enlisted . . . and I thought only of joining my colors to those of the revolutionaries." At age nineteen, Lafayette used his own money to slip the bonds of France and sail to America. He arrived in Philadelphia in time for the fall campaign.

Though some in Congress considered Frenchmen to be arrogant glory seekers, the well-mannered Lafayette seemed different. Agreeing to serve with an honorary officer's commission, he declined a salary and professed to be a genuine believer in the cause of freedom and ideals of America.

Just as French roast coffee was known for its intense taste, so Lafayette was known for his bold decisions. Yet his tongue lacked acidity. Like Washington, he valued manners. While wearing his exquisite glistening, white French uniform, Lafayette rode with Washington to review the troops. Instead of comparing Washington's rag-tag, plainly-dressed, army to the bold blue uniforms of the French dragoons, Lafayette had shown Washington humility, proclaiming, "I am here to learn, not to teach." This Gallic rooster had joined the American brood.

A musket ball had passed through Lafayette's leg at the Battle of Brandywine. Hours later, Washington said something remarkable, especially given his past history of fighting the French military. Well aware of the prejudice against Frenchmen, Washington had told the surgeon taking care of Lafayette to "treat him as if he were my son."

Why was Washington now refusing to see this trained musketeer just three months later? "I see plainly that America can defend herself if proper measures are taken," Lafayette assured Washington in writing on December 30, 1777, after failing to get a meeting with him.

Though thrilled with the outcome at Saratoga, Lafayette was worried about the war brewing within the army. "Now I begin to fear that she could be lost by herself and her own sons," Lafayette wrote, referring to the internal conflict. He was as candid as if he was the only candle burning in a French chandelier.

"There are open dissensions in Congress, parties who hate one another as much as the common enemy, stupid men who without knowing a single word about war undertake to judge you, to make ridiculous comparisons," he wrote, disillusioned by his belief that every man in America "was a lover of liberty and would rather die free than live a slave." He had once believed that Congress's confidence in Washington was boundless. Now he'd changed his mind.

"They are infatuated with Gates without thinking of the different circumstances, and believe that attacking is the only thing necessary to conquer," he wrote. "Those ideas are entertained in their minds by some jealous men and perhaps secret friends to the British government who want to push you in a moment of ill humor to some rash enterprise upon the lines or against a much stronger army."

Convinced that the Commander-in-Chief was too modest, the marquis concluded that the revolution would die in six months without George Washington. No man on the continent who could take his place.

"I should not take the liberty of mentioning these particularities to you if I did not receive a letter about this matter from a young, good natured gentleman at York, whom Conway has ruined by his cunning bad advice but who entertains the greatest respect for you."

Like Gates had done after Saratoga, General Conway bypassed Washington and directly communicated to Congress. He asked Congress's board of war for a promotion. "I have been surprised at first to see the new establishment of this board of war, to see the difference between northern and southern departments, to see resolved from Congress about military operations—but the promotion of Conway is beyond all my expectations," Lafayette wrote, adding that he also wanted a command in the future, but he would ask Washington first.

Lafayette explained that this situation had become personal. Because they had both served in the French military, Conway had also been promoting himself to Lafayette, whose wealth and connections to the King of France were advantageous. Conway had tried to lure Lafayette "with ideas of glory and shining projects, and I must confess for my shame that it is a too certain way of deceiving me."

"The reason of such behavior . . . is that he wishes to be well spoken of at the French court." After Lafayette learned of Conway's letter to Gates, he began to ask questions. "But since the letter of Lord Stirling, I inquired in his (Conway's) character, I found that he was an ambitious and dangerous man—he has done all in his power by a cunning maneuver to take off my confidence and affection for you—his desire was to engage me to leave this country."

Lafayette learned that he wasn't the only one concerned about Conway. General Nathanael Greene and other officers opposed Congress's decision to give Conway a promotion. "Now I see all the general officers of the army revolted against Congress, such disputes if known by the enemy, can be attended with horrid consequences."

"I am very sorry whenever I perceive trouble raised among the defenders of the same cause, but my concern is much greater when I find officers coming from France, officers of some character in my country to whom any fault of that kind may be imputed," Lafayette wrote of the prejudice he faced as a French Catholic from English Protestants. Lafayette had admired Conway for his bravery and skill, but saw him as selfish.

Lafayette encouraged Washington to speak up for himself with Congress and put a stop to these trifling, demeaning disputes. He feared that the Conway cabal would encourage "slavery, dishonor, ruin, and unhappiness of a whole world."

Given this war within, Lafayette felt compelled to affirm his loyalty to Washington. "My desire of deserving your satisfaction is stronger than ever," he wrote, promising to try to succeed wherever Washington placed him.

"I am now fixed to your fate, and I shall follow it and sustain it as well by my sword as by all means in my power," he wrote, pledging his honor and respect. The conflict over Conway had strengthened rather than weakened Lafayette's allegiance to Washington.

Such eloquence and declarations of loyalty won over Washington, who granted Lafayette a meeting. Thinking he was telling Washington for the first time about the cabal, he was relieved to discover that the Commander-in-Chief was already aware of it. After their meeting, Washington knew that Lafayette had chosen him over conspiring with Conway. This was a balm for any emotional wounds that Washington had concealed over the matter.

Lafayette's loyalty had also helped Washington to warm to the possibility of France becoming an ally. "I heartily wish there may be an early declaration of hostilities between France and Britain," Washington had written to the president of Congress in late November 1777. "The political reasons that lead to delay on the part of France, I do not perfectly understand."

Deeply impressed by Lafayette's zeal, Washington also made a recommendation for him. "I should also be happy in their (Congress's) determination respecting the Marquis de la Fayette. He is more and more solicitous to be in actual service and is pressing in his applications for a command." If Congress turned down Washington's request to give Lafayette a direct command, then Lafayette would return to France, which would show King Louis XVI that America wasn't serious about accepting military help from respected Frenchmen.

Washington had noted that Lafayette had fought in New Jersey with General Greene, who wrote that: "The Marquis, with about four hundred militia and the rifle corps, attacked the enemy's picket last evening—killed about twenty—wounded many more and took about twenty prisoners—The Marquis is charmed with the spirited behavior of the militia and rifle corps . . . The Marquis is determined to be in the way of danger."

Congress responded positively: "it is highly agreeable . . . that the Marquis de Lafayette be appointed to the command of a division in the Continental army."

With this star from the east lined up into a strong Continental constellation, it was time for Washington to debate with Gates.

General Washington responded to General Gates's December 4 letter about the Conway matter a month later, on January 4, 1778, from Valley Forge. Perhaps he waited to give himself time to cool down. Washington had tried to keep the matter private. Gates had made it public, involving Congress in the matter, which was another insult to Washington.

Among his admonitions to Gates over the Conway letter, Washington expressed his surprise that "a copy of it had been sent to Congress—for what reason, I find myself unable to account." Washington was "under the disagreeable necessity of returning my answer through the same channel."

Ever the chivalrous knight, Washington didn't want "any member of that honorable body" to suspect him of trying to indirectly make a private letter known outside the military by revealing the "contents of the confidential letters between you and General Conway." He didn't want to involve Congress or cause even "the smallest interruption to the tranquility of this army or afford a gleam of hope to the enemy by dissensions therein."

Washington told Gates that he had always spoken to him candidly and openly. He also expressed confidence in Lord Stirling's motives for showing him a copy of Conway's letter to Gates. A particular word in Gates's December 4 letter had concerned Washington.

Gates had written Washington about the *letters* exchanged between the Irish-French officer and Gates, clearly suggesting that there had been *more than one letter* written between the two officers. The question was why? Why did Conway, who was leading parts of the army in Pennsylvania, need to communicate with General Gates in New York? Did they even know each other?

"I never knew that General Conway (who I viewed in the light of a stranger to you) was a correspondent of yours, much less did I suspect that I was the subject of your confidential letters."

Despite this rebuke, Washington gave Gates a way out by suggesting that Gates's aid-de-camp, Wilkinson, had acted on Gates's behalf by passing the letter to Lord Stirling. He said that he "considered the information as coming from yourself; and given with a friendly view to forewarn, and consequently forearm me, against a secret enemy (Conway)."

By pretending that the letter was not a serious plot or "a dangerous incendiary," Washington gave Gates the benefit of the doubt. The Commander-in-Chief believed that "sooner or later, this country will know [the character or] General Conway." He then ended with some self-doubt. "But—in this, as in other matters of late, I have found myself mistaken." Washington may not have had a big victory on the battlefield in 1777, but with a single stroke of a pen, he'd confronted the war within.

Washington had proven to be the gentleman, who above all others, deserved to be Commander-in-Chief. Congress ended any flirtation they had with replacing Washington with Gates. The Conway Cabal was kaput.

The Conway Cabal, however, left Washington's closest aides furious. Alexander Hamilton fumed in a letter to his friend, George Clinton, in Poughkeepsie, New York. "Since I saw you, I have discovered such convincing traits of the monster, that I cannot doubt its reality in the most extensive sense. I dare say, you have seen and heard enough to settle the matter, in your own mind," Hamilton wrote on February 13, 1778.

"I believe it unmasked its batteries too soon and begins to hide its head; but as I imagine it will only change the storm to a sap," he explained, believing that the cabal was only thwarted for the moment. "Have you heard anything of Conway's history? He is one of the vermin bred in the entrails of this chimera dire, and there does not exist a more villainous calumniator and incendiary."

By this time, Hamilton had returned to Valley Forge. While Hamilton ranted about the vermin Conway in a letter he wrote from his quarters at the forge, another monster, one that had been ongoing for at least a year, reared its head again over the valley, forcing its commander to come face-to-face with the war of lies.

16 FORGERIES AT THE FORGE

L etters flew into the forge about the forgeries. None of them violated rule number 17 of *110 Rules of Civility* which stated "Be no flatterer." The correspondence that Washington received at Valley Forge from his friends about the forgeries was straightforward and made no attempt to flatter Washington.

"Among other tricks, they have forged a pamphlet of letters entitled 'Letters from Gen. Washington to several of his friends in 1776,'" Richard Henry Lee wrote to the Commander-in-Chief from his home in Virginia. Lee sought to inform Washington that the letters weren't just the neurotic inventions of a newspaper publisher. Washington learned that the letters had first been published as a pamphlet, though Lee did not tell him where they were first published.

While not a literal stereotype, which was a mold of a typeset that enabled a printer to quickly reproduce a book, these sham letters were forging a negative stereotype of Washington.

"The arts of the enemies of America are endless, but all wicked as they are various," Richard Henry Lee explained. Because the pamphlet was too large to send with the current post, he promised to mail it to Washington later. How did Washington respond?

"Those contained in the pamphlet you speak of are, I presume, equally genuine, and perhaps wrote by the same author," Washington wrote with sarcasm.

Despite his private denunciations to Richard Henry Lee, the Commander-in-Chief did not make a public reply. His priority was his army, not his reputation. In the mode of King Arthur, a chivalrous leader did not come to his own defense but allowed others to ensure justice over his honor.

On February 23, 1778, Washington rode out of Valley Forge to greet Baron Friedrich Wilhelm Von Steuben, who was thought to be a nobleman from Prussia who'd earned the rank of a lieutenant general during the Seven Years' War. Instead, he was born a commoner, who like Washington, had risen because of his talents and had served as an aide-de-camp to a general.

Nonetheless—or perhaps because of this—Von Steuben's commitment to the cause of liberty endeared him to Washington, who set him to work as drillmaster of his ill clad lackluster army. Rather than trying to teach all of the soldiers in unison, Von Steuben first taught his tactics to a small company of soldiers.

Though Washington had implemented the same discipline and close-order drills he'd experienced as a British colonial soldier, he'd faced unique challenges in forming his force from the start. The Continental Army was made up of men who had initially served in their local militias. Each had different methods for drills and followed different commands.

The large open space in the center of their camp was an ideal parade ground for practicing drills. Von Steuben would soon turn this freezing force into a uniform fighting team. Yet as happy as Washington was to welcome his Prussian God-send, he couldn't escape the fake letters.

★ ★ ★ ★ ★

While his men took refuge from the cold in their huts, correspondence about the forgeries came in hot and fresh. "In a word, having less dependence now on their arms than their arts, they are practicing such low, and dirty tricks, that men of sentiment and honor must blush for their fall," Washington replied in a private letter addressed to his friend Bryan Fairfax on March 1, 1778.

"Among other maneuvers in this way, they are forging letters and publishing them as intercepted ones of mine, to prove that I am an enemy to the present measures of this continent."

Washington concluded that the goal of the false letters was to convince Congress to end the American quest for independence. "Having been deceived, and led on by Congress in hopes that at length, they would recede from their claims and withdraw their opposition to Great Britain."

Around the same time, another friend, Landon Carter wrote Washington about other rumors. "At first your death was circulated by them," he explained.

Yet, Carter was also worried about still other news. Explaining that his hand shook in fear, he knew he needed to pass along sensitive information about the cabal.

"A gentleman ... told me from undoubted information ... that there either was, or would be shortly a great confusion in the army; because the more northern officers in it ... were brewing divisions, and ... that the northern members in congress, either had or would shortly agitate your removal, or supersede you in command with (Gen.) Gates." Carter believed that the motive in the plan to remove Washington was to establish a Northern city as the seat of government after America won independence.

"And let Gates, (former Quartermaster Thomas) Mifflin, and . . . Conway, raise what disturbances they can think of, you have an asylum here in every honest breast," Carter wrote, noting that if he wasn't so ill and old, he would "have been in Congress to have died inch by inch for you."

Despite this, Carter tried to encourage his friend by telling him that those who knew him best, his fellow Virginians, wouldn't believe these letters. "Your local country is unanimously devoted to your protection."

Washington told Carter that the Conway Cabal had been quelled. "With great truth I think I can assure you, that the information you received from a gentleman ... respecting a disposition in the Northern officers to see me superseded in my command by General Gates is without the least foundation," Washington wrote.

Why was he so certain the cabal had collapsed?

"That there was a scheme of this sort on foot last fall admits of no doubt, but it originated in another quarter—with three men (Gates, Conway, and Mifflin) who wanted to aggrandize themselves—but finding no support, on the contrary, that their conduct, and views when seen into, was like to undergo severe reprehension they slunk back—disavowed the measure, and professed themselves my warmest admirers."

Washington was confident that he would remain the commanding general. "Thus stands the matter at present—whether any members of Congress were privy to this scheme, and inclined to aid and abet it, I shall not take upon me to say, but am well informed that no whisper of the kind was ever heard in Congress."

By honorably and privately confronting Gates and Conway, Washington had cast sunlight on the matter, disinfecting the disloyalty.

"I have very sufficient reasons to think that no officers in the army are more attached to me than those from the northward and of those none more so than the gentlemen who were under the immediate command of Gates's last campaign." Washington was correct. The fallout from the cabal fell on General Conway. In March 1778, this Irish-French officer again submitted his resignation, and this time, Congress accepted it. Conway was later injured in a duel with another general who defended Washington's honor. Fearing that he was dying, Conway apologized in a letter to the Commander-in-Chief and then returned to Europe

As far as the forgeries were concerned, Washington shed a little more light on the matter for Carter. He replied that the fake letters were designed "to show that I was an enemy to independence; and with a view to create distrust and jealousy."

Washington decided to defend himself to Congress on the question of the forged letters. Passing along the newspapers that had printed his forged letters, he wrote the president of Congress, Henry Laurens, a private letter on April 18, 1778.

"The gazettes herewith enclosed, if you have not already been furnished with others of as late date, may afford you some amusement, and therefore I take the liberty of sending them," he wrote, trying to make light of the matter while indicating the letters were propaganda. In a postscript, he expressed more emotion.

"Among the many villainous arts practiced by the enemy to create divisions and distrust, that of forging letters, for me, is one."

Washington was correct about Horatio Gates's loyalty to him. Benjamin Franklin eventually weighed in on the cabal by sending Gates a letter.

"The pride of England was never so humbled by anything as by your capitulation of Saratoga. They have not yet got over it," Franklin wrote, praising Gates for his success. But he also gently reminded the general that fractures in the force had a way of reaching the rumor mills of Paris and London.

"The little dissensions between particulars in America are much magnified in England, and they once had great hopes from them. I consider them, with you, as the effects of apparent security; which do not affect the grand points of independence and adherence to treaties; and which will vanish at any renew'd appearance of danger," he wrote

Gates, prodding him to keep his vanity in check.

Despite his admonishment, Franklin was still friendly. "When shall we meet again in cheerful converse, talk over our adventures, and finish with a quiet game of chess."

★ ★ ★ ★ ★

As angry as Washington was about the forgeries, he continued to keep his comments private, not public. In this way, he relied on his friends to defend him. One of his best strengths was keeping his eye on the big picture. He focused on the real mission of Valley Forge: training his men and creating a newfound cohesion. He set Von Steuben up for success in his General Orders.

"Baron Von Steuben, a lieutenant general in foreign service and a gentleman of great military experience, having obligingly undertaken to exercise the office of Inspector General in this Army, the Commander in Chief, 'till the pleasure of Congress shall be known, desires he may be respected and obeyed as such and hopes and expects that all officers of whatsoever rank in it will afford him every aid in their power in the execution of his office."

Timing was everything. "The importance of establishing a uniform system of useful maneuvers and regularity of discipline must be obvious, the deficiency of our army in these respects must be equally so," the orders explained of why obedience to Von Steuben was essential. They only had a few more weeks before fighting would begin again.

"The time we shall probably have to introduce the necessary reformation is short, without the most active exertions, therefore, of officers of every class it will be impossible to derive the advantages proposed from this institution which are of the greatest moment to the ensuing campaign," the orders concluded, exhorting his officers to rekindle their zeal and work for the prosperity of their arms.

Establishing drill and command standards for the Continental Army, Von Steuben taught one company of men his techniques. He showed them how to stand and march with precision using the *common step*, which at the time was seventy-five paces per minute. From Von Steuben, this company learned how to carry and use a bayonet and to quickly respond to orders, such as reforming lines in battle. This company trained another group, that group trained another, and so on until the entire army followed the same standards.

As the spring progressed, Washington's men were gradually put on the same page, both figuratively and literally. Von Steuben put his techniques and commands into written form. Asking Hamilton and Lafayette to simplify some of the wording, Washington produced a new manual for a distinctly American army. The manual received a new name, the Blue Book, once it was printed with a blue cover.

While his men drilled and marched, Washington once again responded to a letter about the forgeries. This time, he replied to his brother, who'd alerted him of the deceit.

"Not one sentence of which you may rely on it, did I ever write; although so many little family circumstances are interspersed through the whole performance to give it the air of authenticity," Washington wrote Jack in an unmistakable denial.

Washington understood that the best forgery was one that mixed truth with falsehoods. So it was in this case.

"The arts of the enemy and the low dirty tricks which they are daily practicing is an evincing proof that they are lost to all sense of virtue and honor, and that they will stick at nothing, however incompatible with truth and manliness, to carry their points."

By the end of the spring, Washington finally received the pamphlet of forged letters in the post from Richard Henry. "'Tis among the pitiful arts of our enemies to endeavor at sowing dissention among the friends of liberty and their country. With me, such tricks can never prevail," Richard wrote Washington on May 7.

The counterfeit letters in this pamphlet were the identical letters that Rivington had published one at a time in the *Royal Gazette* over a two-month span.

Washington replied to Richard on May 25 in a letter "declaring that every word contained in the pamphlet . . . was spurious."

"These letters are written with a great deal of art—the intermixture of so many family circumstances (which by the by wanted foundation in truth) gives an air of plausibility, which renders the villainy greater; as the whole is a contrivance to answer the most diabolical purposes."

Little did Washington know at the time, but before the war ended, each of the four suspected counterfeiters would show their true colors. The culprit would receive justice from Washington in ways neither could imagine.

Though the forged letters did not provoke a public, volcanic eruption from Washington that spring, there was one form of deceit that could and would shortly do so.

While Washington battled dirty tricks and his men worked on their skills, their enemy soldiers kicked back. They partied like it was 1799 while wearing costumes from 1099.

Anyone who submits an article to a newspaper for publication is at risk for rejection. Although they did not have paid reporters, newspaper editors during the war didn't accept every contribution. One British soldier was quite miffed at the rejection he received, especially after the editor initially asked for his report.

"Sir, at the request of the printer of one of the other papers the following description of the Meschianza was hastily penned the day after that celebrated entertainment. The writer readily undertook it, though with inconvenience to himself," the British soldier explained in a letter he wrote to the editor of the *Royal Pennsylvania Gazette*.

"The production was thought too trifling to appear in his paper," the soldier continued. "If you are the same opinion, return it."

The *Royal Pennsylvania Gazette's* editor did not return the article. Instead, he typeset it and published is with the soldier's letter as an introduction to take a stab at scooping his competition. "On Monday, an entertainment was given by the officers of the army to his Excellency Sir William Howe," the soldier's story began.

Why did this event honor General Sir William Howe and his brother Admiral Richard Howe? King George's government blamed General Howe for General Burgoyne's lost at Saratoga and recalled him. In solidarity with his brother, Admiral Howe also requested a recall.

Hence, the king's spy-master John André and other officers decided to send them back to Britain in style. Altering an Italian name for medley, André called this farewell bash the *Meschianza* because it showcased multiple entertainments. More than four hundred loyalist civilians and British military members attended.

The soldier who wrote the article could have been André himself. He declared in the *Royal Pennsylvania Gazette* that the entertainment was so well executed that it "far surpassed anything . . . seen in this or perhaps any other country."

First was a floating parade of decorated barges and ships accompanied by three full bands of music. People crowded the wharves, occupied their balconies, and sat on top of their houses to see General Howell and the parade as they glided along the Delaware River toward town.

When General and Admiral Howe landed, they along with their guests reached a pavilion. Instead of building huts like the Continental Army had for survival, the Redcoats had built a temporary pavilion, two hundred feet in length complete with a vaulted roof covered by a painted canvas and illuminated by chandeliers. This pavilion was turned into a circus, with re-enactors performing like chivalrous knights.

What do you need for a medieval reenactment party if you're a British redcoat in the middle of a war? Why, white knights and a mock jousting tournament emceed by André.

"Seven white knights, completely armed, attended by their squires and pages, enter the lifts as champions to the ladies of the Blended Rose." After parading around, a herald buzzed the sound of a trumpet and announced that the White Knights were ready to prove that "their mistresses are the fairest the world can produce."

A separate trumpet blast ushered in seven Black Knights who "insist[ed] upon the superior beauty of the ladies of the Burning Mountain" the article wrote in a reference to a volcano.

"The contest began with a furious attack with lances, followed by a discharge of pistols, and succeeded by a charge, sword in hand." When the leading knights became embroiled in a dispute over which team won, a stranger knight suddenly entered the arena and announced a compromised outcome, presumably a tie.

"With the knights and squires leading in their favorite damsels" the party-goers enjoyed a ball, fireworks, and a banquet. Even the ladies were dressed in costume, wearing Turkish design. The group adjourned to a tent next to a mansion. Ornamented mirrors filled the space to reflect "the natural as well as the artificial beauties" of the guests and brilliantly illuminated room.

"In short, the powers of description are too languid to do justice to the whole of this singular entertainment, in which British taste was only aided by British magnificence." The officers spent more than three thousand British pounds for the event, and someone paid twelve thousand pounds for the silk costumes.

Not every member of the British military in Philadelphia applauded the extravagance. Admiral Howe's secretary was ashamed of the Meschianza. Likewise, average citizens were appalled. A local civilian and Quaker was offended by the display, not just because of her plain-dressing religious beliefs but because of its insensitivity in the context of war. "How insensible these people appear, while our land is so greatly desolated, and death and sore destruction has overtaken and impends over so many," a Philadelphia Quaker, Elizabeth Drinker wrote in her diary.

She shared the same opinion as the newspaper editor who first rejected the article. Because this event was so extravagant, the story seemed too trifling. Bidding the Howes goodbye was a proper British thing to do. Spending thousands of pounds doing so was quite a contrast to the scarcity facing the Continental Army.

As the leaves turned spring green, several surprises lit up Valley Forge.

17 LUMIÈRE DU SOLEIL

D espite all of the hardships that General Washington experienced at Valley Forge—the lack of resources, the need to train his men, and the forgeries—rays of sunshine, which he called *lumière du soleil*, greeted him and the rest of the patriots at Valley Forge in May 1778.

"The maneuvering of the army is in itself a sight that would charm you," Colonel William Bradford, Jr. proudly wrote from Valley Forge to his sister Rachel on May 14. Bradford had been with Charles Lee at his capture in December 1776. Surviving the shoot-out, Bradford escaped and remained with Washington's troops.

Another bright light was a form of entertainment previously forbidden in camp. "Besides these, the theater is opened. Last Monday *Cato* (May 11) was performed before a very numerous and splendid audience," Bradford continued to his sister.

Among Washington's favorite plays was *Cato*, a true story. It was a biopic and a tragedy written in 1713 by Joseph Addison. It featured Marcus Cato, a Roman senator who opposed Caesar's tyranny and supported republicanism. Following a decisive battle and acting in accord with the tenets of Stoic philosophy, Cato committed suicide. His commitment to dying for republican principles was the message of the production.

Unlike the extravagant British *Meschianza*, this entertainment was simple. "The scenery was in taste and the performance admirable." In other words, Washington didn't spend thousands of pounds to pay for an over-the-top production to reward his troops with some merriment following a tough season.

According to Bradford, the colonel who played Cato at this Valley Forge performance "made an excellent *die*, as they say. Pray heaven, he doesn't die in earnest for yesterday he was seized with the pleurisy and lies extremely ill."

Bradford also knew that the Howes were exiting the stage and returning to London. Would the remaining British army stay or would they go? That was the question. "If the enemy does not retire from Philadelphia soon, our theatrical amusements will continue," Bradford explained to his sister.

Among the brightest of lights came in the form of intelligence from France, not on the pages of a gazette. Before Washington announced the most significant news to arrive at Valley Forge in a letter to his friend Landon Carter, the commanding general gave thanks to God for coming out of the valley.

"My friends therefore may believe me sincere in my professions of attachment to them, whilst Providence has a just claim to my humble and grateful thanks for its protection and direction of me, through the many difficult and intricate scenes which this contest hath produced," Washington expressed his gratitude for God's protection during their quarters at Valley Forge to Carter on May 30, 1778.

Washington believed in Providence's "constant interposition[s] in (on) our behalf when the clouds were heaviest and seemed ready to burst upon us. To paint the distresses, and perilous situation of this army in the course of last winter for want of clothes, provisions, and almost every other necessary, essential to the wellbeing (I may say existence) of an Army, would require more time, and an abler pen than mine."

Washington also wrote Carter that their prospects had "miraculously brightened. Shall I attempt it, or even bear it in remembrance, further than as a memento of what is due to the great author of all the care and good that has been extended in relieving us in difficulties and distress."

Why had their outlook brightened? Not only had Von Steuben trained his men into a strong army, but a king an ocean away also had made a huge decision.

"Authentic accounts have come to my hands of France having declared the United States free and independent," Washington privately wrote, sharing his joy with his brother Jack. Knowing the information wasn't yet public, Washington had received the news from the messenger who was carrying the news to Congress. "That France have done this in the most generous manner, and to our utmost wish. This is great, 'tis glorious news and must put the independency of America out of all manner of dispute."

The greatest interposition of Providence came from France. Gates's victory at Saratoga had given King Louis XVI the confidence that the Continental Army could win. Hence, he was all in. France would officially support the United States of America.

"Give me leave, dear Sir, to congratulate you on the happy event of our treaty with France being so effectually concluded—Congress has ratified on their part and ordered the ratification to be delivered in due form," Richard Henry Lee wrote Washington and explained that Congress would immediately give the news to the public.

"The counsels of France have been governed in this affair by true magnanimity and sound policy . . . Great Britain has its choice now of madness, or meanness." Lee hoped this alliance would end the war with America because he wrongfully concluded that King George III would not want to be at war with both France and the United States. "England alone will pay for her wickedness and folly by the loss of North America."

Hoping the news would "chalk out a plain and easy road to independence," Washington replied to Richard Henry Lee that "the favorable issue of our negotiations with France is matter for heartfelt joy."

Despite this alliance, Washington tried to be prudent and realistic. Recalling his own experience fighting the French as a British subject and volunteer soldier, he believed that the war would continue. "That Great Britain would have submitted to any indignity from France, in order to wreak her vengeance upon America, I have not the smallest doubt, but since the declaration of the King of France through the Marquis de Noailles (the French ambassador to England) they have no choice but war."

Would England give up America to fight France, or would England bolster their defenses in Canada and New York and continue to wage the war on American soil? "But how, under their present circumstances they will conduct it, is a matter not so easily understood, as all their ways have been ways of darkness," the commanding general wrote.

Regardless, Washington mused that the Redcoats would abandon Philadelphia to reinforce the British Army in New York. "They may attempt to hold New York, unless every idea of subjugating America is given up, in that case, their whole resentment will be leveled at France." The King of France's entry into the war would scramble the King of England's chess board. Where the pieces would land, no one yet knew.

Benjamin Franklin had secured the treaty between the United States and France months earlier, on February 6, 1778. This advocate for freedom of speech could hardly wait to rub the noses of his friends in England in the news of this alliance, especially that of an English correspondent who'd recently aggravated him.

"Your 'earnest caution and request, that nothing may ever persuade America to throw themselves into the Arms of France; for that times may mend; and that an American must always be a stranger in France, but that Great Britain may for ages to come be their home,' marks the goodness of your heart, your regard for us, and love of your country," Franklin wrote to his English friend, David Hartley, six days after the treaty with France was signed.

Hartley was a physician who'd written a book comparing Franklin's electricity experiments to another scientist a few years earlier. Though Franklin and Hartley were on cordial terms, Franklin expressed his anger about England's position.

"But when your nation is hiring all the cutthroats it can collect of all countries and colors to destroy us, it is hard to persuade us not to ask and accept of aid, from any power that may be prevail'd with to grant it; and this only from the hope that tho' you now thirst for our blood and pursue us with fire and sword, you may in some future time treat us kindly. This is too much patience to be expected of us; indeed I think it is not in human nature."

Then, as if trying to make his friend jealous, he told Hartley about America's newest friend. "The Americans are received and treated here in France with a cordiality, a respect and affection, they never experienced in England when they most deserved it, and which is now (after all the pains taken to exasperate the English against them, and render them odious as well as contemptible) less to be expected there than ever," he wrote, perhaps referencing the dressing down he'd received at London's Cockpit Tavern by the Privy Council in 1774.

Franklin hinted at his news. "And I cannot see why we may not upon an alliance hope for a continuance of it, at least of as much as the Swiss enjoy, with whom France has maintained a faithful friendship for 200 years past."

Franklin next reversed Hartley's warning for the U.S.A. to stay out of the arms of France. "America has been forc'd and driven into the arms of France. She was a dutiful and virtuous daughter. A cruel mother-in-law turn'd her out of doors, defamed her, and sought her life. All the world knows her innocence and takes her part."

Oh, the irony. The man who'd created the *Join or Die* snake icon to motivate England and America to fight the French had come full circle by achieving a French-American alliance against the British. Hartley had written to Franklin to encourage him to pursue peace with England. Franklin now responded with bluntness tinged with bitterness.

"I know not whether a peace with us is desired in England. I rather think it is not at present, unless on the old impossible terms of submission and receiving pardon. Whenever you shall be disposed to make peace upon equal and reasonable terms you will find little difficulty if you get first an honest ministry," he wrote, referring to the current prime minister, the king, and Parliament.

"The present have all along acted so deceitfully and treacherously, as well as inhumanly, towards the Americans that I imagine the absolute want of all confidence in them will make a treaty at present between them and the Congress impracticable."

How did James Rivington respond to the news that the French alliance was real and not a ruse has he'd previously reported? This advocate for freedom of the press published a notification from the British Navy's viewpoint to reassure his readers.

"As to a French war, be not alarmed, for though it appears probable, and, to my Lord North (the Prime Minister) inevitable..." an article began in Rivington's *Royal Gazette* on May 30, 1778. Rivington had printed an extract of a letter written by a superior officer. This high-ranking British officer was confident that King Louis XVI's infamous bargain with America was not a threat.

"I think, with our present Naval and military force, we shall be able to convince *Monsieur* (King Louis XVI) of his being but a young statesman," the officer wrote, noting that he would defend Britain's rights to trade with Virginia and the Carolinas. He then accused King Louis of deceiving England.

"The duplicity of the court of France is now evident: from the commencement of the present war, they have been amusing the British ministry, with fallacious declarations of their pacific intentions and issuing edicts prohibiting their subjects from trading with the Americans, while, at the same time they were fomenting the rebellion, and clandestinely assisting the rebels," he wrote, promising vengeance for his nation.

This letter was important for another reason. The contents

revealed King George III's next move on his rebel chessboard. Not only had he replaced the Howe brothers with General Henry Clinton, but he was also moving his bishops, knights, rooks, and pawns. "You will soon receive an additional four regiments at New York, three at Halifax." Missing from this list was Philadelphia. If the British government was not reinforcing their soldiers at Philadelphia, then what were the Redcoats there to do?"

There's a reason why journalism is the first draft of history, especially in an era of a partisan press. The fog of war leads to misinformation. When it came to the Battle of Monmouth, whom could newspaper readers trust to find the truth?

18 VOLCANIC ERUPTION

W hen the British Army evacuated Philadelphia and marched to New York City, the Continental Army left Valley Forge and attacked their rear. Who won the Battle of Monmouth in New Jersey? The answer depended on which newspaper you believed. In its infancy in the United States, journalism affirmed the beliefs of readers by informing them with facts clothed in the bias of the citizen or soldier who recorded a battle and reported it to the press. Like dueling chess players, sometimes a battle of words erupted between newspaper editors. Such were the dual articles published after the Battle of Monmouth.

On July 4, 1778, the patriot *Pennsylvania Packet* gave its readers a victory to celebrate on the second anniversary of Independence Day. Henry Laurens, president of the Continental Congress, had received three letters from General Washington and wanted to publish them. With Congress out of session, Laurens made an executive decision and sent the letters to the editor of the *Pennsylvania Packet*, who published them on July 4. "I am now here with the main body of the army and pressing hard to come up with the enemy. They encamped yesterday at Monmouth Court House, having almost the whole of their front," Washington's first letter explained of the Battle of Monmouth that took place on June 28, 1778.

Rivington, not to be outdone by the patriot editor, published a contribution from a British grenadier. This officer was part of the rear guard that had to battle both the high hay crop ready to be cut and the high heat as they marched over seven farms surrounding the Monmouth Courthouse.

"Having seen in a rebel paper the thanks of Congress to General Washington for the important victory at Monmouth, I must use the channel of your paper as the most likely means of conveying to that sagacious body a few remarks on so facetious a performance," the British grenadier derisively penned. He would not be a pawn in this propaganda match. "I am in the first place at a loss to conceive what were their views in that singular publication. They surely could not dream of persuading their army that they had really gained a victory."

A few days earlier, Washington had discovered that the "enemy's intention to march through Jersey (was) becoming serious."

His intelligence was correct. Britain's new commander for its forces in North America, General Henry Clinton, had decided to evacuate his troops from Philadelphia and move them to New York City. Lacking sufficient ships to transport his Redcoats by blue seas, Clinton arranged for eleven thousand British and Hessian soldiers and about a thousand loyalists to travel one hundred miles through emerald forests and muddy quagmires across New Jersey to reach their destination. Their baggage train alone stretched twelve miles.

The new French alliance forced Clinton to reinforce New York in case a French fleet arrived to support the Continental forces. From New York, he could evacuate his troops to Canada if need be.

While he didn't include this off-the-record background, the British grenadier reported his opinion that the purpose of publishing Washington's account by the *Pennsylvania Packet* was to impress the King of France. "Perhaps the intention was to establish themselves in the opinion of the respectable Minister of his most Christian Majesty, whom Congress have lately discovered to be the greatest and most magnanimous of princes."

What neither newspaper account could mention, of course, was the background leading to the battle, to which they weren't privy. Second only to Washington, General Charles Lee had been captured by the British in December 1776. During his imprisonment, he'd received permission from General Howe to write Congress and his Commander-in-Chief.

"I am likewise extremely desirous that my dogs should be brought as I never stood in greater need of their company than at present. God bless you, My Dear Sir, and send you long life and happiness," Lee had written Washington in February 1777. He'd also asked that one of his three aide-de-camps come to New York under a white flag and bring him some of his personal paperwork so he could manage his financial affairs.

After some negotiation with Howe, one of Lee's aides was able to come to him, but he could not bring Lee his dogs because they had been sent to the South.

"Your dogs are in Virginia. This circumstance I regret as you will be deprived of the satisfaction and amusements you hoped to derive from their friendly and companionable dispositions," Washington had replied to Lee.

Washington also had prudently turned down Lee's request to send members of the Continental Congress to him for a conference to discuss peace. Even under a white flag, sending members of Congress to a British prisoner of war was as risky as it was delusional.

"I am to inform you, that Congress not perceiving that any advantage would be derived either to yourself or the public interest from an interview between you and a part of their members, could not consider (them)selves at liberty to comply with your request," Washington had written Lee in April 1777.

Lee's response had shown his disappointment. "It is a most unfortunate circumstance for myself, and I think not less for the public that the Congress have not thought proper to comply with my request—it could not possibly have been attended with any ill consequences, and might with good ones. At least it was an indulgence which I thought my situation entitled me to—but I am unfortunate in all things and this stroke is the severest I have yet experienc'd—God send you a different fate."

By December 1777, Lee had told Washington that the British had paroled him, which had given him a huge advantage. "I think it my duty to inform you that my condition is much better'd—it is now four or five days that I am on my parole, have the full liberty of the City (New York) and its limits, have horses at my command furnish'd by Sir Henry Clinton and General Robinson."

With this freedom he could gallop and gallivant throughout the city. He could dash to the docks and smell the latest catch by fisherman or travel to the Redcoats' favorite gathering place and taste the soft center of fresh baked bread as he took breakfast at Rivington's coffee shop. Not only had Lee enjoyed such freedom at his disposal, but he'd also reconnected with old friends from the British Army.

"I am lodged with two of the oldest and warmest friends I have in the world—Colonel Butler and Major Disney of the 38th Regiment—with the former I was bred up from the age of nine years at school—the latter is a commilito (fellow student) from the time I enter'd the service in the 44th Regiment. In short, my situation is render'd as easy, comfortable, and pleasant as possible for a man who is in any sort a prisoner."

What had Lee done to receive such privileges? Had he given up something to the British military in exchange for these pleasantries? Regardless of his cushy circumstances, he'd told Washington that he wanted to return to his post in the Continental Army in a prisoner exchange.

"I have nothing left to wish for but that some circumstance may arise which may make it convenient for both parties that a general exchange may take place, and I amongst the rest reap the advantage— I have or can have no request at present," Lee had written.

"You may rest assured that I feel myself very much interested in your welfare, and that every exertion has been used on my part to affect your exchange," Washington had assured Lee in January 1778.

"That delay may not produce danger, I shall send in a flag tomorrow for your parole—when obtained, I shall most cordially, and sincerely, congratulate you on your restoration to your country, and to the Army," Washington had written, expressing "my wish of seeing you in camp, as soon as you possibly can make it convenient to yourself, after you are perfectly at liberty to take an active part with us; of which I shall not delay giving you the earliest notice."

General Lee had returned to the Continental Army at Valley Forge by May 30, 1778. He'd spent most of his 18-month imprisonment in New York and had missed many critical changes.

Lee had missed cheering *huzzah* with the troops after the Continental Army had crossed the Delaware River and had defeated the Hessians at Trenton in December 1776. He'd missed feeling the rhythm on the ground from the vibration of the army as they marched in a uniform common step at Valley Forge. He'd failed to witness their transformation from groups of lackluster militia into a uniform, cohesive army. As a result, General Lee still thought of the Continental Army as he'd last witnessed it—the losing team that had retreated from New York in the fall of 1776. He didn't appreciate the new fighting force that they'd become.

Because of this, Washington would soon have a good reason to regret Lee's return.

In late June 1778, at his war council with his officers, which included General Lee, the Commander-in-Chief proposed attacking the British on their way through New Jersey. Ridiculing Washington's suggestion, Lee argued against the odds of confronting Clinton's large army. Lafayette and other officers disagreed with Lee and believed the British were vulnerable because their lines were stretched out like shirts on a clothesline across Jersey for miles on end. Lee objected so strongly that, although he was second-in-command, he refused to lead any troops.

Encouraged by the support of his other officers, Washington detached a brigade to slow the Redcoats' march by obstructing roads, burning bridges, and contaminating water wells. He did this "so as to give time to the army under my command to come up with them and take advantage of any favorable circumstances that might present themselves." Washington explained his strategy at the Battle of Monmouth to the president of the Continental Congress in a letter published in the *Pennsylvania Packet* on July 4.

"The slow advance of the enemy had greatly the air of design, and led me, with others, to suspect that General Clinton desirous of a general action was endeavoring to draw us down into the lower country . . . in order by a rapid movement to gain our right, and take possession of the strong grounds above us," Washington wrote.

"The enemy in marching . . . had changed their disposition and placed their best troops in the rear, consisting of all the grenadiers, light infantry, and chasseurs of the line." When he learned that the enemy was on the road towards Monmouth Court House, he sent Generals Wayne and Lafayette "to take the command of the whole advanced corps . . . with orders to take the first fair opportunity of attacking the enemy's rear."

Though not published in either newspaper, once Lee learned that Lafayette had been given his command, Lee changed his mind about participating. Lafayette acquiesced when Lee arrived to assume his assignment. Washington ordered Lee to engage the Redcoats until he could bring the rest of his newly-trained army three miles away to join him.

"I detached Major General Lee with two brigades to join the marquis," Washington's published letter proclaimed, while noting that Lee now commanded the whole of this detachment of five thousand, about half of the entire Continental Army from Valley Forge. The main body also marched the same day within three miles of Lee's position.

"The enemy were now encamped in a strong position," Washington explained of their location on June 28, noting the natural barriers, such as Jersey's "skirt of a small wood" and other organic obstacles protected the British lines.

Realizing that once the British were twelve miles further down the road, "it would be impossible to attempt anything against them with a prospect of success, I determined to attack their rear the moment they should get in motion from their present ground," Washington concluded. "I communicated my intention to General Lee, and ordered him to make his disposition for the attack, and to keep his troops constantly lying upon their arms, to be in readiness at the shortest notice," he wrote, also issuing the same command to his troops.

"I instantly put the army in motion, and sent orders by one of my aids to General Lee to move on and attack them," Washington wrote, upon learning at five in the morning, that the front of the British line was moving. "After marching about five miles, to my great surprise and mortification, I met the whole advanced corps retreating, and, as I was told, by General Lee's orders without having made any opposition, except one fire given by a party."

When Washington finally met up with Lee near Monmouth Courthouse, he was so upset that he spewed his fury at Lee for his insubordination. Officers who witnessed Washington's volcanic explosion, such as General Charles Scott, reported, that even the "leaves shook on the tree." Lee's defiance had done what the forged letters had failed to do at Valley Forge, provoke a public eruption and response from the man of manners.

What did Washington do with Lee? He arrested him. "The peculiar situation of General Lee at this time, requires that I should say nothing of his conduct. He is now in arrest. The charges against him, with such sentence as the court martial may decree in his case, shall be transmitted for the approbation or disapprobation of Congress."

How did the British grenadier describe Lee's retreat in Rivington's paper? He accused Washington of attempting to "mislead the vulgar" wretches that he governed. Because this grenadier was part of the rear, he claimed he witnessed something opposite in Lee's retreating troops, calling them "the trembling herd who fled four miles before half their number of Britons."

How could Washington claim a victory when half his men under Lee had retreated? The grenadier had an answer. "The idea was possible, but alas they were many foreign officers in the field who know the victories are not gained buy a retrograde motion of four miles; even if though it should be made as Mr. Lee says, without the smallest degree of confusion."

The grenadier observed that Lee had accused Washington of boasting in a newspaper. "It is rather singular that Congress should force Washington to adhere to his story of victory, when the general (Lee) who actually commanded has declared that to call it so would be doing an honorable gasconade," the grenadier wrote, using a French word for extravagant boasting.

How did this British soldier know that General Lee had called Monmouth a gasconade? Despite his arrest after the Battle of Monmouth, Lee had sent notes to newspaper editors to publish his opinion of the battle's outcome. He believed that Washington was overstating the Continental Army's success at Monmouth.

"By the by, Mr. Lee's expression of a handsome check (of Washington) is rather difficult to comprehend. I am yet to learn what check a rear guard can receive, for checks imply that there has been a previous attempt, which is inconsistent with the idea of a rear guard," the grenadier gloated.

"That in consequence of an attack upon it, our rear guard did turn and drive the assailants for four miles must be allowed, for Washington's whole army were witness to it. That success (even if the heat had not forbidden it) would probably not have been followed, for the service was performed, the baggage was safe, and it was the duty of the rear guard to rejoin the army."

This grenadier held a sarcastic theory about Americans claiming victory at Monmouth. "In short, as I cannot but imagine that Congress might have figured to themselves some grounds for their claim of victory, I'm inclined to suppose, that the important success which they talk of, must have been the escape of Washington's whole army from our rear guard."

Why did Washington claim victory? With his battle directions under Lee collapsing, "I proceeded immediately to the rear of the corps, which I found closely pressed by the enemy." Though not reported in this newspaper account, Washington rode Cato-like on a white charger through his ranks, showing his troops that he was willing to risk his life by getting so close to enemy fire. This led

Lafayette to say, "I thought then as now I had never beheld so superb a man."

Washington explained that he "gave directions for forming part of the retreating troops, who by the brave and spirited conduct of the officers, aided by some pieces of well served artillery, checked the enemy's advance." Commanding the left flank, Lord Stirling had posted cannon over an open space unprotected by woods. Part of Lee's original force was under the command of General Wayne in the center. Washington gave the right wing to General Greene. "On intelligence of the retreat, he marched up and took a very advantageous position on the right."

"The enemy, by this time, finding themselves warmly opposed in front made an attempt to turn our left flank; but they were bravely repulsed and driven back by detached parties of infantry. They also made a movement to our right, with as little success." Greene had found a high ground where he placed several cannons that commanded the ground below. This "not only disappointed their design of turning our right, but severely enfiladed those in front of the left wing," he wrote of enfilading or directing a volley of fire along the length of the target.

These actions, along with another advance, forced the British to retire to a position covered by thick forests and morasses. Seeing British campfires in the distance, Washington cooled his boots and stopped fighting with plans to continue the next day. At sunrise, he discovered the campfires were a feint. The British had escaped to New York overnight.

"The extreme heat of the weather—the fatigue of the men from their march through a deep sandy country almost entirely destitute of water, and the distance the enemy had gained by marching in the night, made a pursuit impracticable and fruitless," Washington wrote of his conclusion to halt. "It would have answered no valuable purpose, and would have been fatal to numbers of our men, several of whom died the preceding day with heat." Indeed, Washington's own horse had collapsed because the weather was so hot.

Thanking his men and officers and congratulating their zeal and bravery for this latest match of strategy and skill, he listed the killed and wounded, two officers and twelve soldiers. "The enemy's slain left on the field and buried by us, according to the return of the persons assigned to that duty were four officers and two hundred and forty-five privates."

In contrast, the British Grenadier took aim in Rivington's

newspaper and proclaimed Monmouth, "a laurel which they have not earned." He minimized the significance of the British Army's losses. "Mr. Washington may feel his brows honored with by such a wreath, but victories like that of Monmouth may often befall him and every other enemy of old England, is this nearest wish of a British grenadier."

Ultimately, the facetious British grenadier engaged in a conspiracy theory. "Congress may say that they pinned their faith on their general's letter. I am tempted to indulge a suspicion, that the representation contained in that letter was dictated by Congress," he explained, suggesting that Congress had made up Washington's letter.

"Washington, poor man, never would have had an idea that he had gained so important a success, for though he might not have been forward enough to see truly how the day went, I know of nobody in that army so able in flattery as to have persuaded him against every evidence of his reason that he was victor."

Washington believed that the Battle of Monmouth proved that the newly retooled Continental Army was ready and able to fight and win. The question that neither newspaper account answered was this: Why did Lee defy Washington on the battlefield? His behavior fits the pattern of a man guilty of far more than cheating in a chess match.

Likewise, the truth of James Rivington's activities in London before his return to New York reveals another man guilty of promoting propaganda against Washington.

19 RIVINGTON OR RANDOLPH?

W ho the author of them is, I know not from information or an acquaintance," General Washington had told to Richard Henry Lee about the counterfeit letters at the end of May 1778, a month before he left Valley Forge to fight the Battle of Monmouth.

Who was the real author of the forged letters? Such was the question many of Washington's friends wondered with the curiosity of detectives. This was an important clue: two of the four suspects, James Rivington and John Randolph, were in England when John Bew first published the pamphlet of letters on May 29, 1777.

Knowing what happened to James Rivington when he returned to England in 1776 after being driven from New York sheds light on the possibility that he wrote the counterfeit letters. Stories of exiled Americans devoted to King George III weren't popular fodder for British newspapers, unless that loyalist happened to be a newspaper man with a story to sell as much as to tell. Such was the case with Rivington.

After patriots burned his New York press for a second time in November 1775, Rivington departed America for London aboard the HMS *King Fisher* during the first week of January 1776. Once Rivington stepped off the rocking ship and regained his balance on the land of his mother country, he knew exactly where to go for comfort and sympathy: Paternoster Row, the London street where he once operated his printing press.

Trading the smell of the Atlantic's flounder for the fishy perfume of linseed oil that permeated the air around printing presses, he eagerly visited his publishing friends and his brother's shop, the Bible and the Crown, which was around the corner at the churchyard next to St.

Paul's Cathedral.

Over the next several months, Rivington's plight was the subject of newspaper columns and magazine articles that sought to build sympathy for him. After all, the patriots had "totally destroyed all the types, put an entire stop to his business, and reduced him, upwards 50 years of age, to the sad necessity of beginning the world again."

In the *Gentleman's Magazine and Historical Chronicle,* a writer using the alias Coriolanus, which is the name of a Shakespeare tragedy about a Roman leader, blamed America's preachers for the abuse against Rivington. "The clergy, in the interest of the Congress, made the liberty of Mr. Rivington's press a topic for invective in their pulpits . . . to induce their congregation to stop the circulation of his paper."

Concluding that the rebels were under the influence of passion and prejudice, this magazine article proclaimed that what had happened to Rivington proved that the Revolution was without merit and needed to be defeated. "Dead to the feelings of humanity, and forgetful of the precepts of religion, they [the patriots] seem to delight in the oppression of others, while freedom from oppression is the great object for which they themselves contend."

Hammering on the hypocrisy that Rivington's case revealed, Coriolanus also railed and ranted, writing "while they were declaiming on the sacred nature of property they were destroying the property of their fellow subjects."

Coriolanus added a rhetorical flourish. "While they clamored against tyranny, they were abolishing the freedom of the press whose religion is selfishness, inhumanity and hypocrisy and whose liberty is the power of persecuting others."

The article's goal was to show the abuse Rivington had endured.

"This gentleman, when every other press was under the control of the Congress, with a candor and firmness which will ever do him honor, admitted into his paper the performance of all parties. This impartiality was, however, very displeasing to the leaders of faction," he overstated of his even-handedness as an editor. While Rivington presented both patriot and loyalist viewpoints, he wrote longer pro-British pieces and placed loyalist articles in the best locations of his newspaper. Coriolanus also explained that a mob burned Rivington's house and hung him in effigy. In one of the episodes Rivington hid in a neighbor's chimney.

"By these cruelties he is now driven from America, without business and deprived of the means of maintaining a family consisting of twelve persons whom he left behind him in New York," he wrote, noting that subscribers in America owed Rivington many thousands of pounds.

"Everyone who reads his case, must commiserate the condition of a man deprived of his livelihood and exile from his family for no crime; on the contrary, for the noblest of all principles, that of opposing the torrent of popular delusion, and standing firm in the cause of constitutional freedom and his country."

"We look upon . . . Rivington as a much-injured citizen, and we wish to be instrumental in procuring him redress," Coriolanus concluded. Either this pseudonymous author interviewed Rivington upon his return or Rivington wrote this article and used Coriolanus as his alias, which is the most likely scenario. In this way, Rivington also responded to his detractors like Washington, allowing another identity, in this case a pseudonym, to defend himself.

Someone with much influence and power read Rivington's case: the Earl of Sandwich. Sandwich offered Rivington an opportunity that Rivington couldn't refuse.

John Montagu, the 4th earl of Sandwich, became Rivington's most influential supporter. Far more than the man who became famous for eating beef between two pieces of bread so he could hover over his desk or a gambling table rather than eating at a dining table, Lord Sandwich was the First Lord of the Admiralty. As much as he needed to send every British ship, cannon, and barrel of gunpowder to America, he also needed Rivington for something else, something far more devious. First, he needed Parliament's buy-in for the war within.

"It was seen in the case of Rivington at New York . . . because he printed things not agreeable to the prevailing way of thinking there, had his house entered by an armed force, his types destroyed, and his person abused," Sandwich told Parliament, as the *Morning Post and Daily Advertiser* published on March 18, 1776.

This lord over England's war ships needed Parliament's financial support to "show the strength of the country in the clearest light." Because Rivington was part of the newspaper class, Sandwich explained there was one resource "that was pressing." He meant using the newspaper presses on Paternoster Row to launch a war of lies by shading Britain's successes and failures in the best light to the people of England and portraying the patriots in the worst light. After Rivington's loss in New York, Sandwich feared that England wouldn't succeed in "this war without pressing."

Sandwich ended his speech by observing that "if a push was wanted to be made, it would be an effective one." Push came to print over and over again throughout the conflict, especially in London newspapers when they published propaganda.

"Venal pens . . . were busily engaged in traducing Washington," a British historian wrote about British journalists' first draft of the American Revolution. These reporters working for the crown "made a practice of doctoring for public consumption the news which arrived from America." Though free speech runs the risk of such disinformation and slanted propaganda, attempts to control free speech devolves into tyranny. The remedy for propaganda isn't restraining free speech. The solution is to allow more free speech to counter such lies.

In their morning and evening newspapers, Londoners devoured sensational coverage supposedly arriving by the shiploads. Often the reports made fun of Washington. "A gentleman, who was not long since in America, and who is well-acquainted with General Washington, dined one day with him," one writer had penned for *London's Public Advertiser* in June 1777. Then he suggested that Washington was a fool who didn't know the difference between winning and losing a battle.

Another article spread lies about Washington's wife. "But it is said that Mrs. Washington, being a warm loyalist, has separated from her husband since the commencement of the present troubles, and lives very much respected in the city of New York," *London's Public Advertiser* published on January 11, 1777. In truth, Martha spent more than half the war in camp with her husband.

Still other reports ridiculed Americans. "Two ladies from Boston appear in our circles here," London's *Public Advertiser* told readers on June 11, 1777. After making fun of their clothes and talking to them in the aftermath of the disastrous New York campaign in 1776, a newspaper writer was surprised at how confident these American ladies were in the Continental Army's generals. "We see here with no less satisfaction the portraits of Generals Washington and Lee, the protectors of American liberty."

The forged letters were part of a deliberate attempt to shape public opinion against Washington. Both clear facts and circumstantial evidence created suspicion about the role of Bew and Rivington in the *War of Lies.*

★ ★ ★ ★ ★

The first newspaper publisher to announce Rivington's return to England in 1776 also played a role in publishing the counterfeit letters. A look at this publisher paints a picture of how the fake letters could have come about.

"Mr. Rivington is arrived from New York, who was obliged to leave that place for publishing a paper in favor of government," John Bew published in the *London Evening Post* on February 13, 1776. After keyword searching digitized newspapers, a clear fact emerges: Bew was the first London newspaper printer to publish the news of Rivington's return to London in 1776.

Bew's printing shop was at 28 Paternoster Row, just a long block away from and across the street from where Rivington had once operated his shop. Likewise, the newspaper class frequented London's coffee shops, including the Chapter Coffee House, the premier shop near Paternoster Row. Here newspapers topped the tables and stained the fingers of its patrons. Here, printers could meet with sources.

The fact that Bew was the first to publish Rivington's story shows some relationship between Rivington and Bew, even if it was merely transactional. Bew very likely learned about Rivington's arrival from Rivington himself. Perhaps Rivington walked into Bew's printing establishment and gave him the scoop about being hung in effigy, or maybe the pair met like old friends at the coffee shop where they slurped tea and dished dirt on the Sons of Liberty.

Fifteen months later, in May 1777, Bew published Washington's forged letters as a pamphlet. Rivington became the second person to publish the letters nine months later in February 1778 in weekly newspaper installments after returning to New York as the official printer of King George III. Yet this evidence alone is not strong enough to implicate either one as the author.

Because the Sons of Liberty in New York had burned his shop in 1775, Rivington certainly had a strong motive to retaliate against the patriots by forging letters in Washington's name. Rivington could have written the counterfeit letters in London and given them to Bew, who published them just like he printed the news of Rivington's return to London.

Somewhere in this time period, Rivington joined the payroll and became part of Lord Sandwich's propaganda campaign. These forged letters certainly fit Sandwich's edict that the war wouldn't be won without controlling the message of newspapers. When Rivington returned to New York and reopened his press as the king's printer, he did his best to put a positive pro-British spin on the news, seen in his account of the Battle of Saratoga, where he misled his readers about the true state of the British Army. It wasn't until Burgoyne's capitulation that Rivington printed the truth.

George Washington's friends believed that someone close to him had to have written the letters because they included names of family members. How would Rivington or Bew have known the names of Lund Washington, Martha Washington, and John Parke Custis? Rivington might have learned about John Parke Custis when he reported in 1773 that Washington had attended the New York City shindig for Thomas Gage when Washington took his stepson to King's College in New York.

How would Rivington have known about Washington's wife, Martha, or that his cousin, Lund Washington, was taking care of Mount Vernon in Washington's absence? He would have needed a source to have written letters addressed to these individuals and additional details to make them believable. Who could that have been? George Washington had an idea.

Posing for a painting, no matter the circumstances or the painter, was a test of Job-like patience for George Washington. Yet as there was no technology to quickly capture a visual image, he was left with no alternative but to sit for hours in the same position while a painter went to work. The success of Monmouth in 1778 and the entrance of France into the war gave Washington a little more leisure during winter camp in 1779 than Valley Forge had offered him the previous year, and thus an opportunity to have his portrait painted.

General Washington posed in 1779 for a respected painter and avid collector, Pierre-Eugène Du Simitière. Swiss-born Du Simitière had moved to Philadelphia in 1766, where he had established himself with such distinction that he had been named curator of the American Philosophical Society and later set up a museum. After the Revolution began, he helped Washington to translate a message into French for French-speaking Canadians. He also had submitted a design to Congress for the Great Seal of the United States.

When in 1779 Washington sat for the forty-six-year-old Du Simitière, they talked as the artist studied Washington's left profile and the prominent epaulettes on his shoulders. What the pair discussed as one stood stock still while the other moved his brush in constant motion is lost to history. The results, however, reveal a clue to the author of the forged letter.

Pleased with Du Simitière's portrait, Washington later wrote a friend that Du Simitière "drew many good likenesses from the life . . . I have seen General Gates, Baron de Steuben, &c.—as also that of your humble servant." Du Simitière's painting of Washington was later used on the US one cent coin.

Du Simitière collected Revolutionary War literature and other items for his museum. Within his collection was the handbill of Washington's forged letter to Martha. On it Du Simitière had written "spurious: wrote in London by a Mr. Randolph of Virginia."

Did the forged letters come up when Washington sat for Du Simitière? It is likely. Did General Washington speculate that John Randolph was the author? This is certain, as other evidence supports.

Colonel Tench Tilghman, a military secretary for Washington, wrote a letter to James Tilghman from Valley Forge in April 1778. "The letters published under General Washington's signature are not genuine. They are intended for the purposes you mention. He suspects John Randolph for the author, as the letters contain a knowledge of his family affairs that none but a Virginian could be acquainted with."

Randolph had fled for England in the fall of 1775. Unlike the press coverage that Rivington received when he returned around the same time, Randolph's name is absent from British newspapers. Little is known about Randolph's exile. One of his daughter's married another American exile, a beau she'd rejected and then accepted again, at a ceremony that took place at Lord Dunmore's Scottish castle under a dome carved to look like a pineapple.

Randolph appears to have lived with an enclave of other loyalists along Brompton Row in London, where they formed a loyalist club. Known for his love of gardening, he frequented the Cannon Coffee House at Spring Gardens near Trafalgar Square. Did he meet with Rivington or Bew in the summer of 1776 and dish on all things Washington over a cup of British tea or a stout Irish ale?

Randolph knew the names of Washington's wife and stepson. Lund Washington, his Mount Vernon caretaker, certainly knew Randolph and his character. After all Lund, had reported to Washington in October 1775 of Randolph's suspected whereabouts at the time: "Lord Dunmore will hardly venture himself up this river . . . surely her old acquaintance the attorney (who with his family are aboard his ship) would put him off doing an act of that kind."

Washington's forged letter to Martha references this incident. "I am far from sure, that, that restless madman, our quondam Governor, from the mere lust of doing mischief, will not soon betake himself to the carrying on a predatory war in our rivers."

Washington was correct. Whoever wrote these letters was familiar with some aspects of his life. "He must have had some knowledge of the component parts of my family, but has, most egregiously, mistaken fact in several instances, though the design of his labors is as clear as the sun in its meridian brightness," Washington had written to Richard Henry Lee.

Randolph certainly knew the names of Martha, Lund, and Jackie Custis. He could have been a source for James Rivington and it is possible they could have met after Rivington's return to London. Randolph could have also met with Bew, who first published the forged letters as a pamphlet.

Yet though very little is known about Randolph's time in London, the one surviving letter written by him paints a different picture than a pirate bent on revenge and willing to take a sword to the heart of Washington's character. Instead, this letter depicts Randolph as a man of honor who was heartbroken over the war between the land of his birth and the land of his loyalty.

At the Cannon Coffee House at Spring Gardens on October 25, 1779, John Randolph, picked up a pen and began to write a letter, something he didn't often do. He'd recently heard some exciting news about a beloved family member back in Virginia.

"I must take the liberty to say, that your constituents could not have chosen a man of greater abilities to conduct their affairs, than you possess," John Randolph wrote to his first cousin once removed, Thomas Jefferson, on his election as governor of Virginia. Because of their mutual love of music, Randolph had also left Jefferson his violin in his will. He'd not forgotten Jefferson's kindness in writing to him in 1775 about the death of his brother, Peyton Randolph.

Randolph decided to discuss the politics that divided him and Jefferson in 1779. "If a difference in opinion was a good ground for an intermission of friendship, mankind might justly be said to live in a state of warfare," he explained, noting that "men's minds (were) as various as the author of their being has shaped their persons."

"The man who condemns another for thinking differently from himself, sets up his judgment as the standard of conception; wounds the great liberty we enjoy, of thinking for ourselves," he wrote, adding his opinion on speech intolerance. "And tyrannizes over the mind, which the mature intended should be free and unconfined. That tyrant, I cannot suppose you to be."

Remembering Jefferson for his liberality of sentiment and claiming an uncorrupted heart, he begged Jefferson to give him a fair hearing. "I will allow you . . . to consider them, as the overflowing of a mind, too zealous in the cause in which it is engaged," he wrote.

This exiled Virginian explained that as the tensions escalated before the revolution started, he'd tried to keep an open mind and used his skills as an attorney to logically consider both sides.

"I read with avidity everything which was published on the subject . . . I found myself embarrassed by a thousand considerations, acting in direct opposition to each other." Though conflicted, he followed the most logical, reasonable course of action in his view. "Adversity is a school, in which few men wish to be educated; yet, it is a source, from whence the most useful improvements, may be derived . . . in that school I have been tutored."

Life in England had not been easy. "The insults I received from a people, (whose interest I always considered as my own) unrestrained by the influence of gentlemen of rank gave me much uneasiness: But, the unmanly and illiberal treatment, which the more delicate part of my family met with, I confess, filled me with the highest resentment," he admitted of the treatment he'd received in London.

Rather than being welcomed with open arms upon stepping onto England's shore, he'd been received with the same coolness and contempt as Cinderella by her step-sisters. He'd received only a small stipend from Mother England as compensation for his exile. This amount from the British crown wasn't a widow's mite, but it was hardly enough to sustain him.

In his letter to Jefferson, Randolph suggested that he'd forgiven those who'd insulted his wife and daughters. "As there is nothing which I forget so soon as an injury; and as animosity never rankles in my bosom, I have cast the whole into oblivion. There let it lie buried." This sentiment does not sound like a man driven by revenge.

If Randolph was as quick to forgive as he suggested, he didn't need to participate in Lord Sandwich's propaganda campaign as a source for John Bew or James Rivington. In contrast, he saw through the misinformation and disinformation each time he stained his fingers by holding and reading a newspaper at the Trafalgar coffee house.

"But whoever wishes to avoid error, must steer clear of an English newspaper. There are of daily papers published in the year, 27 million: The types, the ink, the paper and a stamp . . . distinctly pay a duty to government," Randolph wrote.

Unlike someone on the King's propaganda payroll, Randolph railed against the English press war. "Judge then, what a revenue these publications must produce. It is for this reason that ministry throw no impediment in their way."

Randolph's attitude doesn't reflect the tone of a forger. "I have often thought that the toleration of such indecent compositions was a reflection on government, but it is a maxim in England, that as soon as an evil produces good, it ceases to be an evil."

Despite his loyalist leanings, Randolph saw through Lord Sandwich's disinformation campaign. He'd concluded that the liberal press was spewing propaganda rather than seeking the truth. The London press was failing to adhere to the higher ideals of point and counter point as called for by freedom of the press. Despite this realization, he was also appalled by the actions of the patriots.

"Annihilation is preferable to a reunion with Great Britain. To support this desirable end, you have entered into an alliance with France . . . what effect this connection will have on you, or this kingdom, time alone can discover;" he wrote believing that France was a deceitful country. In this letter to Jefferson, he spent several lines criticizing the French for their weak laws and aversion to all things English.

"Yet, I cannot avoid expressing my wish, that you had never entered into any engagements with them . . . But if you are able to discharge the debt, how will you recompense them for the services?" he asked, adding a stern warning. "Nothing but a partition of your country will silence them. When that happens, you may bid adieu to all social happiness; the little finger of France will be more burthensome to you, than the whole weight of George III, his Lords and Commons."

He pinpointed the irony of the French-American alliance. A revolution trying to throw off one monarchy had enlisted the help of another monarchy to do so. "The short representation . . . which I have given you above, is intended to prepare you, for one important question . . . Would it not be prudent, to rescind your Declaration of Independence, be happily reunited to your ancient and natural friend, and enjoy a peace, which I most religiously think would pass all understanding?"

Did Randolph know that Jefferson had actually written the Declaration of Independence? Probably not. Though Jefferson had signed the Declaration during the war, his authorship was not widely recognized. If the British military had known that he'd written it, his name likely would have risen to the top of their most wanted list, next to the names of Samuel Adams and John Hancock, because of their leadership of the Sons of Liberty. Only once the Revolution ended would the public learn of Jefferson's authorship.

"I can venture to assure you, that your independence will never be acknowledged by the legislative authority of this kingdom," Randolph warned, while also expressing distress for Jefferson's welfare.

John Randolph then declared that writing letters was not a common habit of his. "I must now put a period to a long letter, the writing of which is a very unusual labor to me."

Because composing long letters was not a usual practice or passion for this loyalist, he likely would not have had the skill or gumption to pretend that he was George Washington and write letters in his name. Given his knowledge of Washington's family members, he could have been a source for Rivington or Bew, but his distaste of London's newspapers and his opinion that they were full of propaganda suggests that he did not participate in the forgeries.

"Let our opinions vary as they will, I shall nevertheless retain a very sincere regard for you," Randolph wrote in closing, practicing what he preached by showing tolerance for his political differences with Cousin Jefferson. "How you may receive it, I know not. Be that as it will, I shall enjoy one consolation, which is, a quiet conscience."

A man who practiced honor with a clear conscience would be an odd culprit as the counterfeiter behind Washington's forged letters.

The tragedy of Randolph's 1779 letter to Thomas Jefferson is that Jefferson never received it. The letter was found in 1840 among the papers of Sir Edward Walpole, the brother of the celebrated writer Horace Walpole, who was tasked with forwarding Randolph's letter to Jefferson but never did. Dying of a broken heart for his beloved America in 1784, Randolph asked his family to return his remains to Williamsburg for final burial, which they did after the war.

While James Rivington clearly played a role in publishing the forgeries, what mattered most to Rivington? Was it freedom of the press or free-flowing propaganda? How should history remember him?

20 TURNCOAT'S FAKE NEWS

The propaganda war continued in London newspapers, especially in 1780. "It was on Thursday night reported that General Washington had sent notice to Congress of his resolution of resigning his command and retiring to his estate in Virginia," *London's Public Advertiser* reported on July 8, 1780, along with word that Virginia would soon return as a prodigal child to Mother England. This was a lie.

A month later, the news in London was worse for Washington and better for Britain. "A report yesterday prevailed in the city that advice had been received (via Holland) of General Washington being defeated, and that with him upwards of 2,000 rebels were taken, 900 killed and a great number wounded," the *Adams Weekly Courant* published on August 15, 1780.

Yet again, this information was false, although on the next day— August 16—in South Carolina, General Horatio Gates lost more than 2,000 men to death or injury in the Battle of Camden, which gave Lord Charles Cornwallis a victory in their campaign in the South. By this time with territory in New England, New York, and Pennsylvania largely at a stalemate, the war had turned toward the Southern states of Georgia, South Carolina, North Carolina, and Virginia.

Although he didn't want to face checkmate, Gates's strategy had failed. He miscalculated his supply lines, which proved inadequate. The Battle of Camden was one of the largest American defeats of the war. As his Continental troops retreated, Gates fled the battlefield and abandoned his pawns, riding nearly two hundred miles in three days. Accused of cowardice, his reputation was ruined, and Congress removed him from command. Despite the severity of the losses, which knocked hundreds of pawns and one knight off the patriot board, it was not the coup de grâce that Lord Cornwallis had hoped for.

Still another report in London's *Public Advertiser* on August 19 indicated that John Hancock had written to Washington about

Britain's conquest of Charleston, South Carolina, which was a real victory that had taken place in May 1780. However, in the final paragraph, Hancock supposedly wrote that the news would arrive "a day too late for their rejoicing in London."

"Here follow about 20 lines of strange figures, somewhat like Hebrew characters, explanatory no doubt of the intended fire in London," the newspaper editor of London's *Public Advertiser* wrote after quoting Hancock's letter. The editor suggested that this coded message revealed that Washington and Hancock were plotting to burn the entire city of London.

The *Public Advertiser* also reinforced the idea that Lord Sandwich's propaganda war continued by promising benefits to participating newspaper editors, particularly those in America. "It is thought that the exercise of the press by some able writers in America, under the protection of the Royal Army, will claim the honor of sharing in the conquest of America, should that continent be at length subdued."

Presumably, Rivington was among those waiting for this prize. Or was he?

For those reading New York's most prominent loyalist newspaper in August 1781, all seemed lost for General Washington, his army, and the patriots. Rivington painted Washington as a weak man who knew that his French allies and the Continental Congress were beyond anxious for a decisive victory. According to Rivington, Washington knew the stakes. Failure to achieve a game-changing win in the campaign of 1781 would lead the king of France to withdraw his support. Not only that, but the British had also received a big boost through a new alliance.

James Rivington reported on August 25, 1781, in his *Royal Gazette* that: "A gentleman just arrived from Jersey, informs us (and it is on his report we mention) that young Mr. Laurens, lately passed through that province on his return from Paris, and has brought us the following very interesting intelligence, that the Emperor of Germany, has declared himself the ally of Great Britain."

The first fact was true. Washington had sent one of his trusted aide-de-camps, John Laurens, to Paris to ask for money, ammunition, clothing, and other items from the French court. Laurens had recently returned. Mixing fact with propaganda, Rivington gushed that news of the British-German alliance had sent the king of France into a confused tailspin.

"In consequence of this great event, the French nation must withdraw all support from their new allies the rebels of this continent."

That wasn't the best part from Rivington's longstanding loyalist perspective. "And we are informed, that it has, with another concurring circumstance, occasioned Mr. Washington and the Count de Rochambeau [of France] to quit their menacing position at the White Plains (of New York)."

According to Rivington's interpretation, the German emperor's new commitment to England was so powerful, that it had changed George Washington's plans for 1781. Instead of attacking the British army in New York, as so many believed Washington had long been planning to do, he was withdrawing his troops. Rivington reported that Washington and Rochambeau had left New York with Washington's column crossing the North River and camping in East Jersey.

"It is said that the French and rebels left their ground the day after Mr. Washington received the mortifying account of the (German) Emperor's alliance with his Majesty's old and natural friend, the court of Great Britain."

The British were receiving additional help from the Germans but the allegiance would not affect the fall campaign in 1781. Rivington didn't hold back. He threw another dagger at Washington, writing: "We are assured (that) the French and rebel troops did not consort together as men determined either to secure the independence of America or realize Mr. Washington to be a dictator of it."

On that same day, Rivington also published the news that the Comte de Grasse, a French admiral, had left the West Indies (south of Florida) with twenty-four warships and a large convoy of soldiers.

In addition, the *Royal Gazette* reported that Britain's General Lord Cornwallis had relocated his seven thousand Redcoats from Portsmouth, Virginia, to Yorktown, Virginia, because it was "healthier, a place of superior consequence and more eligible for accommodating the army and its followers." Rivington added that Lafayette led a small contingent of men near Yorktown, but didn't think he was a threat.

"The Marquis de Lafayette and the rebel commanders with their troops keep a respectful distance from the Royal Army," he reassured. With such news, his loyalist readers hoped that the war would soon end, and Washington would be tried for treason.

Most patriots by this time, however, didn't believe anything that

Rivington published. One Philadelphia newspaper, the *Freeman's Journal,* called Rivington the mouthpiece of British General Clinton, who was Commander-in-Chief of the British Army in North America. "We can also assure the public from past observation, that Sir Henry Clinton, and his aide-de-camp Mr. Rivington, have long been in the actual service of his most diabolical Majesty, Satan in the first."

The editor of the *Massachusetts Spy* later advertised a special medicine, a warlock's brew. This concoction promised that the user would gain an ability to deceive like Rivington by extracting "a distillation of some hundreds of the *Royal Gazette* of New York." The effect of drinking Rivington's magic tonic was long lasting. "By administering due proportion of this medicine, lies may be formed which are to operate for a day, a week, a month or months, war at hand or at a distance in America or in Europe." Through this satirical article, the *Massachusetts Spy* engaged in the 18th century version of a meme.

To patriots, Rivington, not the editor of the *Massachusetts Spy,* was the king of fake news. Rivington's August 25, 1781, article was a good example because it mixed just enough truth with fiction to confuse and mislead readers. Rivington's name was synonymous with propaganda.

★ ★ ★ ★ ★

No one was more pleased to read James Rivington's August 25 article about George Washington fleeing New York in a panic than Lieutenant General Sir Henry Clinton, who commanded the king's troops in North America. This included twelve thousand soldiers in New York. Rivington's article affirmed Clinton's desire of "wanting to give a mortal stab to rebellion."

Clinton believed that this was his year to shine by ending the nonsense of independence once and for all. He couldn't have been more confident in his conclusion that Washington's greatest desire and plan was to attack him in New York, while the greatest chink in his armor was the lack of resources to do it. Why was Clinton so confident? Intelligence. Seeing the evidence with his own eyes, Clinton was as thrilled and smug as a victorious knight presenting King Arthur with the Holy Grail at his round table.

"I cannot sufficiently express my extreme joy at reading Washington's letter. It is such a description of distress, as may serve to convince, that with a tolerable reinforcement from Europe, to enable your Excellency to determine on an offensive campaign,"

General Phillips had written from his post in Portsmouth, Virginia, to General Clinton earlier in the year on April 16. His intelligence didn't come from revealing the invisible ink used by Washington's Culper spy ring or by using a different language, such as Hebrew or Greek in place of English, to decipher their coded messages. Instead, Phillips had referred to a letter that the British had intercepted between General Washington and Benjamin Harrison.

"I shall give you a short detail of our situation," Washington had legitimately written to Harrison on March 27, 1781. Needing Harrison to understand the dire situation his army faced, Washington had asked him to pass this information to the Continental Congress.

"Of clothing we are in a manner exhausted," Washington had revealed to Harrison. "We don't have more than two thousand stand of arms to spare." Too many soldiers had left the army because their contracts had expired. Washington's Pennsylvania line had dissolved. "Our stock of ammunition . . . is vastly short of an offensive operation of any consequence." Because of General Benedict Arnold's controlled demolition of West Point's defenses as part of his treason, Washington barely had a garrison "sufficient for the security of West Point, and two regiments in Jersey to support the communication between the Delaware and North River."

Seeking to recruit more men in the middle states and bolster supplies, Washington had also relayed hope. "I have hitherto been speaking of our own resources—should a reinforcement arrive of the French Fleet and Army; the face of matters may be entirely changed."

While burdened by the condition of his army, he had also kept his eye on the big picture. Washington had communicated to Harrison that his focus was on New York, and that he saw an opportunity to retake it after their devastating loss in 1776. "You may be assured that the most powerful diversion that can be made in favor of the Southern States, will be a respectable force in the neighborhood of New York."

A British soldier or spy had intercepted Washington's letter to Harrison and had forwarded it to Clinton. Reading Washington's intentions and knowing about his lack of resources had convinced Clinton that he would soon defeat Washington and his rebel army.

Was Washington aware that the British had acquired his letter to Harrison? Yes. He or one of his aides had made a copy of this to Harrison in his letter book before sending it. Washington would often document in his daily diary which letters he'd received that day from his officers or other correspondents and refer to the previous letters he had written to them in his letter book.

When Washington didn't receive a reply from Harrison, he resignedly concluded that the British had intercepted his letter, as he'd indicated in his letter book: "Duplicate. It is feared that the original miscarried with the last week's mail, which is missing and is supposed to have been taken and carried into New York." In fact, this letter could have been a bit of disinformation on Washington's part. He knew the letter could be intercepted. Perhaps he wrote it to make the British think he was myopically focused on defeating them in New York.

General Clinton shared Washington's March 27 letter to Harrison with George Germaine, Britain's secretary of state for the American colonies and coordinator of the war for King George. Germaine was so thrilled at receiving this that he himself wrote a letter on July 14, 1781. "The copies of the very important correspondence which so fortunately fell into your hands . . . show the rebel affairs to be almost desperate, and that nothing but the success of some extraordinary enterprise can give vigor and activity to their cause."

Germaine expressed his joy at Washington's focus on New York: "and I confess I am well pleased that they have fixed upon New York as the object to be attempted, as I have not the least doubt but that the troops you had remaining with you, after the ample reinforcements you so judiciously sent to the Chesapeake (with Lord Cornwallis), would be fully sufficient under your command to repel any force the enemy could bring against you."

This and other information led Germaine and Clinton to conclude that France's Comte De Grasse, who commanded French ships in the West Indies, wouldn't attack Britain's forces in the Caribbean because of Washington's desire to attack New York. They believed that if de Grasse sailed to North America to support Washington and Rochambeau's forces, that his fleet would "join the French forces at Rhode Island," where the other French troops had previously camped. They weren't worried because they doubted that de Grasse would come at all.

"However the present reduced state of General Washington, the little probability there is, I hope, of an augmentation to the French armament," Clinton began in a reply to Germaine. "But, as General Washington's letter to Mr. Harrison (a copy of which your Lordship will see amongst the intercepted letters enclosed) intimates, that there will not be opposed to his Lordship, above two thousand continentals."

Germaine was also happy with Clinton's plans for the British troops under the command of General Cornwallis in Virginia. "It is with the most unfeigned pleasure I obey his Majesty's commands, in expressing to you his royal approbation of the plan you have adopted for prosecuting the war in the provinces south of the Delaware."

No one besides Clinton could have been more pleased to read Rivington's August 25 report than George Washington. The reason? The news was fake, or at least enough of the facts in the article were false to give Washington what he needed most in late August of 1781: a cover story about why he was leaving New York.

The most convincing disinformation or biased news is information that mixes truth with facts. This article by Rivington did just that. Yes, Lafayette was watching General Cornwallis's movements in Yorktown. Yes, one of Lafayette's spies was a twenty-one-year-old slave named James Armistead, who had close access to Cornwallis as a hired servant. Yes, the Comte de Grasse and his fleet were sailing for the East Coast. Yes, Washington had left New York, but not because he feared a new British German alliance. Instead, he was implementing a surprise plan of attack.

A thoroughly romantic glory seeker would have clung to capturing New York no matter the realities on the ground. The worse the odds, the greater the glory. Washington, however, was no Don Quixote chasing Dutch windmills in New Amsterdam. Though Washington had wanted to win the war by defeating the British in New York, where they'd forced him to retreat in 1776, he couldn't succeed there unless several factors fell into place. This included receiving new recruits from the states and reinforcements from the French Navy. As the summer of 1781 progressed, Washington realized that he had a better chance of defeating the British elsewhere.

What had changed his mind? Ever the practical general, Washington had weighed several factors, including the Marquis de Lafayette's intelligence from his post commanding nine hundred men in Virginia. Throughout the spring and summer, General Lafayette had frequently updated Washington on the movements of Cornwallis in Virginia while also giving his opinions on strategy. He wasn't afraid to steer Washington's attention away from launching a battle in New York and choosing the South instead.

"Your first letters, my dear General, will perhaps tell me something more about your coming this way," Lafayette had written Washington on May 24, from his camp sixteen miles from Richmond, Virginia. "How happy I would be to see you, I hope I need not to express."

Tapping Washington's emotional ties to his native state, the marquis had given his opinion that Virginia would be a good place to go fox hunting for Redcoats.

"As you are pleased to give me the choice, I frankly shall tell my wishes. If you cooperate with the French against the place you know, I wish to be at headquarters. If something is cooperated in Virginia, I will find myself very happily situated."

Yet Lafayette knew that Washington wanted to bring men and supplies to New York. "You will then decide, if the upper part of the island, Long Island, Staten Island, or New York Island is to be in our possession," Lafayette had written him again on July 20.

By August 1, Washington concluded that despite all of his diligent efforts and countless commands and requests, he still didn't have the men and supplies necessary to attack the British in New York. Though the one hundred boats from Albany that he'd ordered were ready, along with increased ammunition stores, he still didn't have the number of new recruits that he'd requested from Maryland, Pennsylvania, Virginia, and other places.

"If the states had furnished their quotas of men agreeably to my requisitions, but so far have they been from complying with these that of the first, not more than half the number asked of them have joined the army," he wrote candidly in his diary on August 1.

By this time, Washington had concluded that the plans he'd discussed with his officers and French allies a year earlier wouldn't work in the present circumstances.

"More than these . . . the original plan could not be done without unfolding matters too plainly to the enemy and enabling them thereby to counteract our schemes."

The practical Washington knew that the British had intercepted too many of his letters, including the one he'd sent to Harrison and several more that he'd sent to General Nathanael Greene. As he was playing a game of cat and mouse with Cornwallis in the Carolinas, Greene had not received most of Washington's letters to him.

As much as Washington longed to defeat the British in New York, which would have soothed his bruised ego from losing the city in 1776, he nonetheless prioritized pragmatism over personal glory.

"I could scarce see a ground upon [which] to continue my preparations against New York . . . and therefore I turned my views more seriously (than I had before done) to an operation to the

Southward."

Unaware that Washington was changing his mind about going to Virginia, Lafayette again expressed his opinion on the matter. He wrote Washington on August 6, that instead of taking his ships northward to reinforce Clinton in New York, Cornwallis had not only landed at York, Virginia, but he also had begun building a winter camp. "Should a fleet come in at this moment our affairs would take a very happy turn."

"Had not your attention been turned to New York something with a fleet might be done in this quarter—But I see New York is the object and consequently I attend to your instructions," Lafayette added, frankly expressing his opinion while also showing respect and deference.

"But to return to operations in Virginia, I will tell you, my dear General, that Lord Cornwallis is entrenching at York and Gloucester. The sooner we disturb him the better. But unless our maritime friends (de Grasse) give us help we cannot much venture below. I think his force may amount to four thousand six hundred," Lafayette wrote Washington five days later on August 11.

"In the present state of affairs, my dear General, I hope you will come yourself to Virginia," he added.

By August 14, Washington had received dispatches about Count de Grasse's departure from the West Indies. His convoy included more than twenty-five warships and three thousand two hundred soldiers. Washington was thrilled at the news, despite the change in destination.

Because de Grasse wanted to return and protect his position in the West Indies by November, he didn't want to sail as far north as New York. Instead he had sailed for the Chesapeake Bay. Going to Virginia also kept his ships from being damaged during hurricane season in the Caribbean and West Indies. Though Washington had already begun to seriously consider a campaign in the South, de Grasse's decision struck the final blow against an attack in New York.

"Matters having now come to a crisis and a decisive plan to be determined on—I was obliged . . . to give up all idea of attacking New York," Washington wrote.

In mid-August, Washington then ordered the French and American armies in New York to march toward Virginia. He gave Lafayette the news in a letter on August 15. He asked Lafayette to do everything he could to prevent Cornwallis from marching south and escaping Virginia. Because Lafayette's force was significantly smaller than

Cornwallis's, he couldn't defeat Cornwallis, but he could stall him.

Washington also wrote de Grasse that another reason for abandoning New York was the intelligence he'd received that the British were expecting reinforcements, which Rivington reported on August 25.

"We may add a further inducement for giving up the first mentioned enterprise, which is the arrival of a reinforcement of near three thousand Hessian recruits. For this purpose we have determined to remove the whole of the French Army and as large a detachment of the American as can be spared to Chesapeake, to meet Your Excellency."

The Commander-in-Chief decided to engage in some additional misinformation of his own. Washington was aware that the British knew that he wanted to attack them in New York. Hence, sending his men to Virginia would surprise General Clinton, Germaine, and Cornwallis. The decision would also surprise his army. Without telling his soldiers their ultimate destination, he planned different routes for his army and the French army to exit New York. "As our intentions could be concealed one march more (under the idea going to Sandy Hook to facilitate the entrance of the French fleet within the bay), the whole army was put in motion in three columns."

"With a design to deceive the enemy as to our real movement," Washington ordered wagons to carry flat boats to New Jersey and the construction of French ovens to make it appear that they were anticipating the arrival of the French fleet there. His men signed contracts for food from nearby farmers. In this way, his men made it look like they were planning to attack Staten Island.

The ruse worked. Clinton wrote Germaine in early September that Washington had "crossed the [Hudson] River and by the position he took seemed to threaten Staten Island."

Rivington's August 25 article reported that Washington was fleeing New York in a panic. This description worked perfectly into Washington's plans. When did General Clinton realize that Washington was headed South?

"Early in September, to my great surprise, (for I still considered our fleet as superior) hearing that Mr. Washington was decidedly marching to the Southward, I called a council of all the general officers, who unanimously concurred with me in opinion, that the only way to succor Earl Cornwallis was to go to him in the Chesapeake," Clinton explained.

This British commanding general didn't receive reports until

September 7 that Washington and Rochambeau and their troops were heading south on transport ships.

"Or if I had as many reasons to believe that Mr. Washington would move his army into Virginia without a covering French fleet, as I had to think he would not; I could not have prevented his passing the Hudson under cover of his forts at Verplanks and Stoney Points," he wrote, explaining that he would have arranged for his army to harass Washington's army as they exited New York if he'd known that they weren't just fleeing because Germany was helping King George III but were instead planning an attack.

From his post in Virginia, Lord Cornwallis had a similar reaction. "I never could have the most distant idea that Mr. Washington had the least hopes of a superior French fleet in the Chesapeake; and I consequently never could suppose that he would venture to go there," Cornwallis explained, adding that he believed the British would continue to control the water.

With the surprise of an unexpected shower sweeping down the mid-Atlantic coastline, Washington and Rochambeau led their remaining troops on land to Baltimore, where many of them boarded ships bound for the Chesapeake Bay. Wagons, cows, horses, and cavalry continued by land with Rochambeau and Washington. On September 9, General Washington arrived home to Mount Vernon after a six-year absence and stayed a few days. As it had done years earlier when Washington first became a newsmaker in the 1750s, so Mount Vernon once again offered Washington refuge, a calm before the storm. A few days later, Washington met up with his troops that had gone by ship and thundered toward their final destination, Cornwallis's make-shift castle.

When De Grasse and his fleet arrived in the sea outside of Yorktown, their presence shook Cornwallis with the force of a hurricane. The French fleet engaged and won an ocean battle against the British ships on September 5. After that, the French fleet-controlled water access to Yorktown. Arriving there at the end of September, Washington and Rochambeau joined Lafayette. Together their troops enacted a siege against Cornwallis's position.

For his part, Rivington in New York publicly continued to print that Britain would prevail, even if Washington defeated Cornwallis at Yorktown. "Should this attempt of the French succeed (blocking Cornwallis from escaping by water)," Rivington reported in the *Royal Gazette* on October 3, "the contest may be protracted to a tedious length, and Great Britain might be more beholden to foreign assistance than her real friends wish her to see."

By this time, Washington had given Alexander Hamilton what he most wanted, a light infantry battalion to command. Serving under Lafayette's troops, Hamilton's troops attacked one of the key redoubts protecting the British fort while French soldiers attacked another redoubt at the same time. This approach cornered Cornwallis. Blocked in by both land and sea and unable to receive reinforcements from Clinton, Cornwallis surrendered his men to Washington on October 19, 1781.

"I have the mortification to inform Your Excellency that I have been forced to give up the posts of York and Gloucester, and to surrender the troops under my command by capitulation on the 19th instant (October) as prisoners of war to the combined forces of America and France," Cornwallis wrote to Clinton. To his credit, and as he had done after the British defeat at Saratoga, Rivington published this letter as the authentic news that it was.

A thrilled Washington had now attained what he and the patriots most needed: a decisive victory against the British. This was such a dagger to the British Empire and the core of British identity that it was as if God had struck lightning at Stonehenge. Not everyone could see the big picture, however, at least not publicly.

★ ★ ★ ★ ★

Rivington did what he was expected to do: put a royal spin on the outcome at Yorktown by suggesting that France might soon rule America.

"We can assure the public from recent information, that the whole Continental Army is at this time in the actual service of his most Christian Majesty, Louis XVI, and are paid with French money, which has been for that purpose remitted to Mr. Washington," Rivington published on November 7, 1781. "So that every American soldier of this alliance is now become in every sense a Frenchman."

Suggesting that Congress was subordinate to Washington and the king of France, Rivington declared: "They (Congress) lately felt the humiliating mortification of perceiving General Washington alone entrusted with the cash received from France to pay the army."

Rivington asserted that Washington would be the French king of America. "The people of America, since their revolt from Great Britain, will have no other choice to make a ruler . . . in the Frenchified Mr. Washington alone."

Yes, Washington had defeated Cornwallis with French support, but he was hardly a Frenchmen at heart. Given his experiences in the 1750s, he was not foolish enough to become a French puppet. Lafayette's spy, the slave James Armistead, had fooled Cornwallis. When Armistead later received his freedom, he changed his name to James Lafayette as a tribute to the respected Frenchman.

Likewise, another Frenchman observed that black patriots made up a quarter of Washington's army at Yorktown, with five thousand serving throughout the war. The First Rhode Island Regiment was made up of black soldiers, including slave and free black men as well as native men. The Rhode Island General Assembly granted immediate freedom to slaves who enlisted.

Lafayette had also exposed Washington to moral arguments against slavery, leading Washington to question the practice and make the counter cultural decision to free his slaves years later. Yes, Frenchmen had played a significant role in the Revolution, but Washington was not about to turn into a French puppet.

However, Rivington had something in common with James Lafayette. Accusing America's Commander-in-Chief of being Frenchified wasn't the only fake or faux aspect of Rivington's articles about Yorktown. Was it true, as the rumors after the war suggested, that Rivington was really a spy for Washington? When he reported on August 25, 1781 that poor George had abandoned New York in a panic, had he given Washington cover on purpose?

★ ★ ★ ★ ★

"It is reported as an undoubted fact, that Mr. JAMES RIVINGTON, printer at New-York, was, as soon as our troops entered the city, protected in person and property, by a guard, and that he will be allowed to reside in the country, for reasons best known to the great men at helm," the *Boston Gazette* reported on December 29, 1783, of the shocking news that Washington had sent a Continental guard to protect Rivington from angry patriots when the British military evacuated New York.

After the peace treaty with England was signed in 1783 by Ben Franklin, John Adams, John Jay, and the other peace commissioners, General Washington marched into New York to say goodbye to his officers. Loyalists who didn't want to stay in the United States fled to Canada or returned to England. As surprising as it was noticeable, James Rivington was not among them.

On January 4, 1784, five days after the *Boston Gazette* reported that Rivington was under protection by a Continental guard, a North Carolina lawyer named William Hooper privately relayed some juicy tidbits to his friend, Judge James Iredell. "It has come out, as there is now no longer any reason to conceal it, that Rivington has been very useful to General Washington by furnishing him with intelligence."

A few years earlier, Rivington had brought a partner into his business. Next to his printing shop, Rivington owned a coffee house with Robert Townsend, who spied for Washington in the intelligence circle called the Culper Ring. Because British officers and others frequented Rivington's tavern, the place was a great source for overhearing information under the smothering smoke of cigars and the caramelizing aroma of Madeira wine. A good spy could grow intoxicated with intelligence there—especially if he owned the place. After all, a seemingly innocuous advertisement in Rivington's newspaper might appear frivolous except to the moles who could decode it.

In the 1779 codebook, which was created by Washington's intelligence officer Benjamin Tallmadge, Robert Townsend was listed by a code name and a number, Culper, Jr., 723, while Rivington was listed in the codebook only by a code number and not by a code name. The Culper spies only used Rivington's number to refer to him. This could indicate that he had become a spy in 1779 or it could simply have been a way for Townsend and the other Culper members to refer to Rivington in their coded correspondence.

Additional hard evidence suggests that Rivington had been a spy for Washington since at least the summer before Yorktown. Around the time that Rivington printed the August 25, 1781, article stating that Washington was fleeing New York in fear, a member of Washington's war board passed along key information about the cooperation of the printer and famed loyalist.

Judge Richard Peters reported to General Washington information about Rivington's willingness to help the patriots. "By a channel of intelligence, I have opened I can procure access to Rivington's printing office where there is a person ready to furnish any important papers as intelligence!"

His source was Captain Allen McLane. Washington responded to Peters: "I do myself the pleasure to acknowledge your favor of the 19th instant, Capt. McLane, and thank you for the intelligence you have communicated; The particular mode you have adopted to obtain information, I think may be very usefully employed, and is a fortunate expedient; the necessity of its use to our present operations is happily at an end, if continued, it may be of importance to some future designs." On the reverse of the letter was this inscription: "Genl. Washington, Secret Service, Capt. McLane."

In his reflections, McLane said that he received help from Rivington in August 1781. "I was employed by the board of war to repair to Long Island to watch the motion of the British fleet and if possible, obtain their signals, which I did through the assistance of the noted Rivington," McLane wrote about how he received the Royal Navy signal book from Rivington. McLane then passed the signal book to de Grasse, writing: "Joined the fleet Under the Count de Grasse with the signals."

McLane likely gave the British Navy's signal book to De Grasse around August 30, when Washington recorded his army's position around Sandy Hook. By passing along the Royal Navy's signal book, Rivington took a great risk in order to benefit the patriots and Continental Army. After the Battle of Yorktown, France's De Grasse expressed his appreciation for the British signal book to the board of war. A member of the McLane family later recorded this unsigned document about the transaction:

"On her [the ship's] return he [McLane] was stationed by the Board of War near Sandy Hook to correspond with R of New York, received the signals for the British fleet out of New York (and) delivered them to Count De Grass."

While it is impossible to determine how much Rivington knew about Washington's plans in August 1781, he certainly gave Washington public cover in his newspaper as the general and his troops left New York. Rivington's article clearly fooled British General Clinton. This took place at the same time Rivington passed the Royal signal book to McLane.

Why did Rivington become a spy? One reason may have been his lost income. In 1779, he lost his salary as the King's printer, which could have been a turning point for him, or at least could have given him a reason to seek other sources of income over time. One account proclaimed that Washington gave Rivington a bag of gold at his tavern on his triumphant march through New York in 1783.

Another possible reason that Rivington had turned spy was that his loyalty had genuinely changed. Before the war, he saw himself as the instrument of a free press in British America. This dream was dashed when the mob burned his printing business in 1775, forcing him to take refuge in England. Returning to New York as the mouthpiece for the king in 1777 had forced him to suppress his inclination to present real or neutral news, not news shaded by propaganda.

While he clearly played a role in the *War of Lies* by publishing the forgeries in his newspaper in 1778, he wasn't the first to publish the letters. John Bew published them first. While in England, Rivington or Bew wouldn't have had enough information about Washington's family to write the letters and make them believable unless they had a credible source. John Randolph's disgust for London newspapers and their propaganda made him an unlikely co-conspirator.

After Rivington lost his income from the crown, he may have thought about what would happen to him and to his family at the end of the war. If the Americans lost, he would not have freedom of speech or freedom of the press as a British printer. He preferred living in New York to living in London. He wanted to publish freely. Covertly changing sides gave him the option to engage in freedom of the press after the war. Unfortunately for Rivington, too many people saw him as a biased loyalist for him to succeed as a post-war newspaper man. He continued his retail business.

Years later in 1788, a few months before he became the first president of the United States, Washington reflected on his decision to go to Yorktown instead of New York:

"That much trouble was taken and finesse used to misguide and bewilder Sir Henry Clinton in regard to the real object, by fictitious communications, as well as by making a deceptive provision of ovens, forage and boats in his neighborhood, is certain. Nor were less pains taken to deceive our own Army," Washington wrote to his friend, Noah Webster.

Washington's desire to make people think New York was his end game was purposeful, as he'd indicated in his March 1781 letter to Benjamin Harrison: "You may be assured that the most powerful diversion that can be made in favor of the southern states, will be a respectable force in the neighborhood of New York."

By calling New York a diversion, Washington suggested that he could use New York as either a real objective or a fake pretense, if need be. This is exactly what he did in August 1781. Like any good general who develops contingency plans, he kept his options open, never fully committing until the moment he was ready to move his troops. ". . . Should a reinforcement arrive to the French fleet and army, the face of matters may be entirely changed," he had written to Harrison.

Years later, as Washington shared, "the difficulty consisted more in providing, than knowing how to apply the military apparatus." More important than choosing where to strike in 1781 was bolstering the army. Once he had enough supplies and men, he could choose the best option. He claimed "that before the arrival of the Count de Grasse, it was the fixed determination to strike the enemy in the most vulnerable quarter so as to ensure success with moral certainty."

Though Rivington's decision to spy for Washington doesn't exonerate him as the counterfeiter behind the *War of Lies*, the behavior of another suspect creates a more plausible pattern of culpability. After all, who might believe that treason could be virtuous?

21 "BRAVE, VIRTUOUS . . . TREASON"

While at Valley Forge in 1778, General Washington had received a letter from his friend Landon Carter, who was deeply worried that someone close to Washington had written the forged letters: "So replete with your domestic occurrences, that it deservedly lodges a suspicion of its inventor somewhere near to you."

Who was close enough to Washington in 1775 and 1776 to be the inventor of this scheme? Washington may not have known the identity of the culprit, but his ability to assess character and integrity nonetheless enabled him to outfox a fox and neutralize the counterfeiter.

Could General Horatio Gates have known enough about Washington's family and domestic occurrences to invent the letters? Yes. After buying land in 1773 and settling with his wife into the peaceful countryside of Traveler's Rest in what is now West Virginia, Gates served as a justice of the peace alongside Samuel Washington, one of Washington's brothers.

Once the war broke out, Horatio Gates visited Mount Vernon on May 2, 1775. Though his visit was brief, he likely met Martha Washington and may have met Lund Washington and Jackie Custis. Likewise, from July 1775 until early 1776, Gates was with George Washington in camp, serving as adjutant general. In this capacity, he was present for war council meetings. He certainly had experience writing in Washington's name because he often wrote orders and letters on behalf of his Commander-in-Chief during 1775.

Likewise, because he was in frequent contact with Washington while in Cambridge, Gates would have had an opportunity to learn some of the domestic details included in the counterfeit letters.

However, during this time, Congress promoted Gates again and gave him command of Fort Ticonderoga, New York, with a mission of attacking Canada. Having been overlooked for promotion by the British, Gates had every reason to be pleased with General Washington during the time the counterfeit letters were allegedly written, June to July 1776.

In addition, unlike his friend Charles Lee, Gates did not have an interest in writing letters with the purpose of persuading the public. He didn't pen pamphlets or seek to have articles published in newspapers. When he had conflict with General Washington, especially after the Conway Cabal in late 1777, Gates sought to restore his strained relationship with his Commander-in-Chief. Similarly, Gates's first major conflict with Washington took place after the forged letters were published in England. The timing of Gates's authorship as the counterfeiter doesn't line up.

General Gates's greatest failure was the Battle of Camden, for which he was court martialed. But unlike General Lee, Gates had not disobeyed an order from Washington, who was hundreds of miles away at the time. Instead Gates had mismanaged the troops and supply lines. He'd committed errors in judgment, not deliberate malfeasance resulting from a grudge, like General Lee. Unlike Lee, he didn't use the press to vent his anger and frustration or take jabs at Washington. After leaving the army, Gates continued to write Washington respectful letters.

"The secrecy and expedition of Your Excellency's movement from the North River defeated my wish to have paid you my compliments in person upon your route, as I never knew of your being upon the march until you had passed Alexandria," Gates wrote to Washington on October 7, 1781, upon learning that Washington and France's Rochambeau had marched their troops from New York to Virginia to battle the British at Yorktown.

"Ever willing to give my little aid to serve this our much-injured country, I should rejoice to be instrumental to Your Excellency's success in any way you would please to command, but I think you would not wish me to act under the stigma that has been so ungenerously been laid upon me," he wrote from his home in Berkley County, Virginia. Now identifying as an American, this former career military officer in the British Army now referred to the USA as *our much-injured country*. In this way, he showed that he had fully embraced the cause of independence as his own. Though Gates knew his services would likely be rejected, he offered them anyway.

General Gates still longed for Washington's approval and ended this letter to Washington with a polite, honorable conclusion. "That the Supreme Disposer of events may crown your labors with a glorious, and complete victory, is the earnest request of Sir Your Excellency's most obedient humble servant."

Gates may have been a glory seeker at times, but despite his court martial, he remained devoted to America's cause, unlike Lee. Both of these men were veterans of the British Army who started out as opportunists styled as *friends to America* by Ben Franklin. Eventually, though, Gates embraced the identity of being an American. Did Lee?

Gates had the knowledge of General Washington's family members to write the forged letters, but he lacked a unique skill and experience that Lee possessed. General Lee had forged a letter in someone else's name before.

While Charles Lee has not been previously fingered as the author of the fake letters, he had the means, motive, and moxie to write them. His profile fits a pattern of culpability in several ways. He had a self-centered character, along with more access to Washington than Randolph and Rivington. In fact, evidence before the war started shows that he not only had the writing skills to pull off a forgery—the means—but he also had experience writing as if he were someone else. Whom had he impersonated? None other than James Rivington.

Unlike Virginia loyalist John Randolph, who told Jefferson he didn't often pick up a pen to write, Lee frequently wrote pamphlets and sought to publish them, especially when he arrived in America in 1773. From the South to New England, he toured the colonies and became more acquainted with the rebellion brewing from the merchants who threw tea into Boston Harbor and the farmers who passed resolutions in Virginia.

Lee published a pamphlet on his ideas for a military colony as well as his essays. Carrying on correspondence with the era's most profound thinkers, he'd written Benjamin Franklin about his military plan for America. There was one thing, however, that Lee couldn't stand as a prolific writer. Rejection, especially from of all people, James Rivington.

Before the Revolutionary War started, Mr. Rivington had published a loyalist pamphlet by an anonymous author. An infuriated Lee wrote a counter-pamphlet that Rivington refused to print. Writing a satirical essay called "A Breakfast for Rivington," Lee's vengeance came out in his venal pen. "As Mr. Rivington has given the public to understanding that he does not choose to deal with any writers, but those of the most accurate and elegant kind . . . and as I cannot flatter myself, that I am one," Lee began with as much satire as invective.

"But as I understand . . . that you admit into your paper even the lowest trash, I find myself under the necessity of applying to you." Then Lee showed he had a particular writing skill necessary for committing forgery: the ability to make up a story in the voice of another living person. In this essay, he invented a tale claiming that he'd recently been among the most "flaming factious enemies to all order and government." He then named a few Lords of London and called Rivington a "ridiculous . . . slip-slop coxcomb" who didn't have the decency of the "porter at a bawdy house."

To commit forgery, someone needs the ability to write in first person in someone else's voice. In this satirical essay, Lee wrote in first person and made up a letter that Rivington supposedly had written to his niece.

"My dear Kitty, as you are going to be married, and are so very, young a girl, I would advise you, by all means, at least, at first, to act with a little *cushion*," Lee wrote in Rivington's voice, indicating that the experienced newspaper editor and wordsmith had confused the word *caution* with *cushion*. "Now I would appeal to all mankind, who are not totally blinded by party and faction, whether it is credible, whether it is possible, that a gentleman, who has from his cradle, been in some sort a retainer of the muses, should be guilty of such gross, such ridiculous blunders."

Lee eventually found another publisher for his twelve-page leaflet, which was published February 3, 1776. "A pamphlet entitled A *Friendly Address to all Reasonable Americans*," Lee gave the patriots hope that they could defeat the intimidating British military, which he knew so well.

"For my own part I think there is very great reason to doubt that 7,000 even of the best (British) troops are able to conquer 200,000 of the most disorderly peasantry upon earth, if they are animated in defense of everything they hold most dear and sacred." These words turned Lee's pamphlet into a bestseller that was printed multiple times. Missing from this pamphlet, however, was a call for declaring independence from England. Lee still had hopes that a war would result in a resolution that kept the British empire intact.

Ben Franklin responded positively to Lee's military proposals, which Lee had included in both his pamphlet and a letter to Franklin. Anticipating that King George III would reject Congress's Olive Branch Proposal, Franklin had given Lee hope that his military plans would be used. "Then your proposed solemn league and covenant will go better down, and perhaps most of your other strong measures adopted."

Lee had the means and the artful writing skills to be an imposter of Washington. If he did it, then why? What was his motive?

Leveraging his celebrity as a writer, his knowledge of military strategy, and his career as a British officer who was now a friend to America, Colonel Charles Lee was in Philadelphia when the Continental Congress met in 1775. He'd spoken fawningly to John Adams and other key delegates, and they responded in kind. "Your opinion of my generosity, valor, good sense, patriotism and zeal for the rights of humanity is extremely flattering to me," Adams wrote to Lee. Promoting his military expertise to Congress, Colonel Lee boasted about his exploits in European campaigns, which impressed many of them, raising his hopes of his greatest conquest: becoming Commander-in-Chief of the American forces.

To say he was disappointed when Congress named George Washington as the commanding general instead is an understatement. Congress further insulted Lee by assigning him to the position of second major general, or, third in command, after naming Artemas Ward of New England as the first major general. Though Ward had less battlefield experience than Lee, Ward had been leading the groups of militia that had come together and surrounded Boston in the countryside after the Battles of Lexington and Concord in April 1775. Demoting Ward to third-in-command would have insulted his service, demoralized his men and demeaned his accomplishment of land-locking the British into Boston proper. Naming Ward as second-in-command after Washington but before Lee as third-in-command was a prudent move by Congress at the time.

Lee didn't see it that way. "Did I not consent to serve under an old church warden, of him you had conceived the most extravagant and ridiculous opinion?" Lee complained a year later to a member of Congress. "Your eyes were at last opened, and Deacon Ward returned to his proper occupation," he wrote, referring to Ward's illness that eventually led to his resignation.

Three days after accepting his commission in 1775, the freshly minted General Lee wrote a letter to the British secretary of war to resign his commission as lieutenant-colonel in the British Army, along with the half-pay he'd continued to receive despite professing his support for the patriots for more than two years. Why hadn't he resigned his commission earlier? His malfeasance would come back to haunt him.

Lee's bitterness and jealousy at not being the commanding general grew stronger, especially as the war faltered in the fall of 1776. He'd been with Washington and Gates in Cambridge from July 1775 until the winter of 1776.

At this time, Washington had accepted Lee's plan to raise troops in Connecticut and go to New York. Congress had told Lee that they would soon name him as commander of the Continental forces in Canada. While in New York assessing the city's infrastructure and defenses, Lee learned that Congress was instead sending him to lead the defense of Charleston, South Carolina.

Lee successfully organized and led troops in repelling a British assault force of 2,900 soldiers and seamen on June 28, 1776, at Fort Moultrie on Sullivan's Island. Six days later on July 4, Congress declared independence from England. No fireworks went off in Lee's heart. While in Charleston, South Carolina, this major general responded to a letter from a member of Congress in mid-July 1776. Instead of praising Congress for the Declaration of Independence, which he didn't mention at all, Lee fumed over the news that Congress was considering hiring another general to replace Artemis Ward as the first major general.

"You tell me a dark, mysterious story of a certain great general . . . (who) will, it seems, graciously condescend to serve America, on condition that Congress will give him assurances of stepping over the heads of every officer but one, and this he submits to, only on consideration of the confidence due to an American," Lee wrote on July 19, 1776, angry that "the palpable meaning of your letter is to prepare me for a cession of my rank in favor of some imprudent adventurer." A European prince had recommended this great general, Buckwith.

Buckwith's abilities were so "transcendent, that I [Lee] ought for the public interest to make a second sacrifice." Like Esau's jealousy of Jacob, Lee felt "spurned aside, to make room for so despicable a character as Buckwith, (a) generally reputed coward, and a sycophant, I say, to be kicked out of my station for such a creature as this, would swell a man more humble than myself into a trumpeter of his own merits." His anger thundered to this unnamed member of the Continental Congress.

"What have I done to merit such an indignity? What part of my conduct can justify your harboring such an idea? Have not I staked my fortune, life, and reputation in your cause?" Notice he didn't use the phrases *our cause* or *my cause* but referred to America's cause as *your cause.*

"Great God! Is it come to this? I am not, it seems, an American?" Lee was either very wounded at not being thought of as an American, or he still emotionally maintained his identity as a native Briton instead.

Lee blasted this unknown member of Congress that if this Buckwith was humble and if his motives were pure, then he should accept the rank of third or fourth general. Then General Lee threw down a gauntlet.

"In God's name, if a real genius, or acknowledge hero, favored by heaven with a more than common portion of ethereal spirit, should present himself, . . . receive him with open arms, as an immediate present from god; invest him with the command of the whole."

If Congress thought so highly of this new Caesar that Lee had to step aside as the first major general, then General Washington should also step aside as Commander-in-Chief and give Buckwith the job.

"But if a hero should start up, and down with the attributes which, according to my persuasion reside in the two I have mentioned, and who would charge himself with the mighty task of your political salvation, General Washington ought, and, I am convinced, would resign the truncheon," Lee wrote, pretentiously appearing to praise Washington. "No man loves, respects, and references another more than I do General Washington. I esteem his virtues, private and public. I know him to be a man of sense, courage, and firmness."

While outwardly showing his support for Washington to a member of Congress, within a few months, Lee privately expressed an opposite view to General Gates. "The Congress seem to stumble every step — I do not mean one or two of the cattle, but the whole stable — I have been very free in delivering my opinion to them," Lee wrote on October 14, 1776, to his friend, General Gates, who by this time was leading troops at Fort Ticonderoga.

Lee displayed his moxie by privately fuming that he should be in charge.

"In my opinion General Washington is much to blame in not menacing them [Congress] with resignation unless they refrain from unhinging the army by their absurd interference," Lee wrote, knowing that he had the most to gain if Washington resigned.

Two weeks later, on October 28, 1776, Lee returned to New York as the well-deserved hero for his victory in South Carolina. Lee joined Washington's forces as they struggled to fight the British north of the city. Proud of Lee's triumph in South Carolina but seemingly unaware of Lee's bitterness or that he had the heart of Cain, Washington had named one of the region's forts, Fort Lee, after him.

Meanwhile, General Lee's defiance grew stronger in his letters.

"Let me talk vainly—had I the powers I could do you much good — might I but dictate one week," he fumed in November 1776 to Benjamin Rush. Lee believed that if he could be Caesar and take Washington's job for just one week, he could turn things around.

"Oh, General! An indecisive mind is one of the greatest misfortunes that can befall an army," he derisively wrote about Washington to Joseph Reed, one of Washington's aides, in November 1776. "How often have I lamented it this campaign!" Lee thought so highly of himself, he declared that he was indispensable: "to confess a truth, I really think our chief will do better with me than without me."

Was Lee's moxie enough to turn into malfeasance?

New York's Fort Washington fell to the British on November 16, 1776. Washington and General Greene ordered the evacuation of nearby Fort Lee in New Jersey on November 20. The next day, Colonel Reed, one of Washington's aides, desperately wrote Lee an urgent, secret message. "I do not mean to flatter nor praise you at the expense of any other, but, I confess I do think it is owing entirely to you, that this army and the liberties of America, so far as they are dependent on it, are not cut off."

Reed blamed General Nathanael Greene for convincing Washington that he could hold Fort Washington. He believed that Washington had waited too late to call for an evacuation of Fort Lee. "As soon as the season will admit, I think yourself and some others should go to Congress, and form the plan of the new army," Reed wrote to Lee.

On November 6, 1776, Lee wrote a letter to Benjamin Franklin blaming Congress for their misfortunes. "The spirit of our present troops is upon the whole good, and if America is lost, it is not in my opinion owing to want of courage in your soldiers, but pardon me, to want of prudence, in your High Mightiness's." Perhaps trying to soften this acid blow toward Congress, he added the following, again referring to America as *your country* and not *my country*. "Adieu, God bless you, My Dear Sir, live long and make your country and friends as happy, as you have render'd yourself admirable in the eyes of all good and sensible men."

By late November 1776, the army was divided into two columns as they marched through New Jersey, with General Washington commanding one division and General Lee commanding the other. Through an official message written by Reed, Washington ordered Lee to march his army to rejoin him. When Reed wrote the order to join Washington, his pencil broke, forcing Reed to tell the messenger to relay the rest of the message orally to Lee to push on and join Washington.

At this point, Lee's actions matched his defiant attitude. Interpreting this message as a suggestion, not a command, Lee instead stalled, claiming that he saw an opportunity to annoy the British in Morristown, New Jersey.

"My objections to moving from our present post—are, as I observed before, that it would give us the air of being frighten'd," General Lee wrote to General Washington on November 30, 1776. Eight days later, he assured his Commander-in-Chief that he was following his orders.

"You complain of my not being in motion sooner—I do assure you that I have done all in my power and shall explain my difficulties when we have both leisure," he wrote Washington on December 8. Lee offered an excuse. "If I was not taught to think that your army was considerably reinforced, I should immediately join you, but as I am assured you are very strong, I should imagine we can make a better impression by hanging on their rear . . . It will be difficult, I am afraid, to join you . . . cannot I do you more service by attacking their rear? I shall look about me tomorrow and inform you further—I am Dear General, yours." Around this same time, Lee wrote a letter to the Massachusetts provincial council's president and expressed a diametrically opposite sentiment.

"There are times when we must commit treason against the laws of the state for the salvation of the state. The present crisis demands this brave, virtuous kind of treason." Lee implied that he was deliberately defying Washington to save the army.

Though Washington continued to send Lee messages, each one increasingly more directly and clearly calling for Lee to march his troops to join him, Lee stalled for two weeks. When he did proceed, his troop's progress was slow.

General Lee sent Washington a message on December 11, 1776. Unlike the other messages, this one referred to Lee in the third person, indicating that an aide had written the letter and not Lee himself.

"We have three thousand men here at present but they are so ill shod that we have been obliged to halt these two days for want of shoes—seven regiments of Gates's Corps are on their march but where they actually are is not certain," the note began.

"General Lee has sent two officers this day—one to inform him where the Delaware can be cross'd above Trenton—the other to examine the road towards Burlington as General Lee thinks he can without great risk cross the great Brunswick Post road and by a forced night's march make his way to the ferry below Burlington."

That night, Lee and his small entourage of aides left their army and traveled nearly four miles away to take in the pleasantries of an inn. While his men camped outside in tents, Lee snoozed in a bed at the inn, with the crackling snaps and pops of a fireplace as his lullaby.

He was not enduring the hardships of his men and was not leading by example. The next morning, December 12, the British military interrupted his interlude at the inn and captured General Lee. His patriotic tune immediately changed 180 degrees.

Upon his capture, Charles Lee wrote a letter professing his loyalty to King George III. "You behold me no longer hostile to England, but contemptible and a prisoner!" he wrote to the British captain guarding him.

Because Lee had resigned his British commission three days after accepting his American commission, General Howe at first roughly handled him and planned to try him as a deserter. "He was, besides, persuaded that I was doubly criminal, both as a traitor and a deserter. So totally was he inebriated with his idea, that I am convinced he would have thought himself both politically and morally damned had he acted any other part than what he did," Lee described of Howe's initial treatment.

Then General Howe received a letter from Washington asking to exchange Lee for five Hessian officers. Though Howe rejected the offer, he realized that Washington valued Lee and wanted him back. The British moved Lee to confinement at city hall in New York on January 13, 1777, where he stayed for several months. What did he do during that time? He did what he believed was necessary after the fall of New York. He committed "brave, virtuous treason".

Two and a half months later on March 29, Lee submitted a new battle plan to British General Howe. This was a separate plan to help the British troops gain victory over the Americans. In it, Lee outlined an attack on the Chesapeake Bay. Titled *Mr. Lee's Plan—March 29, 1777*, the treasonous document was in Lee's handwriting and endorsed by Howe's secretary. Hence, when Lee rejoined the Continental Army at Valley Forge in May 1778, he kept quiet about the plans he had given to the British Army. Washington had no idea that Lee had committed treason while he was in captivity—the greatest form of malfeasance.

Within a month, Lee objected to Washington's plan to attack the British as they were marching from Philadelphia to New York. Lee then defied his Commander-in-Chief's orders to attack at the Battle of Monmouth, which led to his arrest and court martial. Lee's secrecy about his actions in captivity lead to an obvious question. What else did Lee give General Howe?

22 PROJECTION

hat else did Charles Lee do while in British captivity from December 1776 until March 29, 1777, when he gave Howe a battle plan? Well supplied with paper and ink, he wrote letters, including correspondence to John Hancock, George Washington, and even his British friends. Despite being caught in a trap, he set his own traps by writing plans for the enemy to use against America.

If General Lee was willing to compose a battle plan to curry favor with Lord Howe, couldn't he have been just as willing to write a counterfeit pamphlet in Washington's name for the British propaganda campaign, while projecting his true opinions? In his jail cell in New York in early 1777, did he write letters pretending he was George Washington in the summer of 1776 and then give them to British authorities to publish them in England, which John Bew did on May 29, 1777? Lee's pattern of life, the timeline, and his malfeasance in defying Washington's orders in the name of treason make his culpability as the counterfeiter highly possible.

Clearly, by the time he was captured at the New Jersey inn, Lee disdained and disrespected Washington. In November 1776, he had proclaimed at least twice in writing that he should have been in charge instead of Washington. He'd also previously forged a letter when he'd written an essay in Rivington's name because he was mad at the newspaper man.

While no hard evidence exists to definitively prove this theory, the pattern of Lee's behavior makes his authorship more plausible than any of the other suspects. Another pattern reinforces his culpability. Several themes in the forged letters line up with statements Lee had made in letters written under his name. In this way, Lee had projected his own feelings and opinions about the war onto Washington by pretending to be Washington and writing the counterfeit letters.

The most obvious connection is the pretense about where the

letters were found. In John Bew's published pamphlet of the forgeries, a preface claimed that the letters from Washington to his friends in 1776 were found in a small suitcase. Where was the suitcase found? At Fort Lee, which was named after Charles Lee, in New Jersey.

"Among the prisoners at Fort Lee, I espied a mulatto fellow, whom I thought I recollected, and who confirmed my conjectures by gazing very earnestly at me," the counterfeiter wrote in the preface to the forged letters. Imagine Lee's delight at choosing the fort named after him as the backdrop for this invented tale.

"I asked him, if he knew me . . . he came and told me, that he was Billy, and the old servant of General Washington," the writer continued of how Billy gave him an almanac that held letters from Washington to his wife, stepson, and Lund.

In reality, Lee had met Billy in late December 1774, when he'd spent six days at Mount Vernon before traveling to Williamsburg. During his time at Mount Vernon, Colonel Lee would have had the opportunity to meet or hear about Lund Washington, Martha Washington, and Jackie Custis, the three correspondents of the counterfeit letters. Also during this time, Washington loaned money to Charles Lee for travel expenses. Lee never paid these loans. His estate paid Washington, without interest, after Lee's death.

Washington knew that neither Billy nor any military aide had been captured by the British. "All the army, under my immediate command, could contradict this; and I believe most of them know, that no attendant of mine, or a particle of my baggage ever fell into the hands of the enemy during the whole course of the war," Washington stated after the war, countering the lie that Billy had been left behind at Fort Lee.

By June 1775, Congress had given Lee something he had long wanted. They had turned him from a colonel into a major general. With his several smelly, yapping dogs in tow, Lee had traveled with his Commander-in-Chief and Billy from Philadelphia to Cambridge, where the rag-tag militias under General Artemis Ward's care awaited them.

Bouncing and bobbing on horses over dusty, rut-filled dirt roads for three hundred miles gave Washington and Lee plenty of opportunities to get to know each other, especially as they stopped and rested their horses. Washington would have learned that Lee loved stroking the fur of dogs as much—if not more—than striking up conversations with average people. "I am like a dog in a dancing school—I know not where to turn myself, where to fix myself," Lee once told Washington.

Once Congress appointed Washington as Commander-in-Chief of the Continental Army while he in Philadelphia, Washington didn't have time to return to Mount Vernon and put his affairs in order back home. From the letters that Washington wrote in June and July 1775, topics topping his mind were concerns about his wife, his stepson, and their farm. Lee could have very easily learned some of the domestic details that were included in the letters while traveling with Washington. Hence, Lee had the opportunity to know enough about Washington's family and life to address letters to Martha, Jackie Custis, and Lund in Washington's name.

Although John Randolph also knew these names, Randolph wouldn't have known some of the topics in the letters that gave them an air of authenticity to the public. When Washington and Lee arrived at Cambridge, they learned that smallpox was raging. The sight of bumpy rashes on the arms and faces of his soldiers alarmed the Commander-in-Chief. He worried about the health and survival of his army. "I have been, particularly attentive to the least symptoms of the smallpox," Washington had written to John Hancock in July 1775. Lee could've easily learned about Washington's desire for Martha to be with him at camp after she was inoculated from smallpox, which is one of the topics in the forgeries.

"But I flatter myself, any further argument will be unnecessary, when I shall add, as I now do, that till you have had the smallpox, anxiously as else I should wish for it, I never can think of consenting to your passing the winter here in quarters with me," Washington's forged letter to his wife declared. Martha was inoculated the first week of June 1776, which is before the date of this false letter, June 24. Lee wouldn't have known this detail because by this time, Lee was in Charleston, South Carolina.

Another theme in the forged letters is Washington's self-doubt about his capabilities, along with a reference to politics as the reason for his appointment. Lee was furious that Congress had prioritized unity and politics over practical experience. At the time, the armed conflict was in Massachusetts. Selecting a commanding general from Virginia signaled that the colonies were now united instead of disconnected.

"In one thing, however, we all agreed, that, as the forces were chiefly to be raised in New-England, it would be extremely rash and imprudent in the southern delegates to leave them in the possession of so formidable a power without any check," Washington's counterfeit letter to Lund complained on June 12, 1776. "I need not tell you, that it was this consideration which, if I am to be credited, sorely against my will, determined me to accept of the command of this army." This, of course, was one of many lies in the letters.

The forgeries frequently painted George Washington as bitter and jealous. "We set out with bad omens. I was mistrustful of them in everything; and they were taught to look upon me with jealousy," Washington had allegedly written to Lund. In reality, Charles Lee was jealous and mistrustful of Washington.

The forgeries also portrayed Washington the way Lee saw his Commander-in-Chief following the fall of New York to the British military in 1776. Though Washington deserved some criticism for his handling of the New York crisis, Lee took this criticism to an extreme and believed that Washington was as incapable as he was inexperienced.

One of the letters portrayed Washington as showing contempt for politicians by claiming that a statesman or a senator could afford to mean well without achieving anything. A general was different and couldn't get away without winning a great battle, much less a glorious war, according to this forged phrase. "But, with a soldier, success alone is merit; and there is nothing that can atone for the want of it. The world is a worse judge of military matters than any other."

Lee saw Washington as a failure, which is how the forged letters painted Washington. In Lee's view, the British officers, many of whom were his friends, were superior in capabilities.

"A man, book-learned only, does very well in the still scenes of marchings and encampments. But when, in the various bustles of actual war, a cause arises, as must often be the case, not described in his books, he is utterly at a loss," Washington's June 18 forged letter to Jackie conveyed. This explains why Lee defied Washington's orders to join him in December 1776 and at the Battle of Monmouth in 1778. He saw Washington as at an utter loss of what to do when it came to actual warfare.

This counterfeit letter also painted Washington as a failure. "But, opposed as I must be by men, probably, of infinitely superior skill, and encompassed moreover with such hosts of other difficulties and discouragements as I am, it is not mine to command success." This letter matches General Lee's opinion of Washington, not the

Commander-in-Chief's view of himself. In this way, Lee projected his opinions onto Washington through his counterfeit identity.

Because the British had captured Lee shortly before Washington's triumph in crossing the Delaware River and attacking Trenton, Lee had missed witnessing one of Washington's greatest victories. He'd not felt the freezing rain on his face while sandwiched in between soldiers into a Durham cargo boat across the icy, inky Delaware River at night or heard the happy huzzahs after capturing hundreds of Hessians the next morning.

The *War of Lies* also presented Washington as obsessed with what others thought of him, a trait which was more characteristic of Lee's personality. One of the forgeries asked these questions: "When either my contemporaries or future historians shall sit in judgment on my conduct" will they focus on "seeing our miscarriages only" and lack the curiosity to investigate the causes? "Am I not too well warranted in concluding, that they will be attributed to mismanagement?" Lee projected his views on Washington through those questions. And there is even more evidence of Lee's feasible malfeasance.

23 FEASIBLE MALFEASANCE

In addition to the *War of Lies* portrayal of George Washington, which was the way Charles Lee viewed him, other thematic ideas in the counterfeit letters—particularly the issues of independence and peace—reflected Lee's actual views, not Washington's. After all, a wolf wrapped in sheep's wool is still a wolf no matter his disguise. One of the major themes of the fake letters is the assertion that Washington opposed independence and wanted to reconcile with England instead. This was not true.

Two weeks after the Declaration of Independence, Lee had not embraced the cause of independence as his own. "Have I not, such has been my zeal for your cause, once already waved my military claims indifferent to the wind and partiality of some of your members?" Lee wrote to a member of Congress after hearing that Congress might replace him. He again referred to the cause as *your cause* and not *my cause* or *our cause*, which showed he didn't embrace independence as his own belief.

Eight months before the Declaration of Independence, while Lee was with General Washington at camp in December 1775, he'd felt the soft prickles of his quill pen as he dipped it hundreds of times in an inkwell to write letters to active British generals. Through these lengthy letters, he had asked them to call on the resignation of the current prime minister to keep the British empire together.

From Cambridge, he wrote an emotional message to British General Thomas Gage, who was commanding the British forces nearby in Boston. "I little thought the time could ever arrive when I should not run with eagerness to embrace General Gage," Lee began before explaining that his disagreement was with King George III and Prime Minister North, not Gage.

"But I hold in such abhorrence the conduct, temper, and spirit of the present court; more particularly their present diabolical measures with respect to this country fills me with so much horror and indignation that I cannot bear to see a man, from whom my affections can never be weaned, in the capacity of one of their instruments," he wrote, politely expressing his disappointment that Gage, who'd led Lee on the battlefield in 1755, had not stood up to Prime Minister North.

"A personal friendship for Mr. Gage has taken too deep a root in my breast; though were you my brother, twinned at birth, I most wish to defeat the purposes by those of whose instructions Governor Gage must act." Lee believed that Prime Minister North was so corrupt and callous that he'd send a force to attack just one single person standing for liberty. "As to North, my opinion of him is this (and I have known him a long time) that did he hear of a single freeman in the remotest part of the world, he would willingly put his country to the expense of furnishing an army for the sole pleasure of destroying that single freeman."

He explained to Gage that he was standing up for the rights of their country, England, by supporting their fellow Englishmen, the Americans. "You have known me long enough, I flatter myself, to be persuaded that zeal for the liberties of my country and the rights of mankind has been my predominant passion."

Around the same time in December 1775, he wrote a letter to his former commander in Portugal, General John Burgoyne, who'd recently written Lee. Burgoyne had inquired to Lee if the Americans were serious about independence.

"You ask me, in your letter, if it is independence at which the Americans aim? I answer, No; the answer never entered an American's head, until the most intolerable oppression forced it upon them." Lee then spoke out for a principle that he believed was a British value. "All they required was to remain masters of their own property, and be governed by the same equitable laws which they had enjoyed from the first formation of the colonies." Lee blamed the two prime ministers under King George III for dividing England from the American colonies.

Lee also compared America to Ireland, which was subordinate to the British empire and Parliament, but it was not then subject to the same taxes as America. Why couldn't the British authorities treat the Americans the same way they treated the Irish? In some ways, Lee acted like a neutral third party, seeking peace.

"But to recur to the question of Americans aiming at independence: Do any instructions of any one of the provinces to their representatives, or delegates furnish the least ground of suspicion?

On the contrary, do they not all breathe the strongest attachment and filial piety to their parent country?" Lee wrote, noting that not one of the colonies or the Continental Congress had called for independence. He then warned the English ministry not to act like a brutal stepmother.

"But if she discards all the natural tenderness of a mother, and acts the cruel step dame it must naturally be expected that their affections will cease; the ministry leave them no alternative."

General Lee then told Burgoyne that he had it in his power to prevent independence. "But the fatal separation has not yet taken place, and yourself, your single self, my friend may prevent it."

Lee believed that the solution for America was not independence, but the resignation of Prime Minister North. With the persistence of Pegasus and the heralding of Hermes, he called on Burgoyne to encourage Parliament to stand up and call for a new prime minster.

"An opportunity is now presented of immortalizing yourself as the savior of your country. The whole British empire stands tottering on the brink of ruin, and you have it in your power to prevent the fatal catastrophe," Lee wrote, perhaps implying that he, too, was seeking to prevent the "catastrophe" of independence. "But it will admit of no delay: exert the voice of a brave, virtuous citizen, and tell the people at home, that they must immediately rescind their impolitic, iniquitous, tyrannical, murderous acts; that they must overturn the whole frantic system, or that they are undone."

Lee concluded his letter with a King Arthur-like loyalty statement for England. "I most earnestly and devoutly love my native country." He encouraged Burgoyne to go public for America's cause, to galvanize political support for the fall of the ministry.

A mere nine days later on December 10, 1775, General Lee sent a different message about independence to Benjamin Franklin in a letter. "I am myself inclined to think that America is not yet ripe for independence, nor am I sure as men's minds are now disposed that it would be for their advantage but at the same time I am persuaded that if you loudly proclaim that nothing shall induce you to break the bands, you risk the total loss of your liberties."

In fact, Lee believed that separating from Britain would undermine his goal of getting Lord North to resign so new policies could be implemented with a new prime minister. "A declaration of this kind will encourage and enable the Ministry to stand their ground, or at least to procrastinate the issue."

Arranging to publish his correspondence to Burgoyne in

newspapers, Lee admitted to Franklin his hopes of saving the British empire through his friend and former commanding officer. "In short, I am conceited enough to wish the continent would adopt the sentiments and language of my letter to Burgoyne, that is, if you choose to declare great affection for the Mother Country, to assure 'em that unless they give up immediately the Ministry and Ministerial system you are determin'd to dissolve the connection. I am much mistaken if this is not the line you ought to pursue."

Despite this, he assured Franklin of his commitment to whatever course Congress took and declared this oracle: "That if Parliament and the people should be depraved enough to support any longer the present ministry in their present scheme, my zeal and reverence for the rights of humanity are so much greater than any particular spot, even the place of my nativity, that, had I any influence in the councils of America, I would not advise not to hesitate a single instant, but to cut the Gordian knot, now besmeared with civil blood." In writing this, Lee told Franklin what he thought Franklin wanted to hear.

Five weeks later, while in Stamford, Connecticut, to recruit soldiers for New York, Lee acknowledged Thomas Paine's persuasive logic by writing George Washington.

"Have you seen the pamphlet *Common Sense*? I never saw such a masterly irresistible performance—it will, if I mistake not, in concurrence with the transcendent folly and wickedness of the Ministry give the coup de grâce to Great Britain—in short I own myself convinc'd by the arguments of the necessity of separation," Lee wrote on January 24, 1776.

Instead of sending him to Canada, Congress assigned a disappointed Lee to a Southern command. While recruiting men in Williamsburg, Virginia, General Lee wrote to Edward Rutledge, a member of the Continental Congress from South Carolina, on April 3, 1776. Unlike his letter to Burgoyne when he suggested that no province in America had called for independence, he curtly scolded Rutledge for not doing so. "By eternal God, unless you declare yourselves independent, establish a more certain and fixed legislature than that of temporary courtesy of the people, you richly deserve to be enslaved, and I think it far from impossible that it should be your lot."

Despite these occasions where Lee seemed to support America's separation from England, in the months that followed, Lee rarely mentioned independence, at least, not in the dozens of his letters that survive. What stands out in his correspondence is that he didn't write a single letter congratulating Ben Franklin, John Adams, Edward Rutledge, or George Washington on Congress's decision to issue the Declaration of Independence.

In contrast to his friend Lee, General Horatio Gates sent John Adams a letter on July 17, 1776, congratulating him on declaring independence. "I am happy to have lived to know that independence is establish'd by the convention of the United States of America, go on and prosper in the glorious work," an elated Gates told Adams.

There is no similar congratulatory letter in General Lee's correspondence. In the only letter from Lee to a member of Congress that survives from July 1776, Lee doesn't mention independence. Instead, on July 19, 1776, from his post in South Carolina, he expressed grievance at the possibility that another bandit general may rob him of his position as first in command after George Washington. News of the Declaration of Independence would have reached him by this time because Congress had sent messengers on horseback and by ship to quickly spread the news throughout the thirteen states.

In reality, declaring independence had destroyed Lee's hope that General Burgoyne or General Gage would stand up to Prime Minister North by calling on Parliament to demand his resignation. Though he had given some support to independence in January and April 1776, his support appears to be tepid. He spoke out of both sides of his mouth on the issue of America's separation from England. He held one position when communicating to his British general friends and a different position when communicating with the patriots.

His letter to Franklin suggesting that Americans weren't ready for independence may have been his true view. His contradictory statements suggest that he was tormented about it. In contrast to George Washington's whole-hearted embrace of independence, Lee's tortured, straddling position more closely resembled the views of the counterfeit Washington in the phony letters.

"I do not really wish for independence. I hope there are few who do," the counterfeiter pretending to be Washington had written to Jackie Custis. "What you say on the subject of independency is perfectly judicious . . . I have no reluctance to confess to you, that the measure (independence) is diametrically opposite to my judgment." This was, of course, a lie about Washington but a truism for Lee.

In reality, independence had been diametrically opposed to Lee's hopes to be the savior of America by convincing Burgoyne or Gage to stand up to Parliament. Washington's forged letter to Martha also carried an anti-independence theme and a pro peace-at-any-cost position. Like a skilled, neutral reporter, Lee had correctly diagnosed the tyranny facing America. However, when Congress actually declared independence, he was too much of an Englishmen to fully transition into an independent American.

"The only true interest of both sides is reconciliation; nor can there be a point in the world clearer, than that both sides must be losers by war, in a manner which even peace will not compensate for." This was also a lie.

Other actions by Lee suggest that he is the author of such forged phrases as this one: "We must, at last, agree and be friends; for we cannot live without them, and they will not without us."

The counterfeit letters also declared that Washington supported a peace treaty a mere ten days before the Declaration of Independence. "For all these reasons, which cannot but be as obvious to the English (peace) commissioners, and ours, as they are to me, I am at a loss to imagine how anything can arise to obstruct a negotiation, and, of consequence, a pacification. You, who know my heart, know that there is not a wish nearer to it than this is," the bogus letter to Martha falsely conveyed as Washington's position.

General Howe's peace commissioners arrived to negotiate with the patriots after July 4, 1776. Though the real Washington didn't believe that Howe's English commissioners were sincere in negotiating peace, the forged Washington elevated peace over independence.

"For I have not yet despaired of an honorable reconciliation; and whilst I can entertain but a hope of that, both interest and inclination lead me to prefer it to everything else upon earth," the June 18 sham letter lied once more, suggesting that Washington wanted peace above all else. This position was closer to Lee's true views.

On several occasions, Lee had tried to encourage peace. Not only had he sought to negotiate an armistice through his letters to Gage and Burgoyne in December 1775, but Lee had also written George Washington on February 19, 1776, to alert him that Howe was sending peace commissioners.

"A captain of a ship from Cadiz, who is a very intelligent person tells us that Lord Howe and Captain Barrington or Admiral Barrington are appointed commissioners to propose terms to the Congress . . . what damn'd fools the Ministry are!"

To Lee, Prime Minister Lord North wasn't a foolish clown for sending commissioners but was foolish for not resigning so someone else could step up as Prime Minister and end the king's abusive policies. Lee most certainly believed that the Ministry was corrupt, but his preferred solution was reconciliation, as his last ditch, down-to-the-wire efforts suggest.

Lee had also tried to implement a plan for reconciliation while he was in captivity as a British prisoner of war from December 1776 to May 1778. He proposed to both General Howe and the Continental Congress that they hold a peace conference in New York. Who would conduct this conference and be the go-between? Why Lee, of course.

In March 1777, the Continental Congress rejected Lee's reconciliation plans for political reasons. Had they agreed, they feared jeopardizing their chances of France becoming an official ally. They also knew that because Lee was a British prisoner of war, he was writing them under pressure. Therefore, they couldn't trust Lee while he was being held captive. Little did they know, but they couldn't trust him when he wasn't a prisoner, either.

Angry that Congress had rejected his peace proposal, Lee expressed his disappointment to John Hancock on March 19, 1777. The slippery Lee also wrote Washington a letter seeking sympathy a week after he had given General Howe a battle plan for capturing the South.

"It is a most unfortunate circumstance for myself, and I think not less so for the public, that the Congress have not thought proper to comply with my request. It could not possibly have been attended with any ill consequences, and might with good ones. At least it was an indulgence, which I thought my situation entitled me to," Lee bitterly and jealously wrote Washington on April 5, 1777. "But I am unfortunate in everything, and this stroke is the severest I have yet experienced. God send you a different fate."

During this time, Lee had also apparently reached out to another British friend on the subject of peace. "I heartily thank you for your letter and regret that cannot I have the pleasure of meeting you in person; the great wish of my life is to see peace between two countries I almost equally love," an English officer named George Johnson wrote Lee on June 17, 1778, while he was with the British Army in Philadelphia and Lee had returned from imprisonment and joined Washington at Valley Forge.

Though Lee's letter to Johnson has not survived, Johnson's letter implies that Lee had written to him proposing some sort of meeting for peace, which was a theme in the counterfeit letters. "I meant in words I had learnt from you, to set before you the many and mutual advantages both would derive from an agreement: and as the terms now offered are more for the interest of your favorite America than you ever hoped to attain, I should have made no scruple to ask your good offices, and to engage my own, to remove any obstacles that obstruct the peace," Johnson wrote, noting that Lee had many friends on both sides of the conflict.

Another strange occurrence took place shortly after Lee returned to the Continental Army at Valley Forge but before the Battle of Monmouth. Writing to Benjamin Rush, a physician in Philadelphia, Lee waxed eloquent on the virtues of Lord Howe, his captor.

"You will think it odd, that I should seem to be an apologist for General Howe: I know not how it happens, but when I have taken prejudices in favor, or against a man, I find it a difficulty in shaking them off," Lee wrote Rush on June 4, 1778, from Valley Forge.

"From my first acquaintance with Mr. Howe, I liked him: I thought him friendly, candid, good natured, brave, and rather sensible than the reverse," Lee wrote, noting that Howe at first viewed him as a traitor and deserter. "He is, besides, the most indolent of mortals: never took farther pain to examine the merits or demerits of the cause in which he was engaged."

Performing his duties to his king and Parliament, Howe rarely read material presented to him but trusted in his aides' conclusions. "But through these absurdities I could distinguish, when he was left to himself, rays of friendship and good nature breaking out." Howe had always been inclined to obey Lord North without question.

"But I believe his eyes are now opened; he sees he has been an instrument of wickedness and folly: Indeed, when I observed it to him, he not only took patiently the observation, but indirectly assented to the truth of it. He made, at the same time, as far as malevolency would permit, an apology for his treatment of me."

Alongside his pattern of behavior which suggested culpability, Lee's true views on peace and his nuanced—if not conflicting—views on independence are reflected in the main themes of the forged letters. He certainly had the moxie, skills, counterfeit experience, and treacherous motive to write forged letters in Washington's name. The timing also lined up.

Lee could have easily written the counterfeit letters in the first four months of his captivity, before or around the same time he wrote a battle plan to curry favor with his British captors. At the end of March 1777, General Howe could have easily sent the forged letters to England on one of the many British ships ferrying back and forth between New York City and London. The counterfeit letters fit into

Lord Sandwich's goal of tapping London's printing presses on Paternoster Row to publish propaganda to sway the public against the patriots and Washington.

London printer John Bew published *War of Lies* as a pamphlet on May 29, 1777. Then Rivington printed the handbill of the Martha letter in December 1777. He subsequently published one letter per week in his new, New York newspaper starting in February 1778. Under this theory, Rivington published the work of General Charles Lee, who'd lampooned him and forged an essay in Rivington's name in 1775 called *Breakfast with Rivington*.

Howe clearly rewarded Lee by giving him privileges while in prison, such as allowing him to gallop on horseback around the city of New York. Lee was released in a prisoner exchange in May 1778. Unaware of Lee's treason, Washington welcomed Lee back and gave him command of troops at the Battle of Monmouth. Lee promptly defied Washington, which was further proof of his treachery and contempt.

Two days after being arrested at the Battle of Monmouth, General Charles Lee wrote two heated letters to Washington on June 30, 1778, which were used against him at his court martial trial as showing disobedience and disrespect to his Commander-in-Chief.

"From the knowledge I have of your Excellency's character—I must conclude that nothing but the misinformation of some very stupid, or misrepresentation of some very wicked person could have occasioned your making use of so very singular expressions as you did on my coming up to the ground where you had taken post," Lee wrote to Washington. "They implied that I was guilty either of disobedience of orders, of want of conduct, or want of courage."

To say that Washington held a different view is an understatement, despite his controlled response in a letter to Lee.

"What I recollect to have said, was dictated by duty and warranted by the occasion. As soon as circumstances will permit, you shall have an opportunity, either of justifying yourself to the army, to Congress, to America, and to the world in general; or of convincing them that you were guilty of a breach of orders and of misbehavior before the enemy on the 28th instant in not attacking them as you had been directed and in making an unnecessary, disorderly, and shameful retreat," Washington replied on June 30.

Convening a twelve-man jury on July 1, 1778, Major General Stirling oversaw the court martial trial that lasted six weeks. Lee was charged with disobeying repeated orders, not attacking the enemy on

June 28, misbehaving before the enemy on the same day, making an unnecessary, disorderly, and shameful retreat, and showing disrespect to the Commander-in-Chief in two letters.

The most damaging testimony came from the written affidavit of Brigadier Generals Charles Scott and Anthony Wayne, who declared that Lee had failed to answer repeated requests to send men to support the front lines as the enemy neared their position. Finding Lee guilty on all charges, the court suspended him from any command in the armies of the United States of North America for twelve months. The last letter between George Washington and General Charles Lee was written in December 1778, when Washington notified Lee that Congress had approved Lee's court martial and sentence. Lee's Shakespearean cautionary tale had one page to turn and one question to answer: To duel or not to duel?

"They approached each other within about five or six paces and exchanged a shot almost at the same moment," Alexander Hamilton relayed of a duel he participated in on Christmas Eve in 1778. Who was the target? Was it Aaron Burr, the man later who took his life? No, it was General Charles Lee.

"His evasions, if known to the world, would do him very little honor," Hamilton had written about Lee to the Baron Von Steuben on December 19, 1778. Just like his assessment of the Conway Cabal, Hamilton knew that this monster had often hidden his head but kept his dagger within reach.

During his court martial, General Lee had questioned Von Steuben's courage as drillmaster and inspector general for the Continental Army. Von Steuben didn't take this stab at his honor lightly. Instead, he wrote Lee a letter and challenged him to a duel. Denying that he had questioned his courage, Lee replied that he was "ready to satisfy you in the manner you desire." Though Lee was ready to pick up a pistol or sword, upon wiser reflection, Von Steuben backed off.

Others would not retreat. Lee's caustic rhetoric against George Washington following his court martial had brought out the worst in one of his top military aides, John Laurens, who was the son of the current president of the Continental Congress. This time the exchange had not led to a cooling off period but instead had led to pistols as the weapons of choice.

Explaining the motive behind the Lee-Laurens duel, Hamilton wrote "that General Lee had spoken of General Washington in the grossest and most opprobrious terms of personal abuse, which Colonel Laurens thought himself bound to resent, as well on account of the relation he bore to General Washington as from motives of personal friendship, and respect for his character."

While Lee claimed that he had always esteemed General Washington as a gentleman, his hidden deeds and private letters had conveyed an opposite sentiment.

"General Lee acknowledged that he had given his opinion against General Washington's military character to his particular friends and might perhaps do it again. He said every man had a right to give his sentiments freely of military characters, and that he did not think himself personally accountable to Colonel Laurens for what he had done in that respect. But [Lee] said he never had spoken of General Washington in the terms mentioned," Hamilton documented.

Hamilton had played the role of second to Laurens while Major Evan Edwards was Lee's second. Edwards and Hamilton's job was to do everything in their power to prevent bloodshed.

Hence, the disgraced former major general Charles Lee and Colonel John Laurens faced each other with their pistols drawn in a remote forest at a quarter past three o'clock in the afternoon of December 24, 1778.

"General Lee proposed, to advance upon one another and each fire at what time and distance he thought proper. Colonel Laurens expressed his preference of this mode, and agreed to the proposal accordingly."

Advancing five paces toward each other and equipped with braces, they fired with one hand at the same time.

"As Colonel Laurens was preparing for a second discharge, General Lee declared himself wounded."

Laurens, Hamilton, and Edwards ran to Lee, who proved true to his temperament. A fight broke out about whether to continue the fight.

"General Lee then said the wound was inconsiderable, less than he had imagined at the first stroke of the ball, and proposed to fire a second time," Hamilton wrote, explaining that both he and Major Edwards believed that the duel should be terminated.

"But General Lee repeated his desire that there should be a second discharge, and Colonel Laurens agreed to the proposal. Colonel Hamilton observed that unless the General was influenced by motives of personal enmity, he did not think the affair ought to be pursued any further; but as General Lee seemed to persist in desiring it, he was too tender of his friend's honor to persist in opposing it."

Major Edwards fulfilled his role as second to Lee. He talked both Lee and Laurens out of firing their pistols again. With the second shot, Charles Lee was slightly wounded on his right side. Despite his wounds, he continued to attack Washington well into 1779.

Though most newspaper editors refused to publish Lee's submissions, he managed to convince the *Maryland Journal*'s editor to publish an article. Questioning Washington's judgment, Lee anonymously suggested that "the loss of the garrison of Fort Washington, and its consequent loss of Fort Lee, with the tents, store & etc." had dampened "the spirits of the people, as to make the difference of twenty thousand men to America." He'd also recommended that a portrait of Gates should be sent when royal courts requested paintings of Washington.

Even Lee's best supporters turned on him and grew tired of the attacks. William Livingston, the governor of New Jersey, told Lee "that I should be extremely unhappy in having reason to believe what is frequently, and perhaps injuriously reported, that you endeavored to lessen the estimation in which General Washington is held by the most virtuous citizens of America." Little did they know the extent of Lee's brave, virtuous treason, as he'd privately called it.

Embarrassed that his sister had read about his court martial in the London papers, Lee revealed that he'd fully returned to England's side. "I feel for the Empire of Great Britain. I feel for the fortunes of my relations and friends, which must receive a dreadful shock in this convulsion," he wrote to his sister in September 1779.

Instead of self-reflection, Lee blamed General Thomas Gage for failing to call for Lord North's resignation. "Had he listened to me, the empire of Great Britain would have stood, the affections and allegiance of this great people continued for ages."

In his last surviving letter, Lee wrote his sister again in June 1782. "For I assure you, that my American enthusiasm is at present so far worn off, that the greatest satisfaction I can receive, is to be informed of the health and welfare of my English friends, who, with all their political sins, corruption and failings, still possess more virtues, at least as individuals, and all the nations of the earth."

Unlike John Randolph, Lee couldn't forgive. Still bitter over his court martial, he accused the Americans of lacking truth, honesty, and sincerity. "All that I shall say is, that, the New England men excepted, the rest of the Americans, though they fancy and call themselves republicans, have not a single republican qualification or idea."

In his final reflection on George Washington in his last letter to his sister, Lee showed his unquenched jealousy: "They have always a god of the day, whose infallibility is not to be disputed: to him all the people must bow down and sing hosannas."

Charles Lee died October 2, 1782, in Philadelphia. *Mr. Lee's Plan— March 29, 1777,* the battle plan he'd written for the British military while in captivity, wasn't found until 1857 in the Howe family papers in England. This discovery shocked many, proving that journalism is only the first draft of history. Historians write the final form.

★ ★ ★ ★ ★

George Washington and his generation never knew about the depth of Lee's treachery, as Lee's letters have shown. They didn't know the extent of his disloyalty or that he'd written a battle plan for Lord Howe, but by court martialing him, they removed him from causing further harm.

"It would be a singular satisfaction to me to learn, who was the author of these letters; and from what source they originated," Washington reflected a decade later in January 1797.

Despite his wishes, Washington never discovered the identity of the counterfeiter of the forged letters. Nonetheless he had assessed the characters of Rivington, Randolph, Gates, and Lee. From turning Rivington into a spy to suppressing the Conway Cabal, and ridding the army of the malfeasance of General Lee, the fully awakened Washington proved that he had the ability to assess someone's true character. In this way, the future First President and First Press-ident eradicated the threat of the enemies within, including the counterfeiter behind the *War of Lies.*

EPILOGUE—FIRST PRESS-IDENT

Each generation has a responsibility to prioritize truth and integrity in government and culture. Honesty should be as widespread as the atmosphere and as natural as taking a breath. Sin stands in the way. The temptation to tyranny is too great. Vigilance, a virtue represented by the color blue field in the U.S. flag, is vital to counter tyranny, whether it is the despotism of King George III the ever-present threat of communism in the culture.

Ben Franklin knew that advances in communication, coupled with the principles of honesty and respect, were essential to the victorious outcome of the war of independence.

"Now by the press we can speak to nations; and good books and well written pamphlets have great and general influence," Benjamin Franklin wrote on June 13, 1782, to a friend in England, Richard Price, a British philosopher who supported the patriots over the British government.

With the final battle completed at Yorktown in October 1781 and the peace treaty seeming nearly as appetizing to the peace commissioners in France as the best Burgundy or Bordeaux, Franklin had time in 1782 to reflect on the printing press's influence in the war for independence.

"The ancient Roman and Greek orators could only speak to the number of citizens capable of being assembled within the reach of their voice: their writings had little effect because the bulk of the people could not read," he explained. In this way, Franklin placed the evolution of the news as a political and influential commodity into historical context.

Because the process of publishing newspapers had become easy by his era's standards, Franklin realized that the availability of news and its commentary had fueled the American Revolution. In fact, the revolution would not have happened or succeeded without newspapers providing crucial information to awaken the public.

"The facility with which the same truths may be repeatedly enforced by placing them daily in different lights, in newspapers which are everywhere read, gives a great chance of establishing them."

The next words he uttered became one of his famous quips. "And we now find that it is not only right to strike while the iron is hot, but that it is very practicable to heat it by continual striking."

Indeed. Although propaganda and disinformation were toxic waste products of the fog of war, people were able to sort through them and ultimately determine the facts and truth for themselves. Freedom of the press and freedom of speech enabled the patriots to create a new government based on representation, not royalty. Fully awakened patriots made sure these rights were protected through the First Amendment to the U.S. Constitution.

The patriots built a new world derived from the Biblical principle that all humans are created in the image of God. As the U.S. Declaration declared, individual rights came from the Creator, not the king or the government. As James Rivington believed, freedom of speech and freedom of the press are the great securities of the other liberties. Without them, despotism and totalitarianism rule.

Would fake news end with the Revolutionary War? Would a new era of freedom of the press begin, one that always focused on truth? No. Each generation must make a commitment to uphold honesty in its culture. Integrity would continue to battle lies, as George Washington discovered in 1797.

"If you read the *Aurora* of this city, or those gazettes which are under the same influence, you cannot but have perceived with what malignant industry, and persevering falsehoods I am assailed, in order to weaken, if not to destroy, the confidence of the public," President George Washington wrote in January 1797, just three months before he left office as the nation's first president.

"Amongst other attempts to effect this purpose, spurious letters, known at the time of their first publication (I believe in the year 1777) to be forgeries—to answer a similar purpose in the Revolution—are, or extracts from them, brought forward with the highest emblazoning of which they are susceptible, with a view to attach principles to me which every action of my life have given the lie to."

President Washington's ire was aimed at the editor of

Philadelphia's *Aurora* newspaper, Benjamin Franklin Bache, the grandson of Benjamin Franklin. Twenty years after John Bew first published the letters, Bache had republished them. Why was Franklin's grandson attacking President Washington?

"But that is no stumbling block with the editors of these papers and their supporters. And now, perceiving a disinclination on my part, perhaps knowing, that I had determined not to take notice of such attacks, they are pressing this matter upon the public mind with more avidity than usual; urging, that my silence, is a proof of their genuiness."

As the nation's first president, Washington had come face to face with the challenges of leading a free people in the context of a free press. Would his final act as a public leader be to disavow fake news?

The next book in this series, *First Press-ident*, will show Washington as he's never been seen before, through the news that covered him during his presidency and called him, of all things, a traitor. Stay tuned.

IF GEORGE WASHINGTON COULD HAVE HAD SOCIAL MEDIA, WHAT WOULD HE HAVE SAID?

If Washington Could Have Had a Facebook Page in July 1776

George Washington
3,000 friends, two million followers

Works at Commander-in-Chief, Continental Army

Studied At: Home Schooled (see book list)
Lives in: Fairfax County, Virginia
Birthday: Feb. 22, 1732
From   Ferry Farm, Fredericksburg, Virginia
                     Pope's Creek, Westmoreland County, Virginia

Married to   Martha Dandridge Custis Washington

Life events   Battle of Dorchester Heights, March 4, 1776
                     Married to Martha, Jan. 6, 1759
                     Battle of Monongahela, July 9, 1755

Sports   Horseback riding, playing cards

Likes   Common Sense

Books

Two Bibles, The Gazetteer's or Newsman's Interpreter, Acts of Assembly Passed in the Colony of Virginia from 1662 to 1715, A Practical Treatise of Husbandry, New Principles of Gardening, A View of the History, Politics and Literature of the Years 1758, 1759, 1760, 1761. History of England, Salmon's Dictionary, Praxis Medica, A Treatise of Military Discipline, Letters of Wit & Politicks, Foster's

Sermons; Blair's Sermons, Collier of the Stage; Bacon's Essays, Cato's Letters, Plutarch's Morals, Paradise Lost, Free Thinker, Pope's Works, Jones of Opium, Lives of the 12 Caesars, Steel's Plays.

Activity/Posts

New York: General Orders, July 9, 1776. "The Honorable Continental Congress, impelled by the dictates of duty, policy and necessity, having been pleased to dissolve the connection which subsisted between this country, and Great Britain, and to declare the United Colonies of North America, free and independent STATES."

Deciding to have a formal reading of the declaration, the general issues this order: "The several brigades are to be drawn up this evening on their respective parades, at six o'clock, when the declaration of Congress, showing the grounds and reasons of this measure, is to be read with an audible voice."

"The general hopes this important event will serve as a fresh incentive to every officer, and soldier, to act with fidelity and courage, as knowing that now the peace and safety of his country depends (under God) solely on the success of our arms: And that he is now in the service of a State, possessed of sufficient power to reward his merit, and advance him to the highest honors of a free country."

July 10, 1776, Broadway show blasted. "Last night, the statue of George the Third was tumbled down and beheaded—the troops having long had an inclination so to do, thought this time of publishing a Declaration of Independence, to be a favorable opportunity—for which they received the check in this day's orders."

General Orders, July 10, 1776. "Though the General doubts not the persons, who pulled down and mutilated the statue in the Broadway, last night, were actuated by zeal in the public cause; yet it has so much the appearance of riot and want (lack) of order, in the army, that he disapproves the manner, and directs that in future these things shall be avoided by the soldiery, and left to be executed by proper authority."

If George Washington Could Have Issued a Social Media Thread after the Battle of Monmouth on June 28, 1778

1/16 The enemy encamped yesterday at Monmouth Court House in New Jersey.

2/16 The slow advance of the enemy had greatly the air of design, and led me, with others, to suspect that General Clinton desirous of a general action was endeavoring to draw us down into the lower country in order by a rapid movement to gain our right, and take possession of the strong grounds above us.

3/16 I am now here with the main body of the army and pressing hard to come up with the enemy.

4/16 The enemy in marching had changed their disposition and placed their best troops in the rear, consisting of all the grenadiers, light infantry, and chasseurs of the line.

5/16 I instantly put the army in motion, and sent orders by one of my aids to General Lee to move on and attack them.

6/16 After marching about five miles, to my great surprise and mortification, I met the whole advanced corps retreating, and, as I was told, by General Lee's orders without having made any opposition, except one fire given by a party.

7/16 The peculiar situation of General Lee at this time, requires that I should say nothing of his conduct. He is now under arrest. The charges against him, with such sentence as the court martial may decree in his case, shall be transmitted for the approbation or disapprobation of Congress.

8/16 I gave directions for forming part of the retreating troops, who by the brave and spirited conduct of the officers, aided by some pieces of well served artillery, checked the enemy's advance.

9/16 The enemy, by this time, finding themselves warmly opposed in front, made an attempt to turn our left flank; but they were bravely repulsed and driven back by detached parties of infantry.

10/16 Were I to conclude my account of this day's transactions without expressing my obligations to the officers of the army in general, I should do injustice to their merit, and violence to my own feelings.

11/16 They seemed to vie with each other in manifesting their zeal and bravery. The catalogue of those who distinguished themselves is too long to admit of particularizing individuals. I cannot however forbear mentioning Brigadier General Wayne whose good conduct and bravery thro' the whole action deserves particular commendation.

12/16 The behavior of the troops in general, after they recovered from the first surprise occasioned by the retreat of the advanced corps, was such as could not be surpassed.

13/16 All the artillery, both officers and men, that were engaged, distinguished themselves in a remarkable manner.

14/16 Congress will be pleased to receive a return of our killed, wounded and missing. Among the first were Lt. Col. Bunner of Pennsylvania and Major Dickinson of Virginia, both officers of distinguished merit and much to be regretted.

15/16 Of the enemy's slain left on the field and buried by us, 4 were officers and 245 privates. In the former number was the Honorable Col. Monckton. 13 exclusive of these they buried some themselves, as there were several new graves near the field of Battle.

16/16 How many men they may have had wounded cannot be determined; but from the usual proportion the number must have been considerable. There were a few prisoners taken.

ENDNOTES

Introduction
p. #, first words
03 "But kings and nobles" John Adams, Notes, Spring 1772, founders.archives.gov.
03 "The preservation" Ibid.
04 "Is not the" Ibid.
04 "But this is" Ibid.
04 "They may be deceived" Ibid.

Part 1:
06 "Be not hasty" 110 Rules of Civility., 7

Chapter 1: Valley Forge Awakening
p. #
09 "increased insult" In Convention May 15, 1776, *PA Ledger,* June 1, 1776, genealogybank.com.
10 "His evasions" Hamilton to Von Steuben, Dec. 19, 1778, founders.archives.gov.
10 "General Gates" Hamilton to George Washington, Nov. 6, year? founders.archives.gov.
11 "How could " Forged Washington to Martha Washington, June 24, 1776, founders.archives.gov.
11 "You, who know" Ibid.
11 "I love my king" Ibid.
11 "see what" Ibid.
11 "It is no easy" Washington to Landon Carter, May 28, 1778. source?
11 "Not one word" Washington to Richard Henry Lee, Feb. 15, 1778, founders.archives.gov.
12 "My attention" Forged to Martha Washington, June 24, 1776, founders.archives.gov.
12 "As the great principles" Peter Labilliere to G. Washington, Nov. 4, 1777, founders.archives.gov.
12 "After a most" Ibid.
13 "A Christian patriot" Ibid.
13 "I trust" Ibid.
13 "P.S. I am" Ibid.
13 "Contains a" Ibid.
13 "Be of good" Ibid.,
14 "As a remarkable" Ibid.

Chapter 2: Join or Die

p. #

15 "that people" *Public Occurences*, Sept. 25, 1690, Boston.
15 "that something" Ibid.
15 "there are many" *Public Occurences*, Sept. 25, 1690, Boston.
15 "false report" Ibid.
15 "reason to" Ibid.15 "best fountains" Ibid.
15 "glut of" Ibid.
16 "memorable occurrence" Ibid.
16 "whom they used" Ibid.
16 "Mr. Washington" *Boston Gazette*, March 5, 1754, p. 1, genealogybank.com.,
17 "is returned" Ibid.
17 "It is undoubtedly" Ibid.
17 "Mr. Washington was" Ibid.
17 "added, that he" Ibid.
18 "Every action done" *110 Rules of Civility*.
20 "any law" Peyton Randolph, Digital Encyclopedia of George Washington.
20 "And they told" Boston Gazette, May 14, 1754, p. 2, genealogybank.com.
20 "And they told" Ibid.
20 "And by G--" Ibid.
20 "Sermons before" *Gentleman's Magazine*, June 1754, p. 255.
21 "Sermons before" Ibid.
21 "Friday last an" *Pennsylvania Gazette*, May 9, 1754, p. 2, genealogybank.com.
22 "Mr. Ward" Ibid.
22 "The Indian chiefs" Ibid.
22 "to join them" Ibid.
22 "The confidence in" Ibid.
22 "In the present" Ibid.
22 "presume that they" *Pennsylvania Gazette*, May 9, 1754, p. 2.
22 "which they are" Ibid.

Chapter 3: Assassination

p. #

25 "Without freedom" *New England Courant*, July 9, 1722, p. 1, genealogybank.com.
25 "Whoever would" Ibid.
25 "Resolved, that" History of Printing in America, 237.
25 "tendency of" Ibid, 239.
25 "For the prevention" Ibid.
25 "every body's business" *The Busy Body, American Mercury* Feb. 4, 1729.
26 "Be not apt" 110 Rules of Civility.
27 "Major Washington had" *Boston Post Boy*, July 1, 1754, p. 2, genealogybank.com.
27 "But the Half King" Ibid.
27 "ambush to" Ibid.
27 "Major Washington interposed" Ibid.
27 "doing any further" Ibid.
27 "However Major Washington" Ibid.
28 "I fortunately" Washington to brother May 31, 1754, *London Magazine*, Aug. 1754, p. 370-1, newspaperarchive.com.
28 "I can with truth" Ibid.
28 "He would not" Horace Walpole *Memoirs of King George II*, Vol 1, p. 400.
28 "We expect every" *London Magazine*, August 1754, p. 370-1.

28 "The third of" *New York Mercury* July 22, 1754, p. 2, genealogybank.com.
29 "Articles of Capitulation" Ibid.

Chapter 4: Colonial Cancel Culture
p. #
30 "Being frequently" Benjamin Franklin, Apology for Printers,
founders.archives.gov.
30 "Men are very" Ibid.
30 "That if they" Ibid.
30 "I request all" Ibid.
30 "That the opinions" Ibid.
31 "That the" Ibid.
31 "suffering the" Ibid.
31 "That it is" Ibid.
31 "Printers are" Ibid.
31 "That when" Ibid.
31 "Hence they" Ibid.
31 "Being thus" Ibid.
31 "They print things" Ibid.
31 "That it is" Ibid.
31 "It is likewise" Ibid.
32 "That if all" Ibid.
32 "do real injury" Ibid.
32 "I consider" Ibid.
32 "Be not hasty" 110 Rules of Civility.
32 "As the articles" *Pennsylvania Gazette* Aug. 22, 1754, p. 1, genealogybank.com.
33 "We were obliged" Ibid.
33 "Every officer" Ibid.
33 "Let any of those" Ibid.
33 "our scalps and spoils" Ibid.
33 "They call it an assassination" Ibid.
33 "That we were" George Washington III, 1757, founders.archives.gov.
34 "But, whatever" Ibid.
34 "And instead of" George Washington, *Expedition to the Ohio*, 1754,
founders.archives.gov
34 "an ambassador *has*" Ibid.
34 "And seeing" Ibid.
34 "It was the opinion" Ibid.
35 "The designs of" *New York Mercury,* July 22, 1754, p. 2, genealogybank.com.

Chapter 5: When False News Is Deadly
p. #
36 "As I have heard" Washington to John Washington, July 18, 1755,
founders.archives.gov.
36 "As I doubt not" Washington to Mary Washington, July 18, 1755,
founders.archives.gov.
37 "But by the all" Washington to John Augustine Washington, July 18, 1755.
37 "When you speak "*110 Rules of Civility*.
37 "I have taken this" Washington to Mary Ball Washington, July 18, 175.,
38 "We were" Washington, Stories of Faith & Courage from the Revolutionary War,
p. 2.

38 "I was the only" Ibid.
38 "In short, the dastardly" Ibid.
39 "We have been most" Ibid.
39 "The general had five" *Pennsylvania Gazette*, July 31, 1755, p. 3,
genealogybank.com.
39 "Mr. Washington had two" Ibid.
40 "The Virginians" *Gentleman's Magazine*, London, Aug, 1755, p. 380,
40 "the regiments" *Pennsylvania Gazette*, Oct. 30, 1755, p. 2, genealogybank.com.
40 "Had these "Ibid,
40 "That our" *Boston Evening Post,* Dec. 15, 1755, p. 1, genealogybank.com,
40 "Your courage" Ibid,
41 "This unfortunate" Washington, *Stories of Faith & Courage* p. 2-3
41"Sir Peter Halkett" Washington to Mary Ball Washington, July 18, 1755.
42"I fance" Renegade Revolutionary, Phillip Papas, p. 29.
43 "By an express just" *Pennsylvania Gazette*, Oct. 30, 1755, p. 2, genealogybank.com.
43 "lately appeared" Ibid.
43 "to take upon him" Ibid.
43 "Last week Colonel" *Pennsylvania Gazette*, Feb. 12, 1756, p. 2,
genealogybank.com.
43 "Last night Colonel Washington" *New York Mercury*, Feb. 16, 1756, p. 2,
genealogybank.com.
43 "Colonel Washington, of" *Pennsylvania Gazette*, Feb. 26, 1756, p. 2,
genealogybank.com.
44 "You may with" Washington to John Washington, May 28, 1755,
founders.archives.com.
44 "Some public" Peyton Randolph to Washington, May 3, 1756,
founders.archives.com.
45 "In regard to" George Washington III, 1757, founders.archives.gov.
45 "some part lefts"Ibid,
45 "point out such errors" Ibid.
45 "Be not hasty" 110 Rules of Civility, number?
46 "Since our last" *Pennsylvania Gazette*, Nov. 30, 1758, p. 2, genealogybank.com.
46 "That on the 12st" Ibid.
46 "false intelligence" Ibid.
46 "forfeited his life" Ibid.
46 "the French were" Ibid.
46 "whole skins and bones" Ibid.
46 "Pittsburgh, formerly Fort Duquesne" *New York Mercury*, Dec. 23, 1758, p. 1.
genealogybank.com,
46 "I have the pleasure" Ibid.
47 "The finest and" Ibid.

Chapter 6: Final Awakenings
p. #
48 "the chief" Recollections & Private Memoirs, George Washington Parke Custis,
314-5.
48 "that hearing" Ibid.
48 "I am a chief" Ibid.
49 "I called" Ibid.
49"Quick, let your aim" Ibid.
49 "He cannot die" Ibid.

49 "Listen! The Great Spirit" Ibid.

49 "Yes, I do" Ibid.

50 "Friends of America" Benjamin Franklin, to William Franklin, March 13, 1768.

50 "Finding that" Benjamin Franklin, to the *London Chronicle* Dec. 25, 1773.

51 "There must" Supplement to the Boston Gazette, June 28, 1773.

51 "Mr. W. could" Benjamin Franklin, to the London Chronicle Dec. 25, 1773.

51 "Their tendency" Ibid.

52 "That I differ" Washington Bryan Fairfax, July 20, 1774, founders.archives.gov.

52 "But as I" Ibid.

52 "that government" Ibid.

53 "For, Sir" Ibid.

53 "fix a stigma" Solicitor General Wedderburn, founders.archives.gov, Jan. 29, 1774.

53 "He has forfeited" Ibid.

53 "Nothing then" Ibid.

53 "fix a stigma" Ibid.

Part Two

55 "Be not apt" *110 Rules of Civility*.

Chapter 7: Suspects

p. #

56 "I yesterday" Von Steuben to Washington, Dec. 6, 1777, founders.archives.gov.

56 "it will be" Washington to Continental Congress, Jan. 29, 1778, founders.archives.gov.

57 "For my own" Ibid.

57 "I have seen a letter" Washington to Richard Henry Lee Feb. 15, 1778, founders.archives.gov.

57 "I have the highest " Forged Washington to Martha Washington, June 24, 1776, founders.archives.gov.

57 "But why should" Ibid.

58 "For I will not" Ibid.

58 "There cannot" Forged Washington to Lund Washington June 12, 1776, founders.archives.gov.

58 "I am not afraid" Ibid.

58 "But we have" Ibid.

58 "Be not apt" 110 Rules of Civility.

59 "Honored with" James Rivington in *Boston Gazette*, March. 22, 1773, genealogybank.com.

59"In short every" Ibid.

59 "integrity and candor" Ibid.

59 "open and uninfluenced" *New York Gazetteer*, Nov. 10, 1774, genealogybank.com.

60 "situation in America" *New York Gazetteer,* April 14, 1774, founders.archives.gov.

60 "fate of America" Ibid.

60 "people of New England" Ibid.

60 "Being much concerned" *New York Gazetteer*, Oct. 13, 1774, p. 1, genealogybank.com.

60 "We also declare" Ibid.

60 "Whereas" *New York Gazetteer*, July 21, 1775, p. 3, genealogybank.com.

61 "Sensible that this" Ibid.

61 "Last Thursday was hung" *New York Gazetteer*, April 20, 1775, genealogybank.com.

61 "the very dregs" Ibid.
61 "flushed with the" Ibid.
61 " pole to pole" Ibid.
62 "that his press has" Ibid.
62 "But the moment" Ibid.
62 "Liberty of the Press" Ibid.
62 "establish a most cruel" Ibid.
64 "Consequently when" *Charles Lee to John Adams*, Oct. 5, 1775, founders.archives.gov.
64 "Cambridge July 6" *Maryland Journal* July 26, 1775, genealogybank.com.

Chapter 8: More Suspects
p. #
65 "I dined" Benjamin Franklin to William Franklin Mar. 13, 1768, founders.archives.gov.
65 "May God give" Benjamin Franklin to Horatio Gates, March 5, 1780, founders.archives.gov.
66 "Tis true many" Lund Washington to Washington, Oct. 5, 1775, founders.archives.gov.
66 "Mr. John" Ibid.
66 "to take her" Ibid.
66 "Lord Dunmore" Ibid.
67 "I am sorry" Jefferson to John Randolph, Aug. 25, 1775, founders.archives.gov.
67 "I have never" Ibid.
67 "I am to give" Ibid.
68 "You will have" Ibid.
68 "Edmund passed" Ibid.
68 "An express arrived" *New York Gazetteer*, Nov. 2, 1775, p. 2, genealogybank.com.
68 "Enclosed information" Ibid.
68 "A ship with sixteen" Ibid.
69 "He continued firing" Ibid.
69 "was ordered to" Ibid.
70 "will have no other" Washington to Joseph Reed. Jan. 31, 1776, founders.archives.gov.
70 "A few more of such" Ibid.

Chapter 9: Independence
p. #
71 "letter and poem such" Washington to Reed, February 26, 1776.
72 "I thank you" Washington to Phillis Wheatley, February 28, 1776.
72 "the world this" Ibid.
72 "If you should" Ibid.
72 "I am with great" Ibid.
72 "The following" Note, Poem to Washington from Phillis Wheatley, Oct. 26, 1776.
72 "Celestial choir" Ibid.
72 "The land" Ibid.
72 "Shall I to" Ibid.
72 "Proceed, great chief" Ibid.
73 "My countrymen I know" Ibid.
73 "Pity this cannot" Forged Washington to Martha Washington, June 24, 1776, founders.archives.gov.

74 "I believe I mentioned" Washington to Joseph Reed, April 1, 1776.
74 "Seamen not being" Ibid.
74 "One or two of them" Ibid.
74 "By all accounts" Ibid.
74 "When the order" Ibid.
75 "I most sincerely" Charles Lee to George Washington April 5, 1776.
75 "Be no flatterer" Charles Lee to George Washington April 5, 1776.
75 "My Dear General" Charles Lee to George Washington April 5, 1776.
75 "cheerfulness and" *New York Gazetteer*. June 3, 1773, p. 3, genealogybank.com.
75 "Yet I love arms" Forged Washington to John Custis June 18, 1776, founders.archives.gov.
76 "I am not" Ibid.
76 "I do not really" Ibid.
76 "What you" Ibid.
76 "For I have" Ibid.
77 "I am" Washington to John Washington May 31-June. 4, 1776, founders.archives.gov.
77 "To form a new govenent" Ibid.
77 "Every man should consider" Ibid.
77 "things have come" Ibid.
77 "The idea was only" Ibid.
77 "still feeding themselves" Ibid.
77 "The colony of" Washington to Fairfax County, May 16, 1775, founders.archives.gov.
78 "The fleet from Halifax" *Pennsylvania Evening Post*, July 8, 1776, p. 2, genealogybank.com.
78 "Monday it came" Ibid.
78 "Tuesday several" Ibid.
78 "swarm of locusts" Ibid.
78 "The *Asia* brought" Ibid.
79 "In Congress July 4, 1776" *Pennsylvania Evening Post*, July 6, 1776, p. 1, genealogybank.com.
79 "We hold these" Ibid.
79 "just powers from" Ibid.
79 "The history of" Ibid.
79 "he has dissolved" Ibid.
79 "He has made" Ibid.
79 "He has affected" Ibid.
79 "cutting off our trade" Ibid.
79 "Has has plundered" Ibid.
79 "He is, at this time" Ibid.
80 "We, therefore" Ibid.
80 "A few hog" Ibid.
80 "children's robes" Ibid.
81 "The Honorable" General Orders, July 9, 1776, founders.archives.gov.
81 "The several brigades" Ibid.
81 "The General hopes" Ibid.
81 "The Brigade Majors" Ibid.
81 "The Honorable Continental" Ibid.
81 "The colonels" Ibid.
82 "attend carefully" Ibid.

82 "The General hopes" Ibid.
82 "Last night the" Washington note, General Orders, July 10, 1776, founders.archives.gov.
82 "Ibid, founders.archives.gov.
83 "received with loud" *St. James Chronicle*, Sept. 26, 1776, newspaperarchive.com.
83 "sons of freedom" Ibid.
83 "is to be run" Ibid.

Chapter 10: Manners & Fodder
p. #
84 "George Washington, Esq" Restate source for first reference in new chapter.
84 "I immediately convened" Ibid.
84 "The officer expressed" Ibid.
84 "Lord Howe regretted" Ibid.
84 "Colonel Reed" Ibid.
85 "punctilio" Ibid.
85 "I deemed it" Ibid.
85 "to distract," Washington to Joseph Reed. April 1, 1776, founders.archives.gov.
85 "No man can wish" Ibid.
86 "After the usual" Washington interview with James Paterson. July 20, 1776, founders.archives.gov.
86 "That Lord Howe" Ibid.
86 "That a letter" Ibid.
86 "The goodness and benevolence" Ibid.
86 "That those who had" Ibid.
86 "This interview was more" Ibid.
87 "I will not" Forged, Washington to John Parke Custis. June 18, 1776, founders.archives.gov.
87 "We must" Forged, Washington to Martha Washington. June 24, 1776, founders.archives.gov.
87 "How often it is" Forged, Washington to Lund Washington. June 15, 1776, founders.archives.gov.
87 "How peculiarly" Forged, Washington to Martha Washington, June 24, 1776.
87 "Suffice it that" Ibid.
88 "We expect " Forged, Washington to John Washington. May 31-June 4, 1776, founders.archives.gov.
88 "However, it is" Ibid.
88 "Unused to the" Forged Washington to Lund Washington June 12, 1776, founders.archives.gov.
88 "At length" Ibid.
88 "I am now embarked" Washington to Burwell Bassett June 19, 1775, founders.archives.gov.
89 "It is an honor" Ibid
89 "a thorough conviction" Ibid.
89 "May God grant" Ibid.
89 "I can answer" Ibid.
89 "If these cannot" Ibid.
89 "I shall not be" Ibid.
90 "this city and province" *Virginia Gazette*, Sept. 14, 1776, p. 2, genealogybank.com.
90 "It is 130 miles long" Ibid.
90 "all good and loyal" Ibid.

90 "By sundry letters" *Virginia Gazette*, Sept. 7, 1776, p. 3, genealogybank.com.
90 "That a reinforcement" Ibid.
91 "Extract of a letter" Ibid.
91 "This afternoon" Ibid.
91 "In the skirmishes" *Virginia Gazette*, Sept. 14, 1776, p. 2.
91 "In a council" Ibid.
91 "Saturday's post" Ibid.
91 "The retreat was" Ibid.
91 "There never was" Ibid.
92 "The manner in which" Ibid.
92 "We learn from New York" *Virginia Gazette*, Sept. 7, 1776, p. 3.
92 "That the enemy ships" Ibid.
92 "They have opened" *Pennsylvania Gazette*, Sept. 25, 1776, p. 3, genealogybank.com.
92 "They have confiscated" Ibid.
92 "I think such acts of" Ibid.
92 "Old Oliver Delancey" Ibid.
92 "Your poor friend Woodhull" Ibid.

Chapter 11: Fort Lee
p. #
94 "The enemy, from there" Ibid.
94 "Their plan" Ibid.
95 "Our garrison at Fort" *Virginia Gazette*, Nov. 28, 1776, p. 3, genealogybank.com.
95 "The garrison must" *The Connecticut Journal*, Jan. 1, 1777, p. 1, genealogybank.com.
96 "You have no doubt" *Pennsylvania Journal*, Nov. 27, 1776, p. 3, genealogybank.com.
96 "We lost some of our" Ibid.
96 "I hope these losses" Ibid.
96 "I still have hopes" Ibid.
96 "Among the prisoners" Forged, Washington Introduction, founders.archives.gov.
97 "asked him a great" Ibid.
97 "contained only" Ibid.
97 "a journal or diary" Ibid.
97 "And in the same" Ibid.
97 "I never knew a man" Ibid.
97 "They contain also" Ibid.
98 "explaining that" Washington to Samuel Washington. Dec. 18, 1776, founders.archives.gov.
98 "pushed us from" Ibid.
98 "less than 3,000 men fit" Ibid.
99 "between you and me" Ibid.
99 "In short the conduct" Ibid.
99 "In a word" Ibid.
99 "Genearl Lee" Nineteenth Century Remembers of Black Veterans, allthingsliberty.com.
100 "However under a full" Ibid.
100 "That early on" *The Connecticut Journal*, Jan. 1, 1777, genealogybank.com.
100 "We had printed off" Ibid.
101 "This moment an" Ibid.

101 "Something was necessary" Ibid.
101 "An on Christmas" Ibid.
101 "A colder or icier season" Ibid.
101 "His Excellency commanded" Ibid.
101 "We intended" Ibid.
101 "the extremity" Ibid.
101 "too much praise" Ibid.
102 "be diligent" *Pennsylvania Evening Post,* Jan. 25, 1777, p. 3, genealogybank.com.
102 "Captain Alexander Hamilton" Ibid.
103 "Alexander Hamilton" *The Pennsylvania Evening Post,* March 1, 1777, genealogybank.com.

Chapter 12: Riveting Rivington & the Ruse
p. #
104 "In the press" *London Public Advertiser.* May 24, 1777, newspaperarchive.com.
104 "Letters from General" *London Evening Post* May 29, 1776, newspaperarchive.com.
105 "It is difficult to" Forged, Washington Introduction, founders.archives.gov.
105 "We cannot look" Ibid.
106 "The printer of" *New York Gazette.* Oct. 11, 1777, p. 1, genealogybank.com.
106 "When he first began" Ibid.
106 "by printing such" Ibid.
106 "Printer to the king's" *New York Gazette.* Oct. 25, 1777, p. 2, genealogybank.com.
106 "Supremely happy will" *New York Gazette.* Oct. 11, 1777, p. 1.
106 "He assures them" Ibid.
106 "quality and quantity" Ibid.
106 "sacrificed their own" Ibid.
106 "by recalling the infatuated" Ibid.
107 "On the same day" *New York Gazette* Nov. 8, 1777, p. 2, genealogybank.com
108 "If Congress" Hamilton to John Hancock, Sept. 18, 1777, p. 2, founders.archives.gov.
108 "by which means" Ibid.
108 "During the" Journals of Continental Congress, Sept. 18, 1777, VIII, 754, loc.gov.
108 "where we had" *New York Gazette* Nov. 8, 1777, p. 2, genealogybank.com.
109 "The Royal Army" Ibid.
109 "The happy prospect" *New York Gazette.* Oct. 11, 1777, p. 1, genealogybank.com.
109 "We have got a" *New York Gazette.* Oct. 18, 1777, p. 3, genealogybank.com.
109 "dawn of day" Rivington's *New York Gazette* Is this the same as the New York Gazette referenced above? if yes, cut "Rivington's". Nov. 8, 1777, p. 2, genealogybank.com.
110 "notice from the French" *New York Gazette.* Oct. 25, 1777, p. 2, genealogybank.com.
110 "that the American" Ibid.
110 "Various reports have" Ibid.
110 "It seems this news" Ibid.
110 "As no accounts, properly" *New York Gazette.* Nov. 1, 1777, p. 3, genealogybank.com.

Chapter 13: Anonymous Sources
p. 3
112 "attack this country" *New York Gazette.* Oct. 11, 1777, p. 1, genealogybank.com.

112 "The power of France" Ibid.
112 "Foreign intelligence" Ibid.
112 "We are assured our" Ibid.
112 "Extract of a letter" Ibid.
112 "Be assured" Ibid.
112 "As to assisting" Ibid.
113 "the present disposition" Ibid.
113 "Her Majesty is" Ibid.
113 "In this divided interest" Ibid.
113 "Notwithstanding the" Ibid.
113 "He never once" Ibid.
113 "that on the contrary" Ibid.
113 "France had never" Ibid.
113 "On Wednesday very" Ibid.
114 "For I" Washington to Richard Henry Lee. April 24-26, 1777, founders.archives.gov.
114 "low arts and dirty tricks" Ibid.
114 "diabolical scheme" Ibid.
114 "virtuous people" Ibid.
114 "to purchase" Robert Morris to John Bradford. May 8, 1776, founders.archives.gov.
114 "it is a fast" Ibid.
115 "further than" Washington to Richard Henry Lee. April 24-26, 1777, founders.archives.gov.
115 "The plan drawn" Ibid.
115 "It may however" Ibid.
115 "Perhaps nothing" *Maryland Gazette* Nov. 18, 1777, p. 1, genealogybank.com.
115 "I observe in your" Ibid.
115 "I mean Lord Stirling's divison" Ibid.
116 "Perhaps the late" Ibid.
116 "Whever this gentleman" Ibid.
116 "The following is" *New York Gazette.* Nov. 8, 1777, p. 3, genealogybank.com.
117 "The troops under" Ibid.
117 "A free passage" Ibid.
117 "To prevent any" Ibid.

Chapter 14: Battling the War Within

p. #
118 "give you a pretty" Washington to Hamilton, Oct. 30, 1777, founders.archives.gov.
119 "I have thought it" Ibid.
119 "What you are chiefly" Ibid.
119 "I arrived here" Hamilton to Washington, Nov. 6, 1777, founders.archives.com.
119 "I used every" Ibid.
119 "The force of these" Ibid.
119 "raised him into" Ibid.
119 "General Gates has" Ibid.
120 "I am afraid" Ibid.
120 "find everything" Hamilton to Washington, Nov. 10, 1777, founders.archives.gov.
120 "Not the least" Ibid.

120 "The plan I" Ibid.
14-14 "My opinion is" Ibid. 120
120 "Tis only wasting" Ibid.
120 "After sending" Gates to Washington, Nov. 7, 1777, founders.archives.gov.
121 "But Colonel Hamilton" Ibid.
121 "With the greatest" Ibid.
121 "I told the" Ibid.
121 "Although it is" Ibid.
121 "Since my arrival" Hamilton to Gates, Nov. 13, 1777, founders.archives.gov.
121 "Is so the number" Ibid.
122 "such wicked duplicity" Stirling to Washington Nov. 3, 1777, founders.archives.gov.
122 "the enclosed" Ibid.
122 "Heaven has been" Ibid.
122 "Sir, a letter" Washington to Thomas Conway, Nov. 5, 1777, founders.archives.gov.
122 "spoke my" Ibid.
123 "I believe I can" Ibid.
123 "My opinion of you" Ibid.
123 "I know, Sir" Ibid.
123 "I shall not attempt" Gates to Washington, Dec. 8, 1777, founders.archives.gov.
123 "in tracing out" Ibid.
123 "Those letters have" Ibid.
123 "The danger" Ibid.

Chapter 15: French Roast
p. #
126 "enthusiastic" Lafayette to Washington, Dec. 30, 1777, founders.archives.gov.
126 "My heart was" Lafayette Memoirs, www.mountvernon.org
127 "I am here" Ibid.
127 "treat him as" Ibid.
127 "I see plainly that" Lafayette to Washington, Dec. 30, 1777, founders.archives.gov.
127 "Now I begin" Ibid.
127 "There are open" Ibid.
127 "was a lover" Ibid.
127 "They are infatuated" Ibid.
127 "Those ideas are" Ibid.
128 "I should not" Ibid.
128 "I have been" Ibid.
128 "with ideas of glory" Ibid.
128 "The reason of such" Ibid.
128 "But since the" Ibid.
128 "Now I see all" Ibid.
128 "I am very sorry" Ibid.
129 "slavery, dishonor, ruin" Ibid.
129 "My desire of" Ibid.
129 "I am now fixed" Ibid.
129 "I heartily" Washington to Henry Laurens. Nov. 26-7, 1777, founders.archives.gov.
129 "The political reasons" Ibid.

129 "I should also" Ibid.
129 "The Marquis with" Ibid.
130 "is it highly agreeable" Ibid.
130 "a copy of it" Washington to Gates, Jan. 4, 1778, founders.archives.gov.
130 "under the disagreeable" Ibid.
130 "any member of that" Ibid.
130 "contents of the confidential" Ibid.
130 "the smallest interruption" Ibid.
130 "I never knew" Ibid.
131"considered the information" Ibid.
131 "a dangerous incendiary" Ibid.
131 "But—in this" Ibid.
131 "Since I saw you" Hamilton to George Clinton, Feb. 13, 1778, founders.archives.gov.
131 "I believe it" Ibid.
131 "Have you heard" Ibid.

Chapter 16 Forgeries at the Forge
p. #
133 "Be no flatterer" *110 Rules of Civility*.
133 "Among other" Richard Lee to Washington, Jan. 2, 1778, founders.archives.gov.
133 "The arts of the enemies" Ibid.
133 "Those contained" Washington to Richard Lee, Feb. 15, 1778, founders.archives.gov.
134 "In a word" Washington to Bryan Fairfax, March 1, 1778.
134 "Among other maneuvers" Ibid.
134 "Having been deceived" Ibid.
134 "At first your" Landon Carter to Washington, March 16-20, 1778, founders.archives.gov.
135 "A gentleman" Ibid.
135 "And let Gates" Ibid.
135 "have been in Congress" Ibid.
135 "Your local country" Ibid.
135 "With great truth" Washington to Landon Carter, May 30, 1778, founders.archives.gov.
135 "That there was" Ibid.
135 "Thus stands the matter" Ibid.
135 "I have very sufficient" Ibid.
136 "to show that" Ibid.
136 "The gazettes" Washington to Henry Laurens, April 18, 1778, founders.archives.gov.
136 "Among the many villainous" Ibid.
136 "The pride of England" Benjamin Franklin to Horatio Gates, June 2, 1779.
136 "The little dissensions" Ibid.
137 "When shall we" Ibid.
137 "Baron Steuben" Washington General Orders, March 28, 1778, founders.archives.gov
137 "The importance" Ibid.
137 "The time we" Ibid.
138 "not one sentence" Washington to John Washington, May 1778, founders.archives.gov.

138 "The arts of the enemy" Ibid.
138 "Tis among the" Richard Lee to Washington, May 7, 1778,
founders.archives.gov.
138 "Declaring" Washington to Richard Lee, May 25, 1778, founders.archives.gov.
138 "These letters are" Ibid.
139 "Sir, at the" *Royal Pennsylvania Gazette*, May 26, 1778, genealogybank.com.
139 "The production" Ibid.
139 "If you are" Ibid.
139 "On Monday" Ibid.
139 "far surpassed" Ibid.
140 "Seven white knights" Ibid.
140 "their mistresses" Ibid.
140 "insist upon" Ibid.
140 "With the knights" Ibid.
140 "the natural as" Ibid.
140 "In short, the" Ibid.
141 "How insensible" Journal of Mrs. Henry Drinker, Sept. 25, 1777-July 4, 1778.

Chapter 17 Lumière du Soleil
p. #
142 "The maneuvering" Bradford, Jared Brown, *Theatre in America during Revolution*, p. 59.
142 "Besides these" Ibid.
142 "The scenery" Ibid.
142 "made an excellent" Ibid.
143 "My friends" Washington to Landon Carter, May 30, 1778,
founders.archives.gov.
143 "miraculously brightened" Ibid.
143 "Authentic" Washington to John Washington, May 1778, founders.archives.gov.
143 "That France have done " Ibid.
144 "Give me leave" Richard Lee to Washington, May 7, 1778, founders.archives.gov.
144 "The counsels of" Ibid.
144 "England alone" Ibid.
144 "chalk out a" Washington to Richard Lee, May 25, 1778, founders.archives.gov.
144 "the favorable issue" Ibid.
144 "That Great Britain would" Ibid.
144 "But how, under" Ibid.
144 "They may attempt" Ibid.
145 "Your 'earnest caution" Benjamin Franklin to David Hartley, Feb. 13, 1778.
145 "But when your" Ibid.
145 "The Americans" Ibid.
145 "But when your" Ibid.
145 "America has been" Ibid.
146 "I know not" Ibid.
146 "The present have" Ibid.
146 "As to a French War" *Rivington's Royal Gazette*, May 30, 177,
genealogybank.com.
146 "I think" Ibid.
146 "The duplicity" Ibid.
147 "You will soon" Ibid.

Chapter 18 Volcanic Eruption

p. #

148 "I am now" *Pennsylvania Packet*, July 4, 1778, genealogybank.com.

148 "Having seen" *Rivington's Royal Gazette*, Aug. 1, 1778, genealogybank.com.

149 "I am in" Ibid.

149 "enemy's intention" *Pennsylvania Packet*, July 4, 1778, genealogybank.com.

149 "Perhaps the intention" *Rivington's Royal Gazette*, Aug. 1, 1778, genealogybank.com.

149 "I am likewise" Charles Lee to Washington, Feb. 9, 1777, founders.archives.gov.

150 "Your dogs" Washington to Charles Lee, Feb. 16, 1777, founders.archives.gov.

150 "I am to inform" Washington to Charles Lee, April 1, 1777, founders.archives.gov.

150 "It is a most" Charles Lee to Washington, April 5, 1777, founders.archives.gov.

150 "I think" Charles Lee to Washington, Dec. 30, 1777, founders.archives.gov.

150 "am lodg'ed with" Ibid.

151 "I have nothing" Ibid.

151 "You may rest" Washington to Charles Lee, Jan. 27, 1778, founders.archives.gov.

151 "I am likewise" Washington to Charles Lee, April 22, 1778, founders.archives.gov.

151 "my wish" Ibid.

152 "So as to give" *Pennsylvania Packet,* July 4, 1778, genealogybank.com.

152 "The slow advance" Ibid.

152 "The enemy in marching" Ibid.

152 "to take the" Ibid.

152 "I detached" Ibid.

152 "The enemy were" Ibid.

153 "it would" Ibid.

153 "skirt of a" Ibid.

153 "I communicated" Ibid.

153 "I instantly put" Ibid.

153 "After marching" Ibid.

153 "leaves shook" Edward Lengel, General George Washington A Military Life, 300.

153 "The peculiar situation" *Pennsylvania Packet,* July 4, 1778, genealogybank.com.

153 "mislead the vulgar" *Rivington's Royal Gazette*, Aug. 1, 1778, genealogybank.com.

153 "the trembling heard" Ibid.

153 "The idea was" Ibid.

154 "It is rather" Ibid.

154 "By the by" Ibid.

154 "That in" Ibid.

154 "In short" Ibid.

154 "I proceeded" *Pennsylvania Packet,* July 4, 1778, genealogybank.com.

154 "I thought then" Jacob Axelrad, *Philip Freneau, Champion of Democracy*, p. 93.

155 "gave directions" *Pennsylvania Packet,* July 4, 1778, genealogybank.com.

155 "On intelligence" Ibid.

155 "The enemy, by this" Ibid.

155 "not only disappointed" Ibid.

155 "The extreme heat" Ibid.

155 "It would have" Ibid.

155 "The enemy's slain" Ibid.

155 "a laurel which" *Rivington Royal Gazette*, Aug. 1, 1778, genealogybank.com.

156 "Mr. Washington" Ibid.
156 "Congress may say" Ibid.
156 "Washington, poor man" Ibid.

Chapter 19 Rivington or Randolph?
p. #
157 "Who the author" Washington to Richard Lee, May 25, 1778, founders.archives.gov.
158 "totally destroyed" *London Craftsman,* Jan. 13, 1776, newspaperarchive.com.
158 "The clergy" *Gentleman's Magazine,* Nov. 1, 1776, newspaperarchive.com.
158 "Dead to the" Ibid.
158 "while they were" Ibid.
158 "While they clamored" Ibid.
158 "This gentleman" Ibid.
158 "By these cruelties" Ibid.
158 "Everyone who reads" Ibid.
159 "We look upon" Ibid.
159 "It was seen" *Morning Post,* March 18, 1776, p. 2, genealogybank.com.
159 "show the strength" Ibid.
159 "the was pressing" Ibid.
159 "this war" Ibid.
159 "if a push was" Ibid.
159 "Venal pens" Trevelyn, *George the Third and Charles Fox,* 279.
159 "made a practice" Ibid.
160 "A gentleman" *London Public Advertiser,* June 11, 1777, p. 3, newspaperarchive.com.
160 "But it is said" Ibid.
160 "Two ladies" Ibid.
160 "We see here" Ibid.
160 "Mr. Rivington is" *London Evening Post* Feb. 13, 1776, newspaperarchive.com.
162 "drew many" Washington to William Gordon, March 8, 1785, founders.archives.gov.
163 "spurious" Washington Collection in Boston Anthenaeum, p. 306.
163 "The letters" Memoir of Lt. Col. Tench Tilghman, p. 165-7.
163 "Lord Dunmore" Lund Washington to Washington, Oct. 5, 1775, founders.archives.gov.
163 "I am far" Forged to Martha Washington, June 24, 1776, founders.archives.gov.
163 "He must have" Washington to Richard Lee May 25, 1778, founders.archives.gov.
164 "I must take" John Randolph to Jefferson Oct. 25, 1779, founders.archives.gov.
164 "If a difference" Ibid.
164 "men's minds" Ibid.
164 "The man who" Ibid.
164 "And tyrannizes" Ibid.
164 "I will allow" Ibid.
165 "I read with" Ibid.
165 "Adversity is" Ibid.
165 "The insults" Ibid.
165 "As there is" Ibid.
165 "But whoever wishes" Ibid.
165 "Judge then" Ibid.

166 "I have often" Ibid.
166 "Annihilation is" Ibid.
166 "Yet, I cannot" Ibid.
166 "Nothing but" Ibid.
166 "The short" Ibid.
167 "I can venture" Ibid.
167 "I must now" Ibid.
167 "Let our opinions" Ibid.
167 "How you may" Ibid.

Chapter 20 Turncoat's Fake News
p. #
168 "It was on" *London Public Advertiser,* July 8, 1780, p. 3, newspaperarchive.com.
168 "A report" *Adams Weekly Courant,* Aug. 15, 1780, p. 3, newspaperarchive.com.
169 "a day too late" *Public Advertiser,* August 19, 1780, p. 3, newspaperarchive.com.
169 "Here follow" Ibid.
169 "It is thought" *Public Advertiser,* July 8, 1780, p. 3, newspaperarchive.com.
169 "A gentlemen just" *Royal Gazette,* Aug. 25, 1781, p. 3, genealogybank.com.
170 "In consequence of" Ibid.
170 "And we are informed" Ibid.
170 "It is said that" Ibid.
170 "Where we are assured" Ibid.
170 "healthier, a place of" Ibid.
170 "The Marquis de Lafayette" Ibid.
171 "We can also assure" *Freeman's Journal,* Nov. 21, 1781, p. 2, genealogybank.com.
171 "a distillation of some" *Massachusetts Spy*, Dec. 6, 1781, p. 1, genealogybank.com.
171 "By administering due" Ibid.
171 "wanting to give " Henry Clinton's Narrative of Fill in name? and throughout? Campaign of 1781.
171 "I cannot sufficiently" Ibid, p. 6.
172 "I shall" Washington to Benjamin Harrison, March 27, 1781, founders.archives.gov.
172 "Of clothing we" Ibid.
172 "have more than two" Ibid.
172 "Our stock of" Ibid, 1.
172 "sufficient for the" Ibid.
172 "I have hitherto" Ibid.
172 "You may be" Ibid.
173 "It is feared" Ibid.
173 "The copies of the" Henry Clinton's *Narrative of . . . Campaign* of 1781, p. 18.
173 "show the rebel" Ibid.
173 "I confess I am" Ibid.
173 "join the French forces" Ibid.
173 "However, the present" Ibid, p. 102.
173 "But, as General Washington's" Ibid, p. 99.
174 "It is with the most" Ibid, p. 18.
174 "Your first" Lafayette to George Washington, May 24, 1781, founders.archives.gov.
175 "How happy I would" Ibid.
175 "As you are pleased" Ibid.

175 "You will then" Ibid.
175 "If the states had" Washington Diary, Aug. 1, 1781, founders.archives.gov.
175 "More than these" Ibid.
175 "I could scarce" Ibid.
176 "Should a fleet" Lafayette to Washington, Aug. 6, 1781, founders.archives.gov.
176 "Had not your" Ibid.
176 "But to return to" Lafayette to Washington, Aug. 11, 1781, founders.archives.gov.
176 "In the present" Ibid.
176 "Matters having now" Washington Diary, Aug. 14, 1781, founders.archives.gov.
177 "We may add a" Washington to de Grasse Aug. 17, 1781, founders.archives.gov.
177 "As our intentions" Washington Diary, Aug. 30, 1781, founders.archives.gov.
177 "with a design to" Ibid.
177 "crossed the" Henry Clinton's *Narrative of . . . Campaign* of 1781.
177 "Early in September" Ibid.
178 "Or if I had as many" Ibid.
178 "Should this attempt" *Royal Gazette*, Oct. 3, 1781, p. 2, genealogybank.com.
178 "The contest" Ibid.
179 "I have the mortification" *Royal Gazette*, Nov. 24, 1781, founders.archives.gov.
179 "We can assure the" *Royal Gazette,* Nov. 7, 1781, p. 2, genealogybank.com.
179 "So that every American" Ibid.
179 "They lately felt the" Ibid.
179 "The people of America" Ibid.
180 "It is reported " *Boston Gazette*, Dec.. 29, 1783, p. 2, genealogybank.com.
181 "It has come out" Andrlik, *Journal of American Revolution*, March 3, 2014.
181 "By a channel" Ibid.
181 "I do myself the" Ibid.
182 "Genl. Washington, Secret Service" Ibid.
182 "I was employed" Ibid.
182 "Joined the fleet" Ibid.
182 "On her [the ship's] return" Ibid.
183 "that much" Washington to Noah Webster, July. 31, 1788, founders.archives.gov.
183 "You may" Washington to Benjamin Harrison, Sr. March 27, 1781, founders.archives.gov.
183 "should a reinforcment" Ibid.
184 "the difficulty consisted" Ibid.
184 "that before the" Ibid.

Chapter 21 "Brave, Virtuous . . . Treason"
p. #
185 "So replete" Landon Carter to Washington, March 10-20, 1778, founders.archives.gov.
186 "The secrecy" Horatio Gates to Washington, Oct. 7, 1781, founders.archives.gov.
186 "Ever willing" Ibid.
187 "That the" Ibid.
188 "A Breakfast" Lee, *Life and Memoirs*, 1813, p. 121-8.
188 "As Mr. Rivington" Ibid.
188 "But as I" Ibid.
188 "flaming factious" Ibid.
188 "ridiculous" Ibid.
188 "For my own part" Ibid.

188 "porter at a" Ibid.
188 "My dear Kitty" Ibid.
188 "Now I would" Ibid.
188 "A pamphlet entitled" Ibid.
189 "Then your proposed" Lee, *Life and Memoirs*, p. 63.
189 "Your opinion" John Adams to Charles Lee, Oct. 13, 1775, founders.archives.gov.
189 "Did I not consent" Lee, *Life and Memoirs*, p. 319.
190 "Your eyes" Ibid.
190 "You tell me" Charles Lee to Unnamed Congress Member, *Life and Memoirs*, p. 318-9.
190 "the palpable meaning" Ibid.
190 "transcendent, that" Ibid.
190 "spurned aside" Ibid.
191 "What have I" Ibid.
191 "Great God!" Ibid.
191 "In God's name" Ibid.
191 "But if a hero" Ibid.
191 "No man loves" Ibid.
191 "The Congress seem" Lee to Gates, Oct. 14, 1776, in *Treason of Lee*, 38.
192 "In my opinion" Ibid.
192 "Let me talk vainly" Lee to Benjamin Rush, Nov. 20, 1776, in *Treason of Lee*, p. 41.
192 "Oh General" Lee to Reed, Nov. 21, 1776, in *Treason of Lee*, p. 41.
192 "How often" Ibid.
192 "I do not mean" Joseph Reed to Charles Lee, Nov. 21, 1776, *Life and Memoirs*, p. 227.
192 "As soon as" Ibid.
193 "The spirit" Charles Lee to Benjamin Franklin, Nov. 6, 1776, founders.archives.gov.
193 "Adieu, God bless you" Ibid.
193 "My objections" Charles Lee to Washington, Nov. 30, 1776, founders.archives.gov.
193 "You complain" Charles Lee to Washington, Dec. 8, 1776, founders.archives.gov.
193 "If I was not" Ibid.
193 "There are times" Charles Lee to Bowdoin, Nov. 22, 1776, in *Treason of Lee*, p. 50.
194 "We have three" Charles Lee to Washington, Dec. 11, 1776, founders.archives.gov.
194 "General Lee has sent" Ibid.
194 "You behold me" Lee to Capt. Kennedy Dec. 22, 1776, in *Treason of Lee*, p. 65-6.
194 "He was, besides" Lee to Benjamin Rush, June 4, 1778, *Life and Memoirs*, p. 340.

Chapter 22 Projection
p. #
197 "Among the prisoners" Forged, Washington Introduction, founders.archives.gov.
197 "I asked him" Ibid.
197 "All the" Washington to Benjamin Walker, Jan. 12, 1797, founders.archives.gov.
197 "I am like a dog" Charles Lee to Washington, April 5, 1776, founders.archives.gov.
198 "I have been" Washington to Hancock, July 21, 1775, founders.archives.gov.

198 "But I flatter" Forged to Martha Washington, June 24, 1776, founders.archives.gov.
198 "In one thing" Forged to Lund Washington, June 12, 1776, founders.archives.gov.
198 "I need not" Ibid.
199 "We set out with" Ibid.
199 "But, with a" Forged to John Parke Custis, June 18, 1776, founders.archives.gov.
199 "A man" Ibid.
199 "But, opposed" Forged to Martha Washington, June 24, 1776, founders.archives.gov.
200 "When either my" Forged to John Parke Custis, June 18, 1776, founders.archives.gov.
200 "seeing our miscarriages" Ibid.
200 "Am I not too" Ibid.

Chapter 23 Feasible Malfeasance
p. #
201 "Have I not" Lee, *Life and Memoirs*, 1813, p. 319.
201 "I little thought" Charles Lee to Thomas Gage, *Life and Memoirs*, 1813, p. 281.
201 "But I hold" Ibid.
202 "A personal friendship" Ibid.
202 "As to North" Ibid.
202 "You have known me" Ibid.
202 "You ask me" Charles Lee to John Burgoyne, *Life and Memoirs*, 1813, p. 279-81.
202 "All they required" Ibid.
202 "But to recur" Ibid.
203 "But if she discards" Ibid.
205 "I am happy" Horatio Gates to Charles Lee, July 17, 1776, founders.archives.gov.
203 "But the fatal separation" Ibid.
205 "I do not" Forged, Washington to John Parke Custis. June 18, 1776, founders.archives.gov.
203 "An opportunity" Ibid.
205 "What you" Ibid.
203 "But it will" Ibid.
206 "The only true" Ibid.
203 "I most earnestly" Ibid.
206 "We must, at last" Ibid.
206 "For all these" Ibid.
203 "I am myself" Charles Lee to Benjamin Franklin, Dec. 10, 1775, founders.archives.gov.
203 "A declaration of" Ibid.
206 "For I have" Ibid.
206 "A captain" Charles Lee to George Washington, Feb. 19, 1776, founders.archives.gov.
204 "In short I am conceited" Ibid.
207 "It is a most" Lee to Washington April 5, 1777, in *Treason of Lee*, p. 109-110.
204 "Have you seen" Charles Lee to Washington, Jan. 24, 1776, founders.archives.gov.
204 "that if Parliament" Ibid.
204 "By eternal God" Charles Lee to Edward Rutledge, *Life and Memoirs*, 1813, p. 290-1.

207 "But I am" Ibid.
207 "I heartily" George Johnson to Charles Lee, June 17, 1778, *Life and Memoirs*, p. 212.
207 "I meant in" George Johnson to Charles Lee, June 17, 1778, *Life and Memoirs*, p. 212.
208 "You will" Charles Lee to Benjamin Rush, June 17, 1778, *Life and Memoirs*, p. 240-2.
208 "From my first" Ibid.
208 "He is, besides" Ibid.
208 "But through these" Ibid.
208 "But I believe" Ibid.
209 "From the" Charles Lee to Washington, June 30, 1778, founders.archives.gov.
209 "They implied" Ibid.
209 "What I recollect" Washington to Charles Lee, June 30, 1778, founders.archives.gov.
210 "They approached" Alexander Hamilton, Dec. 24, 1778, founders.archives.gov.
210 "His evasions" Alexander Hamilton to Von Steuben, Dec. 19, 1778, founders.archives.gov.
210 "ready to satisfy" Alexander Hamilton, Dec. 24, 1778, founders.archives.gov.
211 "that General Lee" Ibid.
211 "General Lee" Ibid.
211 "As Colonel Laurens" Ibid.
211 "General Lee proposed" Ibid.
211 "As Colonel Laurens" Ibid.
211 "General Lee then" Ibid.
211 "But General Lee repeated" Ibid.
212 "the loss of the" *Maryland Journal*, July 6, 1779.
212 "the spirits of " *Maryland Journal*, July 6, 1779.
212 "that I should" William Livingston to Charles Lee, Jan. 16, 1779, *Life and Memoirs*, p. 233.
212 "I meant in" Charles Lee to Sidney Lee, Sept. 24, 1779, *Life and Memoirs*, p. 348-9.
212 "Had he listened" Ibid.
212 "For I assure you" Charles Lee to Sidney Lee, June 22, 1782, *Life and Memoirs*, p. 349-52.
213 "All that I shall" Ibid.
213 "They have always" Ibid.
213 "It would be" Washington to Benjamin Walker, Jan. 12, 1797, founders.archives.gov.

Epilogue: First Press-ident
p. #
214 "Now by the" Benjamin Franklin to Richard Price, June 13, 1782, founders.archives.gov.
214 "The ancient Roman" Ibid.
214 "The facility with" Ibid.
215 "And now we find" Ibid.
215 "If you read" Washington to Benjamin Walker, Jan. 12, 1797, founders.archives.gov.
215 "Amongst other" Ibid.
216 "But that is"Ibid.

BIBLIOGRAPHY

"Copy of a Letter from Major-General Washington to his brother on May 31, 1754." *London Magazine or Gentleman's Monthly Intelligencer,* August 1754. Archive.org.

"Dublin, August 30." *Pennsylvania Gazette,* October 30, 1755. Philadelphia, PA, page 2, Genealogybank.com (accessed May 30, 2019.

"George Washington's Education," Mount Vernon Digital Encyclopedia www.mountvernon.org/digital-encyclopedia/article/education/ (accessed May 23, 2019).

"In Convention Present 112 Members (in Virginia) Wednesday, May 15, 1776." *Pennsylvania Ledger,* June 1, 1776. GenealogyBank.com (accessed Jan. 17, 2022,

"London, Sept. 20," *Boston Evening-Post,* December 15, 1755. Genealogybank.com (accessed October 30, 2010.

"Supplement to the Boston Gazette about Hutchinson Letters." *Boston Gazette,* June 28, 1773. GenealogyBank.com (accessed October 30, 2020.

Andrlik, Todd. "James Rivington: King's Print and Patriot Spy?" *Journal of the American Revolution,* (March 3, 2014) https://allthingsliberty.com/2014/03/james-rivington-kings-printer-patriot-spy/ (accessed May 23, 2019).

Athenaeum, Boston. *A Catalogue of the Washington Collection in the Boston Athenæum, Parts 1-4.* University Press: J. Wilson and Son, The Boston Athenaeum, 1897.

Boston Gazette, March 5, 1754, May 14, 1754, March. 22, 1773, July 20, 1778, GenealogyBank.com (accessed May 23, 2019).

Boston Post Boy, July 1, 1754. www.genealogybank.com, accessed. GenealogyBank.com (accessed May 23, 2019).

Boudinot, Elias. *Letter to George Washington, April 22, 1789;* From National Archives, Founders.archives.gov (accessed May 23, 2019).

Brown, Jared. *The Theatre in America During the Revolution.* New York: Cambridge Press, 2007.

Carter, Landon. *Letter to George Washington, March 10-20, 1778.* From National Archives, Founders.archives.gov (accessed May 23, 2019).

Cecere, Michael. "Washington's Deviation to Virginia," *Journal of the American Revolution,* (Sept. 23, 2013) https://allthingsliberty.com/2013/09/washingtons-deviation-virginia/ (accessed May 23, 2019).

Clinton, Sir Henry. *Narrative of Lieutenant General Sir Henry Clinton Relative to His Conduct during Part of His Command of the King's Troops in North America Particularly to that which Respect the Unfortunate Issue of the Campaign in 1781.* London: J. Debrett, 1783.

Connecticut Journal. January 1, 1777, January 8, 1777, GenealogyBank.com (accessed May 23, 2019).

Conway, Thomas. *Letter to George Washington, Nov. 5, 1777.* From National Archives, Founders.archives.gov, (accessed May 23, 2019).

Cook, Jane Hampton. *Stories of Faith and Courage from the Revolutionary War.* Chattanooga: AMG, 2007.

Custis, George Washington Parke. *Recollections and Private Memoirs of Washington.* New York: Derby and Jackson, 1860.

Daily Advertiser, March 18, 1776, p. 2, July 21, 1787, GenealogyBank.com accessed May 23, 2019).

Drinker, Elizabeth. "Extracts from the Journal of Mrs. Henry Drinker, of Philadelphia, from September 25, 1777 to July 4, 1778" *Pennsylvania Magazine of History and Biography,* Vol. XIII: 1889.

Dunlap's Maryland Gazette, Nov. 18, 1777, GenealogyBank.com (accessed May 23, 2019).

Fiske, John. "Lee, Charles," *Appletons' Cyclopædia of American Biography.* New York: D. Appleton. 1892.

Forged Letter George Washington to John Custis, June 18, 1776. From National Archives, Founders.archives.gov, (accessed May 23, 2019).

Forged Letter George Washington to Lund Washington, June 12, 1776 and June 15, 1776. From National Archives, Founders.archives.gov (accessed May 23, 2019).

Forged Letter George Washington to Martha Washington, June 24, 1776. From National Archives, Founders.archives.gov (accessed May 23, 2019).

Forged Letter George Washington, Introduction, May 31, 1777. From National Archives, Founders.archives.gov (accessed May 23, 2019).

Franklin, Benjamin. "The Busy-Body, No. 1," *American Weekly Mercury*, February 4, 1728/9. Founders.archives.gov (accessed January 7, 2022.

Franklin, _____. "Apology for Printers." *Pennsylvania Gazette.* June 10, 1731. Founders.archives.gov (accessed January 7, 2022.

Franklin, _____. "To the Printer of the London Chronicle, Dec. 25, 1773," *London Chronicle,* December 23, 1773. Founders.archives.gov.

Franklin, _____. *Letter to Richard Price, June 13, 1782.* From National Archives, Founders.archives.gov (accessed May 23, 2019).

Freeman's Journal, Nov. 21, 1781, GenealogyBank.com (accessed May 23, 2019).

Gates, Horatio. *Letter to George Washington, Nov. 7, 1777, Dec. 8, 1777.* From National Archives, Founders.archives.gov, (accessed May 23, 2019).

Gentleman's Magazine and Historical Chronicle, May 1754, June 1754,

November 1, 1776, NewspaperArchive.com (accessed October 30, 2021).

Hamilton, Alexander. Letter George Clinton, Feb. 13, 1778. From National Archives, Founders.archives.gov (accessed May 23, 2019).

Hamilton, ____. *Letters to George Washington, Oct. 11, 1787, Oct. 30, 1787, Nov. 6, 1777, Nov. 10, 1777, note, Oct. 11, 1787, Jan. 19, 1796, July 3, 1787, May 5, 1789, July 30, 1796.* From National Archives, Founders.archives.gov (accessed May 23, 2019).

Hamilton, ____. Letter to Horatio Gates, Nov. 13, 1777. From National Archives, Founders.archives.gov (accessed May 23, 2019).

Hamilton, ____. *Notes on Constitutional Convention, June 1-26, 1787, note June 19, 1787.* From National Archives, Founders.archives.gov (accessed May 23, 2019).

Hancock, John. *Journals of the Continental Congress, Sept. 18, 1777,* VIII, Library of Congress, LOC.gov, (accessed May 23, 2019).

Henry Lee, Richard. *Letter to George Washington, Jan. 2, 1778, May 7, 1778.* From National Archives, Founders.archives.gov, (accessed May 23, 2019).

Howe, William. *Letter to George Washington, Aug. 22, 1775.* From National Archives, Founders.archives.gov, (accessed May 23, 2019).

Humphreys, David. *Life of General Washington,* Athens: University of Georgia Press, 1991.

Independent Gazetteer, May 5, 1787, GenealogyBank.com (accessed May 23, 2019).

Labilliere, Peter. To George Washington, Nov. 4, 1777. From National Archives, Founders.archives.gov (accessed May 23, 2019).

Lafayette, Marie-Joseph-Paul-Yves-Roch-Gilbert du Motier. *Letters to George Washington, Dec. 30, 1777, May 24, 1781, July 20, 1781, Aug. 6, 1781, Aug. 11, 1781, Oct. 6, 1797.* From National Archives, Founders.archives.gov. (accessed May 23, 2019).

Lee, Charles. *Strictures on a Pamphlet Entitled 'A Friendly Address to All Reasonable Americans, on the Subject of our Political Confusions.'* Boston: Isaac Thomas and Booksellers in America, 1775.

Lee, ____. *The Life and Memoirs of the late Major General Lee, Second in Command to General Washington during the American Revolution to Which Are Added his Political and Military Essays and Letters.* New York: Richard Scott, 1813.

Lengel, Edward. *General George Washington: A Military Life.* New York: Random House, 2005.

London Craftsman, Jan. 13, 1776, Newspaperarchive.com (accessed May 23, 2019).

London Evening Post, February 13, 177, May 29, 1776 NewspaperArchive.com (accessed May 23, 2019).

London Public Advertiser, Jan. 11, 1777, May 24, 1777, June 11, 1777, July 8, 1780, August 19, 1780, NewspaperArchive.com (accessed May 23,

2019).

Maryland Journal, July 26, 1775, December 19, 1788, June 2, 1789,

Massachusetts Spy, December 6, 1781, GenealogyBank.com (accessed May 23, 2019).

Middlesex Gazette, September 25, 1786, GenealogyBank.com (accessed May 23, 2019).

Moore, Charles, ed., *George Washington's Rules of Civility, and Decent Behavior in Company and Conversation,* Boston and New York: Houghton Mifflin Company, 1926.

Moore, George H. *The Treason of Major General Charles Lee*. New York: Charles Scribner, 1859.

Morris, Robert. *Letter to John Bradford, May 8, 1776.* From National Archives, Founders.archives.gov (accessed May 23, 2019).

New England Courant, July 9, 1722, GenealogyBank.com (accessed May 23, 2019).

New York Journal, September 6, 1787, September 27, 1787 GenealogyBank.com (accessed May 23, 2019).

New York Mercury, July 22, 1754, February 16, 1756, December 23, 1758, GenealogyBank.com (accessed May 23, 2019).

Papas, Phillip. *Renegade Revolutionary*. New York: New York University Press, 2014.

Pennsylvania Evening Post, July 8, 1776, January 25, 1777, March 1, 1777, GenealogyBank.com (accessed May 23, 2019).

Pennsylvania Gazette. May 9, 1754, August 22, 1754, July 31, 1755, October. 30, 1755, February 12, 1756, February 26, 1756, November 30, 1758, September 25, 1776, GenealogyBank.com (accessed May 23, 2019).

Pennsylvania Journal, November 27, 1776, GenealogyBank.com (accessed May 23, 2019).

Pennsylvania Mercury, October 13, 1786, GenealogyBank.com (accessed May 23, 2019).

Randolph, John. *Letter to Thomas Jefferson, Oct. 25, 1779.* From National Archives, Founders.archives.gov (accessed May 23, 2019).

Randolph, Peyton. *Letter to George Washington, May 3, 1756.* From National Archives, Founders.archives.gov (accessed May 23, 2019).

Rees, Jacob. "Nineteenth Century Remembrances of Black Veterans: Jacob Francis, Massachusetts Continental and New Jersey Militia." *Journal of the American Revolution* (February 2021) https://allthingsliberty.com/2021/02/nineteenth-century-remembrances-of-black-revolutionary-veterans-jacob-francis-massachusetts-continental-and-new-jersey-militia/ (accessed May 23, 2019).

Rivington Royal Gazette, May 26, 1778, May 30, 1778, Aug. 1, 1778, August 25, 1781, October 3, 1781, November 7, 1781 GenealogyBank.com (accessed May 23, 2019).

Rivington, Septimus. *The Publishing Family of Rivington. Rivington's 34 King*

Street, London: Convent Garden, 1919, www.archive.org/details/cu31
92402951 0504 (accessed May 23, 2019).

Rivington's New York Gazetteer, June 3, 1773, November 10, 1774, October
13, 1774, April 20, 1775, July 21, 1775, November 2, 1775, October 11,
1777, October 18, 1777, October 25, 1777, November 1, 1777,
November 8, 1777, GenealogyBank.com (accessed May 23, 2019).

Royal Pennsylvania Gazette, May 26, 1778, November 24, 1781,
GenealogyBank.com (accessed May 23, 2019).

St. James Chronicle and Evening Post, September 26, 1776,
NewspaperArchive.com (accessed May 23, 2019).

Stirling, Lord. *Letter to George Washington, Nov. 3, 1777.* From National
Archives, Founders.archives.gov, May 23, 2019).

Stuart, David. *Letter to George Washington, July 14, 1789*. From National
Archives, Founders.archives.gov (accessed May 23, 2019).

Thomson, Charles. *Letter to George Washington, April 14, 1789*. From
National Archives, Founders.archives.gov (accessed May 23, 2019).

Tilghman, Tench. *Memoir of Lieutenant Colonel Tench Tilghman, Secretary
and Aid to Washington*. Albany: J. Munsell, 1876.

Trevelyan, Sir George Otto. *George the Third and Charles Fox, Vol. I*. New
York: Longmans, Green & Company, 1912).

Virginia Gazette, August 3, 1776, September 7, 1776, September 14, 1776,
November 28, 1776, GenealogyBank.com (accessed May 23, 2019).

Walpole, Horace. *Memoirs of King George II*, London: Henry Colburn, 1847.

Washington, George. "Letter from Major Washington to His Brother, May
31, 1754," *London Magazine*, August 1754, NewspaperArchive.com
(accessed May 23, 2019).

Washington, _____. *Letter to Henry Laurens, General Greene's extract,"* Nov.
26-7, 1777. From National Archives, Founders.archives.gov (accessed
May 23, 2019).

Washington, _____. *Letter to Sir Henry Clinton, April 16, 1781.* From
National Archives, Founders.archives.gov (accessed May 23, 2019).

Washington, _____. *Expedition to the Ohio, 1754.* From National Archives,
Founders.archives.gov (accessed May 23, 2019).

Washington, _____. *General Orders, July 9, 1776, July 10, 1776, March 28,
1778.* From National Archives, Founders.archives.gov, From National
Archives, Founders.archives.gov (accessed May 23, 2019).

Washington, _____. *Letter Noah Webster, July. 31, 1788*. From National
Archives, Founders.archives.gov, (accessed May 23, 2019).

Washington, _____. *Letter to Alexander Hamilton, Oct. 30, 1777.* From
National Archives, Founders.archives.gov (accessed May 23, 2019).

Washington, _____. *Letters to Benjamin Harrison, March 27, 1781, Sept. 24,
Jan. 31, 1788. From National Archives, Founders.archives.gov (accessed
May 23, 2019).*

Washington, _____. *Letter to Bryan Fairfax, March 1, 1778.* From National
Archives, Founders.archives.gov (accessed May 23, 2019).

Washington, _____. *Letter to Burwell Bassett, June 19, 1774*. From National Archives, Founders.archives.gov (accessed May 23, 2019).

Washington, _____. *Letter to Charles Carter, Jan. 12, 1788*. From National Archives, Founders.archives.gov (accessed May 23, 2019).

Washington, _____. *To Continental Congress Camp Committee, January 29, 1778*. From National Archives, Founders.archives.gov (accessed Oct. 30, 2021.

Washington, _____. *Letter to Comte de Grasse Aug. 17, 1781*. From National Archives, Founders.archives.gov (accessed May 23, 2019).

Washington, _____. *Letter to David Humphreys," Oct. 10, 1787, June 12, 1796*. From National Archives, Founders.archives.gov (accessed May 23, 2019).

Washington, _____. *Letter to Fairfax County Commission, May 16, 1775*. From National Archives, Founders.archives.gov, (accessed May 23, 2019).

Washington, _____. *Letter to Henry Laurens, note, Nov. 26-7, 1777*. From National Archives, Founders.archives.gov, (accessed May 23, 2019).

Washington, _____. *Letter to Horatio Gates, Jan. 4, 1778*. From National Archives, Founders.archives.gov, (accessed May 23, 2019).

Washington, _____. *Letters to John Augustine Washington," May 28, 1755, July 18, 1755, May 31-June 4, 1776, May 1778*. From National Archives, Founders.archives.gov, (accessed May 23, 2019).

Washington, _____. *Letter to John Hancock,: July 21, 1775, July 14, 1776*. From National Archives, Founders.archives.gov (accessed May 23, 2019).

Washington, _____. *Letter to Joseph Reed, Jan. 31, 1776, April 1, 1776*. From National Archives, Founders.archives.gov (accessed May 23, 2019).

Washington, _____. *Letter to Landon Carter, May 30, 1778*. From National Archives, Founders.archives.gov, May 23, 2019).

Washington, _____. *Letter to Mary Ball Washington, July 18, 1755*. From National Archives, Founders.archives.gov (accessed May 23, 2019).

Washington, _____. *Letters to Richard Henry Lee, April 24-26, 1777., May 25, 1778*. From National Archives, Founders.archives.gov, (accessed May 23, 2019).

Washington, _____. *Letter to Richard Henry Lee, Feb. 15, 1778*. From National Archives, Founders.archives.gov, (accessed May 23, 2019).

Washington, _____. *Letter to Samuel Washington, Dec. 18, 1776*. From National Archives, Founders.archives.gov (accessed May 23, 2019).

Washington, _____. *Letter to Thomas Conway," Nov. 5, 1777*. From National Archives, Founders.archives.gov, (accessed May 23, 2019).

Washington, _____. *Letter to William Howe," Aug. 23, 1775*. From National Archives, Founders.archives.gov, (accessed May 23, 2019).

Washington, _____. *Memorandum of an interview with Lt. Col. James Paterson, July 20, 1776*. From National Archives, Founders.archives.gov, (accessed May 23, 2019).

Washington, _____. *Expedition to the Ohio, 1754: Narrative.* From National Archives, Founders.archives.gov (accessed May 23, 2019).

Washington, _____. *Diary Aug. 1781.* From National Archives, Founders.archives.gov (accessed May 23, 2019).

Washington, _____. *To Phillis Wheatley.* Feb. 28, 1776. . From National Archives, Founders.archives.gov (accessed May 23, 2019).

Washington, Lund, *Letter to George Washington, Oct. 5, 1775.* From National Archives, Founders.archives.gov (accessed May 23, 2019).

Wedderburn, Alexander, "The Final Hearing before the Privy Council Committee for Plantation Affairs on the Petition from the Massachusetts House of Representatives for the Removal of Hutchinson and Oliver, 29 January 1774." From National Archives, Founders.archives.gov (accessed May 23, 2019).

Wheatley, Phillis. Enclosure, Poem to George Washington, Oct. 26, 1776. From National Archives, Founders.archives.gov (accessed May 23, 2019).

Worthington, Chauncey Ford. *The Spurious Letters Attributed to George Washington.* Brooklyn: Privately Printed, 1889.

Zall, Paul M. ed, *Washington on Washington.* Lexington: University Press of Kentucky, 2003.

ABOUT THE AUTHOR

Jane Hampton Cook's passion is igniting patriotism and making American history relevant to modern life, news, current events, politics and faith. She is an award-winning screenwriter and author of thirteen books, including *Stories of Faith & Courage from the Revolutionary War*. She has written screenplay adaptations for two of her books and is actively shopping them to production companies. SAVING WASHINGTON placed third in ScreenCraft's drama 2018 screenwriting and AMERICAN PHOENIX was a top ten winner in International Screenwriting Associations's Emerging Screenwriters contest in 2020.

A national media commentator and former White House webmaster, Jane has been a frequent guest on the Fox News Channel, SKY News, C-SPAN, BBC, CD Media, WMAL, and other outlets. She has been a cast member and an on-camera storyteller for several documentaries, including Fox Nation's WHAT MADE AMERICA GREAT hosted by Brian Kilmeade and *THE FIRST AMERICAN*, a film about George Washington hosted by Newt and Callista Gingrich. Her YouTube series is called *Red, White, Blue & You*.

Jane received a bachelor's degree from Baylor University and a master's degree (with a minor focusing on communication and journalism) from Texas A&M University. Through a research fellowship from the White House Historical Association in 2003, she launched her passion for biography and history. Jane lives with her husband, John Kim Cook, and their sons in Centreville, Virginia. www.janecook.com.

BOOKS BY JANE HAMPTON COOK
The Submarine & The Spies: Friendship & Vigilance in the American Revolution
Resilience on Parade: Short Stories of Suffragists
and Women's Battle for the Vote

The Burning of the White House: James & Dolley Madison & the War of 1812
American Phoenix: John Quincy & Louisa Adams
America's Star-Spangled Story
Stories of Faith & Courage from the Revolutionary War
Stories of Faith & Courage from the War in Iraq & Afghanistan
The Faith of America's First Ladies

For Children:
First Fireworks for Independence: Virginia's Gift to America
What Does the President Look Like?
B is for Baylor
Maggie Houston

DOCUMENTARIES
Fox Nation's WHAT MADE AMERICA GREAT: THE WOMEN'S VOTE hosted by
Brian Kilmeade

THE FIRST AMERICAN & REDISCOVERING GOD IN AMERICA, II
OUR SACRED HONOR
UNITED STUFF OF AMERICA for the History Channel's H2 network.

www.ingramcontent.com/pod-product-compliance
Lightning Source LLC
Chambersburg PA
CBHW060910120626
46553CB00001B/269